101

ONE WEEK LOAN

finance and taxes in the global economy today. Using a combination of neo-Keynesian economics, critical political theory and a well-grounded perspective on international relations, Patomaki makes powerful and persuasive analytical and normative arguments for the democratisation of globalisation.

Because this book is so clearly written, it will be equally useful for the general reader as well as specialists in money, finance and the political economy of globalisation.

Professor Stephen Gill, author of several leading works on
international political economy

Critical Acclaim for this Book

Heikki Patomaki has produced an extraordinary portrait of finance capital, its irrational behaviour, the endemic instability it introduces in the global economy and its negative consequences for people's wellbeing and the stability of democratic states. His discussion on the prospects of the Tobin tax is enlightening, because he skillfully avoids falling into the trap of those who believe it is either a universal panacea or a meaningless initiative. Instead he realistically explores what the Tobin tax could do to regulate the financial markets and persuasively underlines the political viability of this proposal, dismissing the arguments of neoliberal ideologues who speak of the 'inevitability' of current financial arrangements.

Atilio A. Boron, Executive Secretary, Latin American
Council of Social Sciences (CLACSO)

About the Author

Dr Heikki Patomäki is reader in international relations at the Nottingham Trent University and research director of the Network Instititue for Global Democratisation, NIGD. Prior to this, he was senior researcher at the Finnish Institute of International Affairs, UPI, 1994–97. He is author of a number of books and monographs in both English and Finnish. He is also an active public speaker, contributor to the press and consultant both in his native country, Finland, and elsewhere.

This, his most recent book, emerged as a response to the Asian and Russian financial crises. It has provided the intellectual basis of a campaign organised by the Service Centre for Development Cooperation, KEPA, in Helsinki to get the Tobin tax on to the European political agenda. The campaign has been worked out in cooperation with ATTAC in Paris.

Democratising Globalisation:
The Leverage of the Tobin Tax

Heikki Patomäki

Zed Books

LONDON · NEW YORK

Democratising Globalisation: The Leverage of the Tobin Tax was
first published by Zed Books Ltd, 7 Cynthia Street, London, N1
9JF, UK and Room 400, 175 Fifth Avenue, New York, NY 10010,
USA in 2001.

Distributed in the USA exclusively by Palgrave, a division
of St Martin's Press, LLC, 175 Fifth Avenue, New York,
NY 10010, USA.

Cover designed by Andrew Corbett
Set in Monotype Ehrhardt and Franklin Gothic by Ewan Smith
Printed and bound in Malaysia

A catalogue record for this book is available from the British
Library

Library of Congress Cataloging-in-Publication Data: available

ISBN 1 85649 870 0 cased
ISBN 1 85649 871 9 limp

Contents

Figures, Tables and Boxes

Acknowledgements

No piece of research is a mere individual achievement. Many people have participated in making this book possible. James Tobin, who internationalised an earlier suggestion by John Maynard Keynes, is responsible for the extraordinary idea of taxing currency transactions for global benefit. Roy Bhaskar helped me to articulate the argumentative form and philosophical grounds of this work. Without them, *Democratising Globalisation* would not have been possible.

Many people have also participated in this project more directly. In a Politics of EMU workshop in Helsinki in October 1996, Stephen Gill provoked me to take the Tobin tax more seriously. After the collapse of the rouble in August 1998, Katarina Sehm Patomäki, my wife, strongly encouraged me to engage in a project for the Tobin tax. The first outcome of the project was a Network Institute for Global Democratisation (NIGD) Report entitled 'The Tobin Tax: How to Make It Real', published by UPI, the Finnish Institute for International Affairs, on the eve of the Finnish parliamentary elections, in March 1999. With the help of Kepa, the Service Centre for Development Cooperation in Finland, and Mika Rönkkö in particular, the Report stimulated public discussions in Finland and contributed to the inclusion of a small paragraph about the Tobin tax in the programme of the new government.

Besides Katarina, who helped both to formulate some of the ideas at the core of Chapters 5 to 7, and to refine the original text, I am indebted to the 'Advisory Board' – Christian Chavagneux, Bob Deacon, Adam Harnes, Manuel Montes, Ronen Palan and David Woodward – all of whom provided a brief expert statement to the Report. Bob Deacon also took part in the publication of the Report in Helsinki, together with Syed Mansoob Murshed of UNU/WIDER (World Institute for Economic Research of the United Nations University). Ronen Palan also supported the project after publication, not least by providing material on financial offshore facilities which I have used unscrupulously in some parts of Chapter 3.

Before the Report was written, I received back-up from ATTAC (Association pour une Taxe sur les Transactions Financières pour l'Aide aux Citoyens), a body founded on the initiative of *Le Monde Diplomatique* in June 1998. In early December 1998, Katarina and I (with our new-born baby Anna) attended the founding meeting of International ATTAC in Paris, and six weeks later, again in Paris, we participated in an expert meeting of international economists discussing the feasibility of the Tobin tax with the Scientific Committee of ATTAC. I am grateful to the organisers of these events for the opportunity not only to witness political struggles in the Francophone world, but, more importantly, to have discussions with people such as Bernard Cassen, David Felix, Susan George, John Grahl and Alex Michalos. John Grahl, in many of his e-mail messages since our encounter in Paris, has continued to remind me of the necessity of having capital controls to back up the Tobin tax.

After the publication of the NIGD Report in Helsinki, many Finns helped me to articulate my thoughts on the Tobin tax further. Most important was Monica Ahlstedt, Katarina's mother, a senior economist and risk analyst in the Bank of Finland. In lengthy conversations, she clarified many technical details, provided important material and gave me confidence that my line of argument is both worth pursuing and feasible. Petri Böckerman, a young economist, assumed a more sceptical line on the Tobin tax, and thereby helped me to make the argument stronger. Erkki Tuomioja, a senior MP, promised to do his best to get the idea of the Tobin tax into the government programme – and succeeded. He has done his utmost to promote the idea in the international arena in his present role as Foreign Minister. Two Green Members of the European Parliament, Heidi Hautala and Matti Wuori, have kept me up-to-date on developments in European politics.

The origin of Chapter 1 – and the final structure of the book – lies in the invitation by Hans C. Blomqvist to participate in a seminar organised by the Swedish School of Economics and Business Administration (Helsinki) on financial instability in September 1999. The organisers of the seminar also published in 2000 an earlier and shorter version of Chapter 1 as 'Economics of Financial Instability' in *Ekonomiska Samfundets Tidskrift* 53 (1): 27–42. An article that draws heavily on the present Chapter 7 was published as 'The Tobin Tax: A New Phase in the Politics of Globalisation?' in *Theory, Culture and Society* 17 (4) (August 2000): 77–91; and reproduced in H. Hakovirta (ed.): *Globalism at the Crossroads. Wedges into Global Theory and Policy* (Helsinki: Finnish Political Science Association, 2000), pp. 166–84. A translation of an earlier version was published, in Indonesian, as 'Pajak Tobin: Sebuah Fase Baru dalam Politik Globalisasi', *Wacana* 4 (1999): 96–116. Finally, I am also grateful to the *Eastern Economic*

Journal for permission to reproduce James Tobin's 'A Proposal for Monetary Reform'. It was originally published in the *Eastern Economic Journal* 4 (3–4): 153–9. In spring 2000, Anna Leander gave me very useful and profound comments on drafts of the Introduction and Chapters 1 and 2. (Still, I doubt whether she will be happy with the final outcome.) Most importantly, Pauline Eadie, my research assistant, has patiently photocopied thousands of pages of material; helped to draw many of the figures and compile many of the tables of the book; composed the indexes and the list of abbreviations; and, with Katarina, checked the language and references of the work. The final touches to the manuscript were given by Jeff Fry, who copy-edited the version sent to Zed Books in August 2000. Last but not least, I would like to thank Robert Molteno from Zed Books for his patience and discerning comments on the original proposal, Report and Introduction to this book.

This book is dedicated to Anna, my two-year-old angel, who deserves to live in a globalising world with hope, not dominated by unconcerned neoliberalism or the postmodernism of despair.

Heikki Patomäki
Nottingham, 2001

Abbreviations

ASEAN	Association of South-East Asian Nations
ATTAC	Association pour une Taxe sur les Transactions financières pour l'Aide aux Citoyens
BBA	British Bankers' Association
BIS	Bank of International Settlements
CEED	Center for Environmental Economic Development
CIDSE	International Cooperation for Development and Solidarity
DWS	Dollar–Wall Street (regime)
EC	European Commission
ECOSOC	Economic and Social Council (of the United Nations)
EEC	European Economic Community
EMS	European Monetary System
EMU	Economic and Monetary Union
ERM	Exchange Rate Mechanism
EU	European Union
FIRE	Finance, insurance and real estate (activities)
FSF	Financial Stability Forum
G-5	Group of Five
G-7	Group of Seven
G-8	Group of Eight
G-10	Group of Ten
G-77	The largest Third World Coalition in the UN, established 15 June 1964 by seventy-seven developing countries, signatories of the 'Joint Declaration of the Seventy-seven Countries' issued at the end of the first session of UNCTAD in Geneva
GDP	Gross Domestic Product
GIF	Global Intervention Fund
HSBC	Hong Kong and Shanghai Banking Corporation
IBF	New York International Banking Facilities
ICBL	International Campaign to Ban Landmines

IIF	Institute of International Finance
IMF	International Monetary Fund
IOSCO	International Organisation of Securities Commissions
ISDA	International Swaps and Derivatives Association
ITO	International Trade Organisation
LIBA	London Investment Banking Association
LTCM	Long-term Capital Management
MAI	Multilateral Agreement on Investments
MEP	Member of European Parliament
MNC	Multinational Corporation
MP	Member of Parliament
NATO	North Atlantic Treaty Organisation
NESC	(US) National Economic Security Council
NGO	Non-governmental organisation
NIGD	Network Institute for Global Democratisation
NIC	Newly Industrialising Country
NTM	New Transatlantic Market (agreement)
OECD	Organisation for Economic Cooperation and Development
OTC	Over the counter
TEU	Treaty of the European Union
TTO	Tobin Tax Organisation
TTZ	Tobin tax zone
UCITS	Undertakings for Collective Investments
UN	United Nations
UNCTAD	United Nations Conference of Trade and Development
UNDP	United Nations Development Programme
UNESCAP	United Nations Economic and Social Commission for Trade and Development for Asia and the Pacific
US$	United States dollars
VAT	Value Added Tax
WIDER	World Institute for Development Economics Research
WTO	World Trade Organisation

Preface: Is the Tobin Tax Feasible?

An article on the Tobin tax was published in the August 1999 issue of *Le Monde Diplomatique*. It was accurately reported that the manifesto of the then new Finnish government included a passage on the necessity of studying the possibility of introducing a Tobin tax-like measure in order to reduce the instability and volatility of international financial markets. I was identified as one of those responsible for this commitment and, as a result, was flooded with complimentary e-mail and letters encouraging me to pursue the cause.

As nice as it is to receive thanks and encouragement, I have to admit that I have been somewhat embarrassed by the response. Unfortunately, there is not too much substantial collateral for this effusive praise. The only action by the Finnish government so far on the subject has been the commissioning of an expert study by the Ministry of Finance. The study concluded that the Tobin tax is neither necessary nor workable. Given the neoliberal bias of the professors involved, this was not unexpected. So far, the government has not discussed the report or the issue in general.

Had the Ministry of Finance first read this book on how to implement the Tobin tax, written by Heikki Patomäki, they might have come to slightly different conclusions. The book is a ground-breaking work, the first of its kind. It is not content merely to state the case for the Tobin tax, but also strives to give concrete answers to the question of what could and should be done to implement the Tobin tax and how this could take place.

The proposal for a currency transaction tax (CTT) is now more generally known as the Tobin tax after its first proponent James Tobin, who first proposed such a tax almost thirty years ago. Even if nothing has been done to contribute to the implementation of such a tax – on the contrary, the liberalisation of capital markets and financial transfers has continued at an accelerated pace – the proposal remains valid and has gathered more support than ever before, particularly through the efforts of NGO networking.

Parliamentarians in many countries - not only in Europe but particularly in Canada – and in the European Parliament have embraced the proposal, but governments have been more circumspect. The most visible have been a number of NGOs, with ATTAC the most prominent, which have created an international network of activists committed to the Tobin tax proposal in particular, and to combating the negative effects of globalisation in general.

The Tobin tax is an almost deceptively simple idea: a tax levied on every currency exchange, set at a level low enough not to hinder any transactions needed to finance real trade in goods and services or long-term capital investment, but high enough to discourage the bulk of de-stabilising speculative money movements. Given the vast amount involved in daily currency transactions – around US$1,500 billion – a tax of just 0.5 per cent would, in theory, generate far more income than the total amount of official development aid from the industrialised countries to the less-developed countries. Thus the introduction of a Currency Transaction Tax could, at a stroke, solve all the problems of development financing.

Why has such a self-evidently wonderful idea not been put into practice? Could it be because it is, alas, too good to be true?

Usually the proposal is dismissed by referring either to the undesirability of intervening in international financial transactions, the technical difficulties and unworkability of such a tax, or to the lack of universal support for the idea, which makes it unenforceable, or to all of these.

For James Tobin and the success of the CTT, it is essential that the tax be applied universally by all the most important players in the global economy. Given the fact that the US administration has adopted an entirely negative attitude towards the proposal and that no signs of real enthusiasm for it are evident either in Japan or the Euoropean Union, it would appear that it is not realistic to proceed in the implementation of the proposal.

Heikki Patomäki attempts to circumvent this conclusion by suggesting that the tax be introduced by either the EU or a group of 'like-minded' countries acting as an advance guard. He envisages a new international organisation, to be called the Tobin Tax Organisation, which would administer the Tobin tax and decide on the use and distribution of the income it generates. The proposal sounds attractive, but is this really any more feasible, either technically or politically?.

Given the wide scope of the popular debate on the Tobin Tax, surprisingly little research has actually been done or published on the practicalities of it. To the best of my knowledge, no international financial institution or other international organisation has, in the recent past, produced any published study (as distinct from limited-circulation intra-organisation papers) on a Tobin tax-style international currency transaction tax. Patomäki's book is thus a valuable and welcome contribution to the debate.

The demand for a Tobin tax is concerned not only with stability in international financial markets. The Tobin tax has become a powerful symbol of efforts to find new and effective means to combat the negative consequences of globalisation and to regain democratic and social control over market forces running wild.

I very much share these concerns and I am in favour of the Tobin tax. At the same time, I do not want to see the Tobin tax end up as a historical curiosity, cultivated by a faithful group of followers such as the proponents of Henry George's Single Tax. Thus we should avoid transforming the demand for the tax into a mantra, the repetition of which stands as a measure of one's commitment to the General Good.

The Tobin tax should not be understood as a single issue. It is rather the tip of an iceberg consisting of a wide range of measures needed to make globalisation serve the general interest. And should it appear that the tax might, in any of the forms in which it has been put forward so far, prove to be technically unfeasible and/or politically unrealistic, we must not despair but define and propose other means that can be used to further the same aims of managing globalisation and diminishing the instability of international financial markets.

And if we have to conclude that it is not possible to bypass the Bretton Woods institutions (the IMF and the World Bank), we must reform them and their rules and policies and endeavour to establish more effective democratic control and regulation of international financial markets.

Patomäki does, in fact, address these issues also, because many of the examples he refers to, such as the unilateral measures to control capital movements, adopted by Chile and Malaysia and generally deemed to have been successful, are precisely the kind of surrogate measures that can be used in the absence of a Tobin tax.

I hope that this important book on a most important subject will be read by all those who want to see effective measures taken to counter the negative effects of globalisation in general and the instability of international financial markets in particular.

Erkki Tuomioja PhD,
Minister for Foreign Affairs

Introduction

This book project began after the Asian and Russian financial crises in early October 1998. In the numerous discussions on what must be done, the Tobin tax clearly emerged as the prime reform proposal. James Tobin first made the suggestion for a low-rate tax on financial transactions of currencies in 1972. A quarter of a century later, the proposal seemed well worth serious consideration.

Soon I realised that the Tobin tax is a more complex idea than I had originally thought.[1] And the more I have studied it in 1999 and 2000, the more it brought previously hidden aspects and layers of global realities to the fore. Many economic activities and political aspirations have been subordinated to the power of the increasingly global financial markets. The Tobin tax provides emancipatory potential that goes far beyond simply stabilising the foreign exchange markets or, for that matter, taxing transnational hot money.

The first chapter analyses the problem of financial instability, in particular focusing on the foreign exchange markets. These markets are characterised by daily and weekly volatility, steep longer-term fluctuations and sudden full-fledged crises. Since the collapse of the Bretton Woods system, volatility and fluctuations have increased. It also seems that out of the almost eighty currency crises which have taken place since the late 1970s, the most far-reaching ones have occurred since 1990. The Asian crisis, which spread to Russia and Brazil, in particular alarmed the world. Many of these crises have been connected to developments in bonds, equities and loans markets, themselves crisis-ridden.

Chapter 1 argues that at the heart of the problem lies the *growing power* of market movements, stemming from the process of financial multiplication. This process is the collective consequence of leverage building, mutual indebtedness and rising prices. The socio-economic consequences of crises are upsetting. A crisis is produced in the secondary markets, where foreign exchange contracts, stocks and bonds are being exchanged. Yet, the unexpected implosion of the values of assets, and/or the flight of funds, also have an effect on the primary markets of savings, loans and currencies. The primary markets, in turn, co-determine the conditions for many other economic activities. The total cumulative loss of output for a combined banking and currency crisis has been, on average, some 15 per cent (see Figure 1.4). The effects on the weakest sectors of the population include unemployment, marginalisation, poverty and illness. Given the current global financial system and the principles of governing it, those who suffer the most have typically had the least to do with producing the crisis.

Chapters 2 and 3 attempt to uncover less visible aspects and effects of the global financial markets. Chapter 2 provides a power analysis that focuses on private financial actors and their resources. Financial actors have direct transformative capacity both individually and collectively. The financial markets tend to allocate capital collectively on the basis of shared neoliberal frameworks of analysis of financial prospects. The heavyweights and market leaders can manipulate markets for their own benefit, even orchestrate attacks against the currencies of major states. Moreover, the individual and collective financial actors are not just market players; they have also created collective associations to pursue issues of common concern and interest. These associations claim to have privileged access to governments all over the world.

Despite the importance of these features, perhaps the most far-reaching conclusion of Chapter 2 is that when we look at wider developments more closely, there seem to be, in fact, a number of on-going processes that draw resources from the non-financial sphere to the financial markets. Financial multiplication would be impotent without the *continuous movement of further resources* into the system.

Chapter 3 looks at global power relations from a different angle. The re-emergent global financial markets have played a pivotal role in the relations between *territorially organised states*. Since the 1960s, the eurodollar markets in London have been the response of the British governments to the country's declining position and economic difficulties. The establishment of the eurodollar markets was also an attempt to reinstate the City of London as the world's financial centre. With the support of the US, it was a success. At the turn of the 1970s, the US decided to allow itself more freedom of action by renouncing the Bretton Woods system, and in the 1980s, it learnt to use the financial markets more systematically to reinforce its hegemony. Furthermore, the rise of offshore facilities was, mostly, initiated or encouraged by the UK and the US. Once established, global financial markets tend to undermine the basis of democracy and welfare states. They underpin the hegemony of neoliberal ideology, and stimulate a partial return to the nineteenth-century-style *laissez-faire* governance and, simultaneously, rapidly increasing transnational criminal activities and networks. They also contribute to growing global disparities.

Arguably, the power of financial markets distorts investments, subordinates firms to financial interests and draws increasingly more resources from consumption, investments and public spending to mere hedging and speculative searches for financial gains. The winners at this casino, in turn, receive excessive rewards, amounting to hundreds of billions of dollars, or more. These practices also tend to raise the real interest rates and force states to follow deflationary policies. Collectively, this seems to mean inefficiency and declining global demand, and may help to explain the gradually deepening stagnation of the world economy.

According to IMF's *World Economic Outlook* for October 1999, in the 1980s 'advanced economies' grew at the annual rate of 3.1 per cent, which was much less than in the previous decade. In the 1990s the growth rate has been only 2.4 per cent. Outside the OECD area, economic growth has occurred mainly in Asia, in particular in China and the Asian 'tigers'. Following the Asian crises, the growth rates of the Asian tigers have not yet recovered their previous levels, and the cumulative output loss has been considerable.[2] In the late 1990s, more than eighty countries have lower per capita incomes than a decade or more ago, and at least fifty-five countries had consistently declining per capita incomes.[3] The power of global finance seems to have contributed to these developments.

Chapter 4 makes a *normative* case for a low-rate tax on financial transactions involving currencies. The Tobin tax addresses the power of speculative financial markets and their socio-economic consequences. James Tobin's original case was based on the ideals of the autonomy of states and their economic stability. Although his general case is more valid today than ever, it fails to address wider issues of economic efficiency, justice, democracy and human emancipation. In a nutshell, instead of letting globalisation take us back to the nineteenth-century principles of economic governance, we should democratise globalisation and facilitate the setting up of more efficient and just practices.

Justice as fairness would dictate, as a bare minimum, that, if someone accepts the benefits of a practice, he should not refuse to do his part in maintaining it. The current system of 'individual profits, socialised risks' fails to meet even this minimalist criterion of justice. The Tobin tax is a way to make the participants pay their fair share in maintaining the global financial system. Further, justice as fairness would seem to imply some compensation for past, present and future injustices for those affected by the financial crises. The Tobin tax can be seen as a practical way of collecting resources for this compensation.

Moreover, a generalised commitment to enacting principles of justice in a world of disparate agents, many of them vulnerable to others' powers, must also be a commitment to transforming the powers of agents and the structure of institutions, so as to reduce powerlessness and vulnerability. Similarly, going beyond Tobin's argument for a somewhat increased autonomy for states in their economic policy, the generalised ideal of democracy seems to point towards enlargement of the real possibilities for self-determination. Like the argument for human emancipation, the comprehensive argument for democracy also suggests a more *democratic system of global governance* than the present one.

Chapter 5 discusses the technical and economic problems of realising the Tobin tax. These include the problems of tax evasion and the effectiveness of the tax in alleviating economic instability. Tax evasion is potentially a serious problem, and a wide variety of currency substitutes have to be covered. What is more, a systematic policy to deal with offshore tax havens has to be agreed upon, a policy that should be part of any project to tackle the problems created by global financial markets.

The fear of the technical failure of the Tobin tax seems to be greatly exaggerated. When the installation of the tax is seen as a step-by-step progression, and the idea of the tax is slightly modified, *not all* major financial centres have to be within the taxation system from the outset to make it practicable. Chapter 5 therefore goes on to suggest that the Tobin tax could be realised in two phases. In its first phase, the system would consist of a grouping of interested countries, preferably including the EMU countries. This grouping could establish an open agreement – any state can join at any time – and a supranational body orchestrating the tax and collecting the revenues. It should also take measures to prevent actors from relocating their financial activities, such as a high tax on lending to outside actors. In the second phase, which should be carried out when all major financial centres and most other countries have joined the first phase, a universal and uniform Tobin tax at a higher rate would be applied, with an increased surcharge triggered by exceptional fluctuations. This arrangement would solve the tax evasion problem. Following the amendments of Spahn (two-tier system) and Woodward (global fund to support currencies), it should also be more sound, efficient and just than Tobin's original proposal.

The problem of the Tobin tax has always seemed to be the lack of realistic political possibilities. Tobin and his followers have assumed that 'universal' consent would have to precede workability. Since major states and powerful organisations are opposing the idea, this appears unrealistic. It is possible that a Big Crash will come and change the global political landscape, but the political consequences of that would be unpredictable, possibly dangerous. *Democratising Globalisation* makes an argument for building a better system before (in the absence of) a major global crisis.

Instead of speculating on universal consent, *Democratising Globalisation* builds more realistically on the possibilities opened up by the two-phase approach. Any significant grouping of countries can proceed quickly, despite the resistance of some of the major centres. Since this model empowers actors to work for the tax even without the support of the US, the UK, the International Monetary Fund (IMF) or any given actor deciding to oppose the idea, it is emancipatory in its implications.

Thus far, only Canada has been actively promoting the Tobin tax. This indicates that even outside the heartland of the global financial system, it is likely to take intense political struggles and the input of a wide global social movement before countries will start joining the regime. But a worldwide campaign for the Tobin tax has already emerged, and things *can* change. The anti-landmines coalition offers an example of how momentum can build without getting everyone on board from the beginning. Indeed, it is very important to underline that the two-phase model does not compromise the aim of a universal system of taxation: it is devised in such a manner that it will build up pressure for the outsiders to join.

Another ethico-political problem concerns the outcome of the process of establishing the tax regime. Very little serious consideration has been given to this matter. A global tax regime with sanctions and surveillance systems and potential for huge revenues raises the whole issue of political theory in the global context: what are the principles of legitimation of collective organisations? Following the normative argument for the Tobin tax, it is argued that we should democratise global governance and facilitate the setting up of more efficient and just practices.

Tobin and many of his followers have assumed that the task of orchestrating the tax should be given to the IMF. For Tobin, in the 1970s, there were tactical reasons for this assumption; he thought that a universal tax could be imposed via the IMF. For the representatives of the Washington consensus – should they come to consider the implementation of the proposal seriously – this is likely to be the preferred solution both for ideological and power-political reasons. However, I make an argument for *not* giving the IMF this role, and for *not* subordinating the proposed Tobin Tax Organisation (TTO) to the Bretton Woods institutions.

Instead, I suggest that, in the first phase of establishing the Tobin tax regime, a new supranational body must be founded for orchestrating the tax. I have here called it the Tobin Tax Organisation. It is a two-phase model that allows the interested states to take the initiative in devising the TTO without the consent of all the economic 'great powers'. The TTO should also be independent of any existing organisational structure. Given that it will also have a role in collecting and allocating the revenues, the question is: how can we guarantee a fair democratic representation in its

of other exchange controls and regulations over the stock market (e.g. against short-selling and insider trading).

In February 1999, however, 'in view of increasing concerns raised by foreign investors over the twelve-month holding period requirement' as well as to facilitate portfolio investment from abroad, the Malaysian government revised the exchange controls. Consequently, the twelve-month holding period requirement was replaced by a graduated exit tax (levy on the repatriation of portfolio capital).[32] Since the imposition of the controls, the exchange rate of the ringgit has remained fixed to the US dollar. Moreover, almost all the economic indicators improved: exports, reserves and domestic demand are up and both inflation and interest rates are down. The 6.7 per cent decline in GDP in 1998 was turned into positive growth again.[33]

Box 1 Paradoxes of Malaysia

The policies of Prime Minister Mahathir of Malaysia seem to be paradoxical in many ways. His defence of 'Asian values' appears to be in conflict with human rights and liberal-democratic aspirations in Malaysia, yet in the West it is often the democratic Left that seems to be more empathic towards his position of cultural relativism and relatively independent, state-based economic policies. The financial crisis of 1997–98 occurred simultaneously with fierce power struggles and campaigns in semi-democratic elections in Malaysia. In September 1997, in the World Bank meeting in Hong Kong, he 'compared today's global capital markets to "a jungle of ferocious beasts", and implied that they were directed by a Jewish cabal' (T. Friedman 1999: 93).

Mahathir's strong attacks against the external speculators and his resort to re-regulatory measures have, in turn, provoked a fervent reaction from the neoliberal and liberal-democratic circles of the West against him. He has been accused of a contradictory anti-globalisation rhetoric and *de facto* reliance on the benefits of globalisation (ibid.). Malaysia had chosen an export-oriented development strategy based on attempts to attract foreign capital, also by means of establishing export-processing zones and, even, an offshore financial centre. However, Malaysia has always set strict conditions to foreign investors. Also the Labuan offshore centre, which was inaugurated in 1990, has been carefully regulated and does not, for instance, allow money launderers in. Nevertheless, it also represents a strategic move in the competitive game of regulatory laxity. (See Abbott 1999.)

As the insistence of Malaysia's prime minister that he will lift the capital controls only when there is a new global financial architecture indicates, the call for *international reforms* became particularly strong after the series of crises that started from Asia in 1997. This call has led, in the practices of global governance, to a slight theoretical transition from the orthodoxy towards a Polanyi.[34] Or, more precisely, the multilateral organisations and Western leaders have started to emphasise the importance of constructing and regulating the markets in the right way, as defined by them.

In his seminal book *The Great Transformation*, Polanyi criticised the liberalist faith in the naturalness of self-regulating markets and spontaneous progress. The role of the modern European state was decisive in the eighteenth- and nineteenth-century socio-historical construction of the capitalist *laissez-faire* market economy. This 'great transformation' brought about the conditions for a self-regulating market economy: 'The gearing of markets into a self-regulating system of tremendous power was not the result of any inherent tendency of markets towards excrescence, but rather the highly artificial stimulants administered to the body social [...]. Only in the institutional setting of market economy are market laws relevant.'[35]

In the regime centred on the Bank for International Settlements (BIS), the central bankers have met since the mid-1970s to construct a set of norms, rules and regulations and decision-making procedures for preventing and handling financial crises. In response to the Latin American debt crisis of the early 1980s, which shook the US banks in particular, the Basle Committee, under the auspices of the BIS, eventually agreed in the late 1980s on uniform rules on banking, including the risk-adjusted capital/asset ratio of 8 per cent. The Basle Accord applies to G-10 countries (G-7 plus Sweden, Belgium, Holland, Luxembourg and Switzerland).

Similarly, the attempts of the late 1990s to relieve the tendency for currency and financial crises presuppose that the conditions for properly self-regulating markets have to be artificially created. It does not suffice simply to deregulate and liberalise; new mentalities, administrative bodies and regulations have to be produced as well. In line with the orthodoxy, however, the idea is that only such policies and regulations which help to ensure the self-regulation of the market are in order.

The IMF, in collaboration with the World Bank, has in the late 1990s been championing what it calls 'second-generation reforms' in its member countries, enacted through its surveillance, technical assistance and financing. These include a demand for more transparency in economic policies (the investors must know what the states are doing); and for the establishment of a simple and transparent regulatory environment and a professional and independent judicial system that will uphold the rule of law, including property rights (this is intended to facilitate and simplify financial trans-actions).[36]

The idea seems to be that by giving investors better and more accurate information about the economic conditions of states and by establishing simple, well-functioning and unchanging rules of the game, the laws of the market will finally start to work as they should (efficiently and optimally, guaranteeing stability). However, unlike the regulations introduced by Chile and Malaysia, these rules are meant, first and foremost, to guide states rather than investors and traders in the forex and stock markets.

Will the 'second-generation' reforms help to reduce fluctuations in the forex markets? Apart from the major problem that the emphasis is on regulating states, not the market actors, the answer depends on how we explain the recurrence of financial crisis.

Explaining the Recurring Financial Crises

One of the first crises hit the Southern Cone of Latin America in the early 1980s. Another well-known crisis is that of the Black Monday of October 1987, when the Wall Street stock exchange went down for a while. Europe was struggling with a series of crises in the early 1990s (both the EMS and the Nordic countries). Soon it was the turn of Mexico in 1994–95. The most recent series of well-known crises started in Asia in 1997, spread to Russia in August 1998, and finally to Brazil in late 1998, with repercussions elsewhere in Latin America. Japan has been delving deeper and deeper into a deflationary spiral, also because of its banking crisis. And these are only examples of some seventy banking crises and ninety currency crises since the 1970s. The next major crisis may well occur again in the US, given that a collapse of its stock markets is already long overdue.

In the North, including Japan, these episodes have often involved either banking or currency crises (although there have been cases of both occurring simultaneously); but in the South they have typically been a combination of the two. They have been associated with borrowed funds based on financial multiplication of (typically short-term) investments in assets and real estate. This multiplication can be created within a national banking and investments funds system itself, and/or can be based on the leverage of global financial markets, assuming the form of short-term capital inflows. These developments can also be interrelated. Thus, the transformations and increased competition of commercial banking in the major industrial countries has created, in the context of financial liberal-isation, much of the impetus for the increased capital inflows in the South.[37]

The value of paper or electronic money and assets is based on *trust*.[38] At the heart of all financial crises is the sudden disappearance of sufficient trust or confidence on a bundle of assets (including currency, bonds, equities, etc.). Somebody takes a lead and starts to sell in large quantities, others follow. Suddenly, the previously shared – and often taken-for-granted – trust disappears and panic hits those who still hold these assets, particularly so if they have them in large quantities and are existentially dependent on their values. Disappearance of trust is often contagious, particularly if reinforced by complex investment strategies, which may make values of seemingly separate assets strictly interdependent. Everything that is associated, for one reason or another, with a bundle of assets suddenly becomes quite suspicious and uncertain as well. And so it goes on until some kind of a bottom is reached or the authorities start to do something decisive (if they can).

The disappearance of trust or confidence is at the heart of the problem. Suppose that it was X that collapsed this time. We have two possible, different *ex post actu* (after the event) explanations:

(1) Blame the victim.[39] Disappearance of trust or confidence in X was due to the problems with the economic fundamentals of X. Had X lived up to the criteria of correct fundamentals, there would have been no disappearance of trust and confidence.

(2) Blame the system.[40] In a system constructed like the powerful global financial markets, confidence in X, Y, Z etc. is bound to disappear every now and then, perhaps with an increased frequency; the constellation of more or less arbitrary factors, including the highly speculative decisions of many investors, determined that it was X's turn this time.

There are thus two possible ways of approaching the problem of explaining these crises. In fact, a number of syntheses are possible as well.

Blaming the victim The first explanation obviously assumes that the investors are rational in the very strong sense that they react correctly and responsibly to the changes in *objective* economic conditions and developments. This assumption is perhaps the essential element of orthodox economics.

The 'blame the victim' explanation raises a number of questions. First, if the explanation is always constructed *ex post actu*, and if the perception of the 'real problems' and the reactions to them are not separable, this explanation becomes conceptually tautological. Had there been no collapse of X, would there still have been a fundamental problem with X? The argument becomes, indeed, easily circular (cf. Figure 1.3 above). Quite correctly, Krugman warns about the seduction of 'twenty-twenty hindsight'. For example, 'now that we know that Japan and Korea have experienced a devastating economic setback, we start to imagine that we always knew that they had feet of clay'.[41]

As always, orthodox theory dictates that any deviation of practices from the ideals it has set is a problem, not for the theory but for the practices. At some point, this fundamentalist belief should be allowed to be problematised, too. Tautological *ex post* determinism imposed upon episodes that have already taken place does not do.

Second, in the 'blame the victim' explanation, there is a fundamental ontological problem: there is no explication of the *mechanisms* that would mediate between the supposed economic 'fundamentals', however specified, and the concrete reactions of the actors in the financial markets. More realistically, we should ask how the contextual realities of dealers, bankers and fund managers are in fact constructed.

Constitution of actors First, we should have an understanding of the actors. Most importantly, the financial actors and their powers are based on a complicated *process of multiplication* of loans, assets and transactions. Many investors are investing for very small margins. Often they have obtained loans on their assets in order to be able to invest more to yield bigger revenues from the small margins. This is called *leverage* in the jargon of financial markets. In the US, the financial sector debt relative to GDP had risen from the negligible 2–3 per cent in the early 1950s to 60 per cent by the mid-1990s. Presumably, the development has been similar elsewhere in the OECD area.[42] The borrowed funds have been invested, in turn, in other assets, possibly in shares in other investment funds such as investment banks (many of them brands of established commercial banks), mutual funds or hedge funds. Often these promise much higher rates of return than any companies producing non-financial goods or services. These higher rates of return are, in turn, a consequence of the financial multiplication process.

A large part of the accumulated debt remains serviceable only as long as there is no major downturn in any of the crucial areas of the financial markets. Many assets remain valuable only as long as other, cross-invested assets remain valuable. That is, the same actors can be, as debtors or investors, dependent on the yields of other actors in the financial markets. Like the value of money itself, the whole financial system is based on *trust* (confidence) that the prices of most assets will rise or at least remain relatively stable; also, in the future, that the values do not disappear. The quite rational fear of sudden major fluctuations or collapses, once materialised, can be existential for small and big investors alike, and consequently lead to a chain-reaction, which, if it is a far-reaching one, constitutes a crisis.[43]

So the actors are themselves products of the rules, options and inter-dependencies of the financial markets and the consequent process of financial multiplication. But more concretely, who are the actors in the global forex, bond and equities markets? (For a more systematic analysis of the actors and their resources, see Chapter 2.) Markets of both currency exchanges and OTC derivatives are regulated by states, although the OTC derivatives market is less standardised and thus more lax in its rules. In the context of most countries, including at least some offshore centres,[44] only exchange brokers and the dealers of the banks are authorised to make wholesale forex deals, and they have to keep accounts on their transactions and positions. They also have to report all their activities to the central bank and/or to the Bank of International Settlements. They can implement the orders of their customers or make transactions on their own initiative.

In fact, most forex transactions are short-term dealer-to-dealer trans-actions made in major international currencies and geographically located in major financial centres. Bahrain, Singapore, Luxembourg, the United Kingdom and Hong Kong have clearly specialized in global foreign exchange trading. In contrast, in markets where domestic currency business accounts for around 70 per cent or more of turnover, this may be due partly to the use of domestic currency as a vehicle (United States, Germany, Japan) and partly to the greater prominence of transactions driven by cross-border trade and financial flows rather than cross-currency arbitrage and hedging (Italy, South Africa, Canada, Portugal, Spain).[45]

Almost $1,000 billion is processed daily as dealer-to-dealer transactions, a large part of it for very small and very short-term margins. Of the outright forwards, however, more than half take place between a dealer and a customer; these 'customers' play a role also in other OTC derivatives markets.[46] The customers – such as multinational corporations or invest-ment funds, which are not authorised to make deals themselves – may, however, be deeply involved in financial activities, and in the markets on outright forwards, futures, options and swaps the line between hedging and speculation is a thin one. Many corporations have their own financial offices and, despite their claims to the contrary, seem not only to engage in costly hedging operations but also to take risks and speculate with currency fluctuations, anticipated devaluations and changes in interest rates.[47] Mostly, they have to operate through banks.

Apart from dealers spreading risks and speculating with currencies among themselves, a large part of the forex markets transactions stem from movements originating in the decisions of institutional investors such as investment banks, mutual funds or hedge funds. The biggest of them belong to Switzerland, the US, Japan and the UK. In 1997, the world's top ten fund managers controlled $4,220 billion worth of assets.[48] Sometimes the currency transaction is only an intermediate process, a step between, say, liquidating a US Treasury bond and buying shares of Matsushita in its place. However, banks, mutual funds, hedge funds and other institutional investors have increasingly been treating forex as an asset class in itself, separate from any underlying asset or bond.[49] They seem to have become prominent players also in the forex derivatives markets.[50] It is also the case that, more and more often, investments are also complex hybrids, with a forex transaction as an element of the overall cross-border investment deal.

The flows and assets of global financial markets are themselves products of the multiplication process. In 1999, world GDP was about $30,000 billion. That is, currency dealers exchange among themselves an amount equivalent to the world GDP in fewer than thirty trading days. Largely this is not real, in the sense that these funds could be materialised in any more concrete form, that is, in terms of turning them into money that can be translated into production of goods and services or their consumption. Or, in more technical terms, these assets are mostly liquid for any given (insignificant) participant in almost any given time, but not for a large number of them simultaneously.[51]

The same assets may make many across-the-borders round-trips a day, in some cases with practically no risk and minimal margins (these flows can be considered as insignificant in their consequences). Many of them can be and are used as underlying assets for derivatives, and derivatives of derivatives, all with different maturities, etc. And they can be, and are, used also as collateral for loans, which in turn can be invested in assets. Yet, these figures are indicative of the magnitude and power of these flows.

It is also noteworthy that the ten top fund managers control assets equivalent to 13 per cent of the world GDP. This is approximately the combined GDP of France, Germany and the UK, or the combined GDP of the world's eighty poorest countries, including China, India, Indonesia, Nigeria and Russia, the five countries which together account for almost half of the world population.

Modelling the system The being, actions and contexts of the financial actors are constituted (i) by the interdependent resources they command; (ii) by the trust in the persistence of the value of assets and liabilities; (iii) by the rules and regulations of the markets within which they act; and (iv) by the reflective rules of rationality that guide their anticipations, strategic calculations and actions. In general, it can be claimed that the more liquid the assets and the shorter the time horizon, the less the decisions have to do with the economy of production, consumption, trade and state budgets, and more with the internal dynamics of the financial markets themselves.

Of course, if we, again tautologically, *assume* that the prices of these assets *must* correspond to developments in economic 'fundamentals', however specified, there can be no problem of mediation or detachment. Yet,

---

Box 2 Keynes's 'beauty contest'

J. M. Keynes himself was an active participant in the speculative game of stock exchange in the 1920s (when he lost his fortune) and the 1930s (when he rebuilt it). In his analysis of financial markets, he was not content with abstract and unrealistic assumptions about the nature, rationality and knowledge of financial actors. Rather, he started with an understanding of the practices of financial markets as he had experienced them. As a participant in these markets, what is the rational way to make money? In his *The General Theory of Employment, Interest and Money* (1961/1936), Keynes says there are in fact two ways: *enterprise* and *speculation*. Enterprise is 'the activity of forecasting the prospective yields of assets over their whole life'; whereas speculation is 'the activity of forecasting the psychology of the market'. He argues that 'as the organisation of investment markets improves, the risk of the predominance of speculation does increase' (p. 158).

Implicitly on the basis of his own experiences from the 1920s and the 1930s, he claims that in 'New York the influence of speculation is enormous'. This is simply because liquid investments – 'hoarding or lending money' – often pay better, at least in the short-run, than real long-term investments in production. He also claims that this is 'an inevitable result of an investment market organised' in a manner making investments liquid (p. 155).

He likens the behaviour of investors in these kinds of markets to 'newspaper competitions in which the competitors have to pick out the six prettiest faces from a hundred photographs, the prize being awarded to the competitor whose choice most nearly corresponds to the average preferences of the competitors as a whole'. However, in this strategic game, everybody knows that everybody else is looking at the problem from the same point of view. 'It is not the case of choosing those which, to the best of one's judgement, are really the prettiest, nor even those which average opinion genuinely thinks the prettiest. We have reached the third degree where we devote our intelligences to anticipating what the average opinion expects the average opinion to be. And there are some, I believe, who practise the fourth, fifth and higher degrees' (p. 156).

contra orthodoxy, we should study the *mechanisms* that produce the outcomes. Even in what Keynes calls 'enterprise activities' – dealing with financing productive, non-financial investments – in the financial markets, there must be a mechanism of mediation between the material economy of goods and services and the financial markets' decision-making. This entails the possibility of a relative detachment, even without the prevalence of speculation. As far as speculation is concerned (covering in fact both the hedging against risks and gambling on risks), Keynes's analogy to a beauty contest (see Box 2), in which each player tries to guess or anticipate the preferences of the others, knowing that everybody is doing the same thing, helps to understand and explain why financial activities are partially detached from the reality of production and exchange of goods and services.

The few available accounts of the global financial market *practices* of the turn of the century indicate at least the following points:[52]

- Normally, there is an indirect link to the material economy of work, production, consumption, trade and state budgets through the assessments of the IMF or the rating agencies such as Standard & Poor's Ratings Service and Moody's Investors Service.[53] Also, the reports and actions of the IMF and BIS play a role in constituting actions. These private or public expert systems are highly dependent upon mathematical models, available statistical data, and computer systems – but they also rely on news and other qualitative information. With the exception of a broad outline of the development of a few variables under 'normal' circumstances, *the expert systems cannot predict* any more than any economic theory can; typically these models have been built on unrealistic orthodox assumptions.[54] As Keynes has already made clear, 'human decisions affecting the future, whether personal or political or economic, cannot depend on strict mathematical expectation, since the basis for such expectation does not exist'.[55]

- Decisions must be based on anticipation of the (immediate) future in the context of high uncertainty, and they have to acquire information from anywhere they can. For dealers and investors with short-term horizons, whatever happens to the largely fictitious prices of assets for whatever reasons is in fact quite real, and they have to act consequently. Fortunes may come and go with these fluctuations. The more prevalent the perception that these fluctuations have only little to do with non-financial activities and processes, the less there is reason to care about the assessments of the non-financial developments.[56] The public assessments of rating agencies etc. are thus not sufficient (and sometimes not even considered relevant or read). For traders and investors, shared moods about the overall situation; partially shared, partially private analyses of uncertain political situations; rumours about economic and political developments and other investors' decisions; as well as assessments about the possibility of speculative attacks and self-fulfilling prophecies; are all very real, with potentially far-reaching consequences.

• Therefore, what matters for financial decision-making on assets that appear liquid is – given a sufficiently deepened and extended process of financial multiplication and, also, laxity of regulations – anticipation of the moves of other players *within* the financial markets. In most contexts, the concerns of exporters, importers and those making direct foreign investments, or, more generally, the prospects of the firms producing goods and services, whose shares are sold in stock exchanges, are quite secondary. In some segments of the financial activities, they may not enter the decision-making process at all.

• However, it is often better to be a step ahead of the others – although not too much, for then you would lose as well. The more professional macro hedge funds, for instance, may base their strategies on macro-economic models, which try to anticipate devaluations or drastic changes in interest rates. If depreciation of a currency is expected, they may, for instance, sell that currency forward or buy a put option. Anticipation of changes – particularly if many others follow the market leaders' actions – may in fact contribute to bringing about those changes; this is the phenomenon of self-fulfilling prophecies. However, whatever happens at least partially of one's own accord, is, in many situations, potentially profitable, certainly more profitable than simply reacting, after others, to episodes and developments that have already taken place. For the latecomers, prices have changed already, occasionally with dramatic consequences.

• The stories actors tell about the market situation – possibly partially based on sophisticated models of market developments – and their choices constitute the strategic game they are playing (within the rules and regulations of the market). This strategic game is typically highly reflective, partially communicative and often also self-referential. Yet, however sophisticated and leveraged the markets, these stories continue to make – even if only vague and ambiguous – references to the non-financial world (to the economic prospects of X; changes in economic policies of X, etc.). Thus an external process, whether a swindle uncovered, an unexpected political desicion or a sudden turn in economic development, may trigger a downward process. At a certain point, the game may turn out to resemble a Prisoner's Dilemma game.[57] If the confidence on the prospects of X is gone, the individually rational choice of 'sell as quickly as you can' amounts to a collectively catastrophic outcome of a collapse, although collectively most actors would be better off by not selling for the time being. For any individual actor the worst outcome is to co-operate now while (most) others defect. By not selling as quickly as they can, they would be easily left with nothing. Hence the occasional bursts of panics.

For a country or a group of countries to get into trouble, it is in principle enough that a minuscule part of the global flows and funds is diverted from its currencies, bonds and assets, typically after an undue expansion. What exactly will be the geographical space and context in which, at least in retrospect, there has occurred an undue and untenable process of financial multiplication? It is part of the nature of these crises that the bubbles are difficult to identify beforehand – given the ubiquity of financial multiplication – and their bursts are unpredictable in any precise, scientific sense of the term. A credible assessment of a 'bubble' would in itself be a likely cause of a run away from those assets/markets. In a sense, the global financial markets as a whole are a big bubble, and it is possible also that the global financial system as a whole may one day collapse: 'A local monetary system may collapse completely, as happened in Germany in the 1920s; in some circumstances which we might not envisage at all, this might perhaps happen to the global monetary order, with disastrous consequences for billions of people.'[58]

In open systems, precise predictions are in principle always impossible (for methodological details, see Appendix 1). Anticipations of futures are possible, but they are also very much part of the game in financial markets. Also, learning takes place, perhaps in cycles of myopic optimism, associated with excessive leverage-building and indebtedness, until a bad financial crisis scares players into prudence – for a while.[59] National, regional and global authorities do their best to assure the trust and confidence of investors. Typically, it is very hard to do this without creating 'a game of heads I win, tails the taxpayer loses'.[60] This game will encourage 'morally hazardous' lending and investments and then counter-productively stimu-lates undue expansions. From the perspective of political authorities, this may be a Catch-22 situation. If you do not back the financial actors up, crises are more likely and also likely to be more severe. If you back them up, you are encouraging them to take excessive risks, thereby creating conditions for crises (besides paying for the gambling of these financial actors).

In addition, there are particular actors – rating agencies, investment consultants etc. – who make their revenues by assessing the prospects of countries, markets and assets. If believed by a sufficient number of actors, any prophecy about the doom of a given market can trigger exactly what it predicts and become self-fulfilling. These prophecies are believed more easily if the actions of the market leaders are decisive enough, and if other processual elements of the overall context appear sufficiently – given the *shared conceptual framework* of explaining economic developments – to support the interpretation on which the prophecy is based.

Contingency of agents, actions and structures Quite obviously, this argument seems to be in line with the 'blame the system' explanation. Yet, the systemic explanation is also somewhat problematic. It is, first of all, too deterministic. With a Polanyin insight, it is possible to argue that rules and institutional settings constitute the system. Thus by reconstructing these rules and settings, it is indeed possible to eliminate some of the obvious possibilities for the emergence of financial bubbles and crises, and thereby make them less likely (in the absence of counter-tendencies, that, again, would make them more likely).

Although Europe, North America and Japan have experienced crises as well, many crises in different geographical spaces and contexts have thus far occurred soon after liberalisation and deregulation of the financial markets. These experiences have led to learning and also partial re-regulation of the markets. It seems that it is particularly crucial to regulate the *process of financial multiplication*. In particular, it is essential to control the level and quality of risks, indebtedness (leverage), and the chains of interdependencies between actors. Moreover, all the options of selling something that one does not have or manipulating and orchestrating fluctuations for one's own benefit must be closed as well, to the extent possible.

The less one wants to problematise and/or study concretely the elements of a given context, the more in line with theoretical expectations these factors may appear (at least *ex post actu*). It is, on the one hand, highly plausible to interpret the Asian crisis as a mere product of the global financial system, because almost all the 'usual macroeconomic suspects' seem to have been absent. All the main East Asian economies displayed in 1994–96 low inflation, fiscal surpluses or balances, limited public debt, high savings and investment rates, and substantial foreign exchange reserves, with no signs of significant deterioration before the crisis. The only worrying sign was the mounting trade deficit, mostly ignored by analysts. Just before the crisis, both the IMF and the World Bank praised these countries for 'sound macroeconomic fundamentals'.[61] Despite the strength of 'Asian tigers', somehow the global financial system seems to have produced the crisis.

Yet, there are always actors and their practices and choices involved. The causal responsibility may be located in different ways. The Asian financial crisis may also be presented as a crisis of the Asian developmental model. Opacity of information, over-investment and loan-funded

---

Box 3 LTCM and 'crony capitalism'

As unregulated speculative vehicles for 'high net-worth individuals' and institutional investors, hedge funds are free to hold whatever financial instruments they wish and to pursue whatever investment or trading strategies they choose. LTCM (Long-term Capital Management) is an investment partnership started in 1994. It was very successful, having annual returns in excess of 40 per cent in 1995 and 1996, although somewhat less in 1997. Aided by the reputations of well-known economists (including two Nobel prize-winners) and traders, it was able to raise its leverage up to forty times its original funds, or more. Relying on insights generated by sophisticated mathematical models, and by building complex investment strategies, LTCM made bets on the changes in the relative prices of bonds in the US and abroad due to changes in the risk premia. (See Edwards 1999.)

The announcement of devaluation and a debt moratorium by the Russian government on 17 August 1998 triggered a massive flight to safer assets. Top economists and sophisticated models notwithstanding, this surprised LTCM. Very high leverage and large open positions of US$200 billion produced losses that the fund could not sustain. In two weeks, LTCM had to send a letter to its investors revealing that it had lost 52 per cent of its value. It had lost its original funds and emerged suddenly as a systematic risk to a number of financial actors.

The Federal Reserve Bank of New York orchestrated a private rescue operation by fourteen banks and other financial firms. LTCM was recapitalised by a total amount of US$3.5 billion. Soon this led to a reversal of accusations of 'crony capitalism'. World Bank chief economist Joseph Stiglitz stated: 'While South Korea, Thailand and Indonesia were heavily criticized for acquiring mountains of debt, the magnitude of debt at LTCM was unbelievable' (AFP News, 1998). Martin Khor (1998) went even further: 'This episode brings to light Western banks' reckless lending practices and the substantial use of leverage by these funds giving them considerable power to move financial markets. The bailout of LTCM has, in turn, left US financial authorities open to accusations of practising the very "crony capitalism" they have often attributed to the afflicted Asian countries in crisis.' Indeed, the LTCM bailout was a matter of a small circle of friends and high officials of banks who had also invested their personal money in the LTCM.

investments in non-productive assets, real estate, etc., may look as if they stemmed from the Asian model leaning towards 'crony capitalism'. Indeed, the rationale of the (mostly speculative) finance companies that boomed before the crises in Thailand and elsewhere seem to have been based on political connections.[62] On the other hand, the money to finance these companies was pumped in from abroad (see also Box 3). Consequently, it has been claimed that the bubble was in large part produced by Western and Japanese banks operating in South-East Asia, partially outside the normal regulations of the Basle Agreement. Before the crisis that started in summer 1997, there was a rise in short-term lending (up to and including one-year maturity) to Asians and East Europeans. The banks were active in acquiring 'non-traditional' assets such as in higher-yielding local money markets and other debt securities. There was also an increase in lending to the private non-bank borrowers, the finance companies and the like, with this share rising to 45 per cent at the end of June 1997. Increased competition and relatively low interest rates had driven the Western banks to search for new, profitable opportunities. Already before the beginning of the crisis, the Bank for International Settlement had drawn attention to the way funds were being lent to 'emerging' economy borrowers, with little or no premiums, and had raised questions about this.[63]

Any crisis, including the Asian one, occurs at a highly complex intersection of different processes. This makes different theoretical interpretations possible. It is telling that economists looking for regularities in closed systems have in fact followed the real world historical developments. First they developed the so-called first-generation explanations of financial crises on the basis of the Latin American experiences in the early 1980s ('crises are due to irresponsible macroeconomic policies').[64] After the European experiences of the early 1990s, they constructed the second-generation theories ('a speculative attack on a currency can develop either as a result of a predicted future deterioration in fundamentals, or purely through self-fulfilling prophecy').[65] In the later 1990s, after having found these to be inadequate to explain the Asian, Russian and Brazilian crises, they are in the process of devising more complicated explanations combining different elements of earlier models with the peculiarities of the Asian crisis.[66]

An attempt to tackle real world complexities is certainly an improvement. However, these economists would do even better by acknowledging that a constellation of processes and highly reflective and often overtly self-referential reactions to them, leading to a particular financial crisis, is unpredictable, although not unexplainable. This despite the possibility of identifying certain characteristic signs of local and perhaps also global developments towards crises, such as rapid increase in short-term indebtedness. As explicated above in the conceptual model of the functioning of the global financial system, what is crucial – besides the quality of the financial multiplication process – is the way economic and political developments are *interpreted* by different actors in highly interdependent strategic contexts of financial markets, and how these interpretations are acted upon. In principle, any development can emerge as a trigger for a series of downward processes. The emergence of a trigger becomes easier the more cross-invested and leveraged the financial markets, and the more weight a handful of market leaders have assumed.

Because the systems are open and there are always many actors playing a role, it is true for any narrow explanation that the processes leading to a financial crisis can always be equally well understood in terms of a competing theoretical framework. This is not necessarily irrational. It is a consequence of the openness of systems and contextuality of action that many things could have been otherwise in any given episode. Any of these elements can then be taken up as *the* explanation; the rest of the context is, then, either reified as exogenous 'facts' or misrepresented. The attempt to stick to one simple explanation only is not always totally wrong, just short-sighted and narrow-minded. From a more holistic perspective, however, *cause* is an insufficient but necessary part of a *complex* which is itself unnecessary but sufficient for the *production* of a result, i.e. the INUS-condition.[67] That is, there are always many elements taking part in producing the outcome; and many of these elements could, in any given context, have been otherwise.

Take again the Asian crisis. From a novel theoretical perspective, it may turn out, against the 'blame the victim', 'blame the financial actors' and 'blame the system' explanations, that the crucial factor was, after all, the transformative capacity of the Asian states. The states that faced the crisis had either failed to develop or, in many cases, renounced their industrial planning capabilities and, in particular, controls over financial markets (in fact, they also did this in response to the pressures coming from the Washington consensus). Had they *not* failed to develop or maintain these crucial transformative capacities, the path of economic development in the second-generation NICs would have been different and they should have been able to avoid the crisis.[68] It is noteworthy that Taiwan and China did not liberalise, kept capital controls and avoided the crisis (although Taiwan's currency, too, depreciated during the crisis).

Actors, including states, can act otherwise and systems can be reformed. Yet, despite its limitations, *the systemic explanation of financial crises is strong* in a sense that it reveals something essential about the power and functioning of global financial markets. The growth of the global financial markets and their power is based on the financial multiplication process, which tends to grow mostly with indirect and typically rather vague and ambiguous connections to the world of economic developments in production, exchange, distribution and consumption. The global financial markets should be seen as a *system of social relations* that creates particular resources, facilitates certain kinds of actors and actions and makes possible certain kinds of interdependent episodes. As it had developed by the mid-1990s, the characteristic functioning of the system based on financial multiplication was a *necessary* – although not in itself sufficient – *part* of a complex, that was *sufficient* but not necessary for the production of the Asian crisis. In other words, it was a crucial cause of the crisis.

The Socio-economic Consequences of Financial Crises

After a sudden turn or a crisis, the recovery or stabilisation may also appear as relatively quick. Return to the previous values – or to an approximation of them, or to new relatively 'stable' values – of exchange rates or bonds and equities have been in some cases only a matter of a few months, although sometimes it takes years. Obviously, the depth and length of crisis also depends on the relative capabilities and actions of the authorities; in the 1990s on the increasingly sizeable mobilisation of financial resources by the OECD countries, the IMF, the World Bank and regional organisations.

However, even in the case of apparently quick recovery or stabilisation, financial crises tend to have far-reaching socio-economic consequences. In the process of the financial reorganisation of an economy, many activities and the life prospects of millions of people are seriously affected, in many cases for a long time or permanently. The crisis has been produced in the *secondary markets* in which stocks, bonds, forex contracts, etc., are being exchanged. Yet, the unexpected reversal of financial multiplication – the implosion of the values of assets, and/or the flight of funds – also has an effect on the *primary markets* of savings, loans and forex. The primary markets, in turn, co-determine the conditions for many other economic activities. The recovery of the economy as a whole takes usually between one and a half and six years. The links are always dependent on the institutional arrangements of the countries and regions concerned. The following list should thus be read merely as indicative of the mechanisms that we should be looking for:

• Interest rate: higher interest rates mean that debts become (much) more expensive; in some cases, after a crisis, the interest rate has been raised to 40 per cent or more (and for a short while, it could have been even thousands of per cents). Since most households and firms in (late) modern capitalist economies are indebted, this, by raising the costs of debt-servicing, restrains their economic activities and tends to contribute to redundancies, unemployment and bankruptcies. Consequently, fewer new loans are taken under the strained conditions. Hence, there will be fewer investments and less demand for investment goods.

- Value of property such as real estate: not all assets are 'just paper' (or signs on a screen); a sudden drop of the value of these assets may contribute to the *de facto* insolvency of many actors.

- Price and demand for products: within a national economy, the demand for goods and services will be reduced because of the consequences of high interest rates and the implosion of the value of assets. Suddenly, many people and firms have much less money to buy things with. Since other actors are dependent on their investment and consumption decisions, the conditions of the dependent actors will get worse as well, further reducing demand. Output goes down significantly and unemployment increases. However, externally the devaluation of a currency in particular, but also the implosion of values, will increase demand. For the outsiders, the goods and assets, including firms, of a crisis-ridden country have suddenly become very cheap. But for the consumers inside, the imported goods become much more expensive, which means declining real income and less domestic demand.

- State budget: because of the cost of attempts to defend the value of currencies or bailout banks and other financial actors, the state is already short of money before the secondary impacts of a crisis. The secondary impact translates into a reduction of tax revenues and increase in the state social expenditure, etc. If the IMF and other multilateral organisations and/or states condition their rescue packages and loans on balanced state budgets, the tertiary impacts, too, will be far-reaching, and typically include privatisation and, perhaps most importantly, reductions in social expenditure, health and education. It has been claimed that the severity of the Asian crisis was mostly due to the IMF response of tightening budget and drawing liquidity away from the markets, *when, given the Asian institutional arrangements, it should have been exactly the opposite.*[69] Moreover, the loans of the rescue packages have to be paid back with interest, which creates a long-term constraint on state actions.

- 'Confidence' of potential direct investors: not only will the short-term funds flee the country (or the affected sectors), but also potential long-term investors will have to rethink, given the tendency to a downward spiral and reduced demand. However, simultaneously, the fall of prices will make the purchase of already existing means of production and assets much cheaper, including the privatised sectors and firms. These investments may not add to the productive potential of the country, but

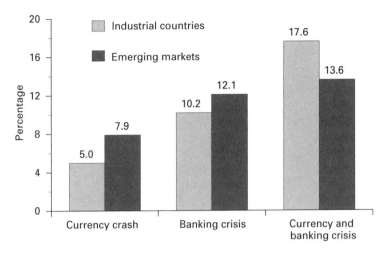

FIGURE 1.4 Cumulative loss of output due to crises
Source: IMF 1998b: 79.

do bring in money and, most far-reachingly, change the ownership and control structure of the economy.

There is no mechanism that would compensate for the lost growth and its socio-economic consequences. The 1997–98 crisis, for instance, meant by year 2000 a short-term loss of some 10–20 per cent of GDP for Thailand, Indonesia, Korea and Malaysia (assuming that the growth of 1996–97 would have continued otherwise). The long-term cumulative loss is bigger. The Asian crisis was deeper and more severe than financial crises usually are. Figure 1.4 summarises the estimations of the IMF on the cost of almost 200 crises in lost output relative to trend. The total cumulative loss for a combined banking and currency crisis has been, on average, 14.4 per cent for the countries concerned. It has been estimated, however, that the Asian crisis and its global repercussions cut *global* output by US$2 trillion in 1998–2000.[70] This is perhaps 6 per cent of the global GDP; by far, the worst crisis thus far.

It has also been estimated that the Asian crisis made 10 million people officially unemployed. Many others became either under-employed or lost their jobs without leaving a mark in the official statistics (in addition to ubiquitous attempts to colour statistics, immigrant workers, many of them illegal, fall into this category). Moreover, some 50 million people in Asia alone fell under the poverty line; the emergence of malnutrition and hunger has been reported. In Russia, *most* people's salaries are now below the absolute minimum cost of living, after the 40–50 per cent drop in real incomes due to the crisis; that is, tens of millions of Russians suffer acutely from the collapse of the economy, which has been reinforced by the financial crisis. Many more people in Asia, Russia and Brazil are facing the long-term effects of declining public health care, education, pensions and social benefits.[71] The striking fact is that, given the current global financial system and the principles of governing it, those who suffer the most have typically had the least to do with producing the crisis.

Not everybody in the global political economy suffered, however. The few speculators who played smart may have benefited from the fluctuations. Most of the Western financial actors involved in the Asian markets were eventually bailed out by the governments of the crisis-ridden countries, with funds borrowed from the IMF, other multilateral organisations, and Western and Japanese governments (i.e. from the taxpayers of the OECD countries, but to be paid back by the crisis-ridden countries, which will ultimately bear the costs).[72] Despite some losses due to exposure to the Russian market, the fluctuations of, and flights from, the 'emerging markets' also induced forex trading. This kept many Western banks busy and their profits high. The remark in the Annual Report for 1998 of HSBC (a major transnational bank operating from Hong Kong, Shanghai and the UK – the second largest in the world – which made US$1 billion from forex dealing in 1998) is typical: 'Dealing profits increased in 1998 as the Asian currency turmoil continued through the first half of 1998 and wide margins and high volumes in customer driven business continued to underpin foreign exchange revenues.'[73]

Half of the major banks' profits are made in forex markets. The Asian crisis also had positive effects on some countries. Demand for the safe, less risky, 'high quality' assets increased. This helped Wall Street to boom during the crisis. The moments of uncertainty about the possibility of contagion to New York were precariously managed and quickly buried in the unconscious. The US economy in particular succeeded in benefiting from two consequences of the crisis: increase in the demand for US assets and the cheapening of South-East Asian imports.[74]

Conclusion

It is commonsensical to distinguish between the 'real' economy of production and exchange of goods and services, and the 'paper' economy of financial markets. The distinction is clear – and critical. Although there is a need for a system generating savings and allocating credits, the secondary financial markets do not necessarily produce wealth any more than a casino does, particularly if speculation prevails over enterprise. The problem with this distinction is, however, that it seems to deny the reality of financial markets occupied with both speculation and hedging. The social relations of the system of globalising financial markets are causally powerful: they empower actors positioned in these structures with transformative capacity. The collective outcomes of their interdependent actions may be typically unintended, yet no less causally efficacious. On the contrary, they have far-reaching causal consequences. The global financial markets are real.

In this chapter, I have argued that since the collapse of the Bretton Woods systems there appears to have been a jump to a new level of volatility. Statistics do not appear to show any radical changes in volatility or fluctuations since the mid-1980s. However, these statistics hide two important factors. The exponential growth of the global forex markets indicates the *growing power* of these markets to shake and undermine any given currency or asset. Moreover, there have been four tendencies and *processes intervening* in the functioning of global financial markets. First, there has been a greater frequency of crisis interventions by G-5 and G-7 monetary authorities and an attempt to increase forex reserves on a par with the rapid growth of forex markets. Second, regional monetary integration in Europe in particular has reduced the intra-OECD fluctuations. Decisions to peg currencies to the dominant ones – also by reinventing the colonial practice of currency boards – has had a similar, albeit more fragile and ambiguous, effect. Third, according to the dominant neoliberal discourse, the homogenisation of economic policies should have had a stabilising effect as well, although in reality this is doubtful. And finally, there has been a resort to re-regulation, both in some of the crisis-ridden countries and globally.

The bulk of this chapter has been dedicated to building a model about the characteristic functioning of the financial markets. The point of departure is that financial agency is inter- and system-dependent; and that financial decisions must be explained in terms of sensitive trust or confidence in developments and reflexive strategic considerations. The model is also based on the notion of radical uncertainty due to the openness and unpredictability of the future. The emergent game is based on storytelling about strategic moves and market developments. It is also typically highly reflective about the anticipations of the moves of the others. And it tends to be self-referential, in a sense of being at least partially detached from assessing the prospective long-term yields of assets conceived as forces of production. In many respects, it is like Keynes's famous beauty contest.

Financial actors and their powers are based on a complicated process of multiplication of loans, assets and transactions. The systemic explanation

in the 'Washington consensus'. Soon it became the basis of the Western response to the crisis. See A. Singh 1999: 9, 18–20.

40. In the context of the Asian crisis in particular, the systemic interpretation has gained more ground. Many Asian political leaders, most notably Mohamed bin Mahathir, the prime minister of Malaysia, blamed the activities of foreign speculators and the structure of the international financial system; ibid.: 19. Also some of the well-known investors, including George Soros, and economists involved earlier in championing neoliberal models, such as Jeffrey Sachs, began to support the view that the global financial system itself is unstable and prone to crises. In addition, a number of Keynesian economists and many leftist intellectuals and movements adopted this view. The story is told, with references, in Patomäki 1999a: 17–31; see also Chapter 6.

41. Krugman 1999a: xii–xiii.

42. Watson (1998: 2) claims that 'overall systemic debt burdens within the western economy are no lower today than they were in the Keynesian era of budget-deficiting. The only significant difference is that debt-financed growth within the western economy has become increasingly privatised.' In fact, however, it seems that the overall debt ratio to GDP has constantly risen. Although in Europe the Maastricht Treaty has stabilised the public debt ratio, the US state has taken more debt in the 1990s, and in particular the debt ratio of both financial firms and households has risen sharply. For the US figures, see Henwood 1997: 59–60. Even in consultation with the Bank of Finland, I have not been able to acquire systematic European figures; the Finnish ones are rather peculiar. In Finland, in the 1980s, there occurred a rapid process of private indebtedness, due to the liberalisation of the financial markets; after the major financial crisis in the early 1990s, this debt was in effect transformed into public debt. With the return of exceptionally high growth in the late 1990s, Finland has been rapidly paying off the debt (in line with its traditional, Protestant 'no-indebtedness' policy of public finance).

43. See Grahl 1991.

44. Most offshore centres are not sites of forex dealing activities, except perhaps notionally. About offshore activities, see Chapter 3.

45. BIS 1996: 15.

46. For the exact figures, see BIS 1999a: 16–27.

47. Veseth 1998: 71; Chavagneux 1999.

48. K. Singh 1999: 27.

49. Henwood 1997: 41.

50. BIS 1999a: 25.

51. To think otherwise would imply a commitment to the *fallacy of composition*; what is possible for one actor is not always possible for many or all of them simultaneously.

52. Unfortunately, there have been only few studies of this kind. Doug Henwood's *Wall Street* (1997) is perhaps the best account, although it focuses only on the stock and bond markets in the US. Leyshon and Thrift (1997) take a few preliminary steps towards this direction as well, but eventually they shy away from doing any proper empirical research; see particularly Chapter 9. There is plenty of material for this kind of scrutiny in the almost 200-pages-long chronology of the Asian crisis 1997–98, collected by Professor Roubini, based on information from several news sources (Reuters, *Wall Street Journal*, *New York Times*, CNNfn, *Financial Times*, Bloomberg, etc.) and available online at http://www.stern.nyu.edu/~nroubini/ asia/AsiaChronology1.html.

53. Before the Asian crisis, not only did the IMF and the rating agencies generally

praise the performance of the second-generation NICs, but the few signs of weaknesses that were reported by the BIS in particular were simply not read by the market participants; A. Singh 1999: 25.

54. By creating certain kinds of expectations, they tend to have disciplinary effects on states. See above the section on 'homogenising economic policies'.

55. Keynes 1961/1936: 162–3.

56. Speculation proper or derivative markets would not exist without radical uncertainty; there must be an abundance of contradictory assessments of future developments for these kinds of markets to exist in the first place. Cf. Tobin 1978: 157–8.

57. Despite my original intentions, in this book there is no space to discuss this argument further. Suffice it to say that the Prisoner's Dilemma is a game-theoretical model in which individual utility maximisation appears to be self-defeating, or at least contradictory to some kind of social or collective rationality. In the technical terminology of the game theory, one says that in the Prisoner's Dilemma game the outcome of the individually rational choices is Pareto inferior (or is not Pareto optimal), that is, there is an outcome in which both (or all) players simultaneously could do better (for moving towards a Pareto optimal state, it would be enough for there to be one player who could do better while all others would do as well). In financial markets, under the conditions of radical uncertainty and fear of unexpected losses, every single actor may suddenly face a Prisoner's Dilemma (PD) kind of a situation: for everybody, it is rational to take their money away from X, but thereby the value of X collapses, and everybody is much worse off than they would have been had they kept their money in X. One crucial difference to the real world story is, of course, the fact that usually the players in the PD-game of the world financial markets are bailed out, while it is the outsiders who bear the main burden of the consequences of these losses. This would seem to aggravate the problem to a great extent, since, counting on a bailout, the collectively disastrous outcome may still be individually bearable. Another problem is more methodological, and works in the opposite direction: despite the standard account that there are dominant strategies (= 'do not co-operate' or 'defect') for rational players, the actors can and do co-operate and organise *collective action*, particularly if they are made to communicate in a sustained manner, and if there is a leader or a vision capable of showing the direction. For instance, in the 1907 Crash in New York, Pierpont Morgan launched a series of rescues and eventually invited the leaders of the financial community to his library; 'he locked the doors and pocketed the key'. By early morning, Morgan had made the others sign a collective rescue package deal, with substantial commitments from each trust (Plender 2000: 30). This episode has been repeated a number of times in the twentieth century, for instance in the contexts of the British banking crisis of the 1970s and the LTCM debacle of the late 1990s.

58. Giddens 1991: 136.

59. Cf. Minsky 1982: 90–116.

60. Krugman 1998. But for a crucial qualification in the global political economy context, see note 72, below.

61. See Bustelo 1998.

62. See the discussions in Bello et al. 1999; and Krugman 1999a: 83–101.

63. Raghavan 1998.

64. Krugman 1979; and for a survey of related models, Agenor et al. 1992.

65. Obstfeld 1996; and for a survey of related models, Eichengreen et al. 1996.

66. See Krugman 1998 and 1999a; Bustelo 1998.

67. See Patomäki 1991: 223, 239.

68. Weiss 1998: x–xv, and Weiss 1999, argue that the second-generation NICs which were involved in the financial crises have in fact been characterised by a weaker transformative capacity of the state than in Japan and Taiwan, and that, in some cases, the weakening of state capacities was deliberately manufactured by the main actors of the Washington consensus earlier in the 1990s. Had they had (or kept or developed) more state capacity in crucial areas, they should have been able to avoid the financial crises.

69. Krugman 1999a: 103–4 and 111–12, tries to explain why Washington dictated a total 'inversion of the Keynesian compact' in terms of a double standard and 'the perceived need to win market confidence at all cost'; and, more technically, Hirst and Thompson (1999: 161–2), who also say that because of the differences in institutional arrangements, the response that might have been adequate for the Anglo-American type of economies was actually causing the severity of the crisis in the Asian context (but note Krugman's point about double standards!).

70. This estimate is from UNDP 1999: 2.

71. These figures are based on UNDP, UNESCAP, World Bank, IMF, Asian Development Bank and Russian State Statistics sources, as put together and summarised by Hayward: 2000a (mimeo).

72. Gowan (1999: 29) claims that the US had already discovered a way of combining unregulated financial markets with minimal risk to the US banking and finance in the early 1980s. 'Using its control over the IMF/World Bank and largely with the support of its European partners, Washington discovered that when its international financial operators reached the point of insolvency through their international activities, they could be bailed out by the populations of the borrower countries at almost no significant cost to the US economy.'

73. Many other similar statements from the Annual Reports of different banks, and detailed figures of the profits of British banks, can be found in Hayward 1999 (mimeo). American and British banks alone made nearly US$10 billion profit from forex trading in 1998.

74. These connections have been spelled out by, for instance, Soros (1998: xii–xiii).

2

The Power of Global Financial Actors

The growth and globalisation of financial markets have consequences that go far beyond economic instability. For instance, the increased power of finance contributes to the current process of redistribution of resources and wealth in favour of the well-off, while simultaneously facilitating transnational criminal activities. The financial actors have power both individually and collectively. This chapter forms the first part of my analysis of the power of global finance.

Power is the transformative capacity of agents, based on their resources and social positioning. Resources include competencies (practical and systematic knowledge about 'how things are to be done') and facilities (e.g. equipment and money). In the following, I explicate the origin and development of financial actors and their resources. Who are these actors, where do they come from and what exactly is their transformative capacity? First, I discuss the historical emergence and development of financial actors and markets until the establishment of the Bretton Woods system. Second, I sketch a contemporary typology of the main actors and of the constantly changing rules and technologies that both aid and constrain their activities. Simultaneously, I explicate their aggregate resources as facilities in terms of basic capital, assets and available leverage. As a by-product of this analysis, the (hypo)thesis emerges that there are a number of processes that draw resources from the non-financial sphere to the financial markets.

Following this, I examine the process of formation of the individual agents that in their everyday practices reproduce these collective actors, namely, individual managers of investment funds, or dealers at banks and broking houses. Financial markets consist of a stream of interventions by these corporeal, concrete human beings in the on-going process of events in the markets, thus producing various outcomes. In particular, I discuss the knowledge of 'how things are to be done' of these actors, focusing on the role of orthodox economics as the basic frame of interpretation; and their organisational structures of accountability and incentives, which in many ways seem to encourage extreme short-termism.

Last but not least, the individual and collective financial actors analysed in this chapter are not just market players; they have also created collective associations to pursue issues of common concern and interest. These associations claim to have privileged access to governments all over the world. Hence, the last section attempts to shed some light on the activities and aims of these powerful lobbying organisations.

The Emergence of 'High Finance'

Many banking terms and practices originated in Renaissance Italy. Financial markets developed further on a par with the modern state and corporations, and their attempts to find ways of raising funds. Joint investments in trade companies had already begun by the sixteenth century. In the early seventeenth century, the Dutch and East India Companies issued shares to the public to fund their early imperial enterprises, closely linked to the Dutch and British state imperialism. The share certificates were made freely transferable, and hence a secondary market to claims to future income was established.[1] Amsterdam opened a stock exchange in 1611.[2]

In 1694, the same year in which the Bank of England was founded, English governmental lotteries were re-established through an Act of Parliament. The lottery tickets that were an indispensable part of government finance in England between 1694 and 1826 were early forms of government bonds. They were used to finance colonial expansion, wars and other major areas of state expenditure. In many cases, ticket-holders were entitled not only to a possible prize but also to a periodic payment. From 1710 onwards, English state lotteries were organised by the Bank of England. A lively secondary market in lottery tickets emerged, and it became possible to make side bets on the outcome of the draw, which were known as insurance.[3] Many coffee houses provided the sites for trading. In 1760, after being kicked out of the Royal Exchange because of their rowdiness, a group of 150 brokers formed a club at Jonathan's Coffee House where they met to buy and sell shares. In 1773, the members of this club voted to change the name of Jonathan's to the Stock Exchange.

Paris was the early financial centre, but the Revolution of 1789 ended that. The formal and regulated New York Stock Exchange was founded in 1792 and the official London Stock Exchange was opened in 1802. In the early nineteenth century, English state lotteries were eventually abolished and replaced by the more modern-sounding financial practices of the City of London. At first, railway shares and bonds assumed a central place in these markets. Hence, the expansion and intensification of capitalist markets was also funded with new financial instruments. Although there had been precedents in medieval Europe, Japan and elsewhere, the *futures market* seems to have been an American, mid-nineteenth-century innovation, originally devised to counter the impact of long distances and unpredictable weather. Also the modern joint stock company was a American innovation of the same era; in Europe, established structures tended to slow down these legal developments, despite their apparent attractiveness.[4] The joint stock company legislation clarified the distinction between the owners and managers of a corporation, and was also a reason for the rise and growth of the American stock markets in the late nineteenth century. The innovation was, however, soon replicated in other parts of the English-speaking world and Continental Europe.

By the latter half of the nineteenth century, financial actors and markets had assumed a prominent place in capitalist economies, world markets (which were still based on the gold standard) and international relations. These developments evoked a number of commentaries and analyses. For instance, it is telling how Friedrich Engels wrote in an addendum to Marx's *Capital 3* about the changes that were taking place in the late nineteenth century. In that addendum from 1895, he says that since 1865, when Marx wrote the main text, a most important change has taken place. The stock exchange has assumed a much bigger and more significant role than before. Engels claims that there is a tendency that every sector of production, exchange and communications will be concentrated in the hands of financial investors. Therefore the stock exchange becomes 'the most conspicuous exponent of the capitalist mode of production'.[5] Nevertheless, Engels seemed to follow Marx in assuming that this development is also a step from capitalism proper – based on the direct control of means of production by individual capitalists – towards a system where the control over means of production will be socialised.[6]

In his complex and sophisticated analysis published in 1946, Karl Polanyi argued that *haute finance* ('high, mighty finance') came to occupy a central role in European civilisation in the late nineteenth and early twentieth centuries. Nineteenth-century European civilisation itself rested upon four institutions: (i) the balance of power between the Great Powers; (ii) the international gold standard; (iii) a self-regulating market; and (iv) the liberal state. Towards the last quarter of the nineteenth century, the emergent monetary system underpinned the functioning of power-balancing policies, because (although the Rothschilds and other important bankers were ready and willing to finance small wars for all kinds of purposes) the stock markets and international banking, that is, the international monetary system itself, was dependent on peace between the European Great Powers. Furthermore, according to Polanyi, the combination of the globalising financial markets and the gold standard left, in fact, very little room for manoeuvre for (particularly smaller) states in their economic policies. The monetary system had disciplinary power:

> Finance – this was one of its channels of influence – acted as a powerful moderator in the councils and policies of a number of smaller sovereign states. Loans, and the renewal of loans, hinged upon credit, and credit upon good behavior. Since, under constitutional government [...], behavior is reflected in the budget and the external value of the currency cannot be detached from the appreciation of the budget, debtor governments were well advised to watch their exchanges carefully and to avoid policies which might reflect upon the soundness of budget position. This useful maxim became a cogent rule of conduct once a country had adopted the gold standard, which limited permissible fluctuations to a minimum. Gold standard and constitutionalism were the instruments which made the voice of City of London heard in many smaller countries which had adopted these symbols of adherence to the new international order. The Pax Britannica held its sway sometimes by the ominous poise of heavy ship's cannon, but more frequently it prevailed by the timely pull of a thread in the international monetary network.[7]

Yet, according to Polanyi, the economic basis of the nineteenth-century system eroded rapidly: increasing tendencies towards cartelisation and monopolisation of production were antithetical to the laws of a self-regulating market; the possibilities for territorial expansion of markets by means of building and enlarging empires came to an end; the rise of national protectionism tended to limit the size of world markets; and, eventually, the consultations-based power-balancing policies of the Concert of Vienna were replaced by a system of two competing European blocs.[8] It appeared that neither capitalist modernisation/enlightened reason nor 'high finance' was powerful enough to prevent the Great War from breaking out. The war fragmented the globalising economy and its rising financial system.

After the war, there emerged a nostalgia for the relative peace and stability of the nineteenth century, and, consequently, attempts to restore that order (for Polanyi, the League of Nations was essentially an enlarged and improved version of the Concert of Europe, a facility for consultation and joint action).[9] London and New York re-emerged as financial centres and, because the attempts to reinstate the gold standard were at best only partially successful, foreign exchange markets proper also emerged.

The financial booms of the 1920s resulted in the Great Crash of 1929. As a consequence, the stock exchanges and other sites of financial activities were viewed with increasing suspicion, and some of them were eventually either closed down or regulated meticulously. Indeed, the 1930s transformed radically the legitimate options of economic policies. It also led to the rise of economic nationalism and a global war of revanche and counter-imperialism. These strengthened the case for new international institutional arrangements. Finally, in 1944, the Bretton Woods system was created to replace the nineteenth-century institutions with a system of capital controls and collective management of exchange rates that were tied indirectly, via the dollar, to gold. The Bretton Woods system represented a partial victory of productivism over financial capital; it imposed significant constraints on the freedom of movement of financial capital.[10]

This short history of the power of finance should illustrate the historical specificity of global financial markets and, simultaneously, the fact that the post-Bretton Woods era has, in some respects, a precedent. But only in some respects. There is no gold standard or nostalgia for it and the rules, options, technological facilities and actors of the financial markets have changed as well. Also, because of many transformations, no strict historical analogies are possible. More loosely, however, the historical analogy can be taken as a warning of the destructive political forces that may be unleashed by financial instability and its socio-economic consequences.

The Re-emergence of 'High Finance': Financial Actors in the Post-Bretton Woods Era

The golden age of 'high finance' was between the 1870s and the 1930s. World War I and the Great Crash drastically interrupted this era; it came to an end with the advent of World War II. High, mighty finance started to re-emerge in the 1960s, with the appearance of the eurodollar markets, hedge funds and offshore centres. These developments had the explicit backing of the US and the UK. Soon, the unilateral US decision to go for a system of freely floating exchange rates in 1971, and the consequent rounds of deregulation, ended the era of 'financial repression' (as it came to be seen by the new actors whose agency and activities were 'liberated' from the constraints of capital controls and fixed exchange rates). Indeed, the global financial markets re-emerged quickly.

The post-Bretton Woods context is none the less very different to the 1870–1930s era. States are much bigger and engage in, often multilateral, 'lender-of-last-resort' activities. There are rules and regulations partially inherited from the Bretton Woods era, partially created by the central bankers within the Bank for International Settlements (BIS)-centred regime. There are also international multilateral arrangements such as G-7, and organisations such as the IMF, which play an important role in managing the system. These elements constitute the context of contemporary global high finance. Moreover, it is crucial to understand that in a world dominated by liberal-democratic welfare states, the institutional arrangements favouring global finance have to ensure sufficient electoral support or, at the very least, passive consent (possibly based on a 'there-is-no-alternative' view) in many of the countries concerned.[11] In other words, the problem of legitimisation is also historically specific. And finally, the actors and activities are also not the same: legal options and technological possibilities have enabled innovations of financial actors and instruments, and new 'emergent markets' in Asia have come to the fore. Who are the actors of the post-Bretton Woods global financial markets? What is their transformative capacity? Despite deregulation and the rise of offshore centres, the access to wholesale forex or bond and equities markets remains for the most part regulated. Only particular institutional actors with an authorised permit may participate directly. Others have to pay the brokers and dealers to make the transactions for them. A large proportion of the transactions are made in particular sites called *exchanges*, in which brokers communicate and bargain on a face-to-face basis. Many other contracts to sell and buy are made between bank-dealers, increasingly by

---

Box 4 The Bretton Woods system

The Anglo-American agreements reached during the dark days of World War II were different from anything that the capitalist world had seen before. They established rules for a relatively open and multi-lateral system of trade and payments, but they did so in a way that would reconcile openness and trade expansion with flexibly fixed exchange rates, capital controls and commitments of national governments to full employment and economic and political stabilisation.

The Bretton Woods system was a compromise between various positions. Most notably, Keynes and the British wartime cabinet emphasised imperial preferences, full employment and state-interventionist policies for stabilisation. The US State Department favoured a traditional, *laissez-faire* free trade position.

At one point in the course of complex and controversial negotiations, Keynes retreated to the countryside, where he developed an ambitious plan involving mechanisms for both the orderly adjustment of exchange rates and the mobilisation of credit that would prevent countries from resorting to deflation as a means to correct maladjustments. The International Clearing Union would have the authority to create and manage US$25–30 billion of a new international currency to correct payment imbalances. It would also have the authority to tax the excess reserves

using electronic trading networks. Indeed, in the US and the UK in particular, there have also emerged stock markets that have granted – with the permission of state authorities – direct access also to non-institutionalised actors via the internet. Also, in the wholesale forex markets, access to markets and practices has changed:

> The arrival of electronic brokers in foreign exchange enabled almost any bank [including investment banks], however small, to find the best exchange rate in the market. That cut margins on trades, so that commercial banks could no longer simply turn a profit by offering prices and taking a cut. They therefore began trying to sell more high-margin, sophisticated products to their clients. The US investment banks, meanwhile, decided to beef up their currencies business. [...] the investment bank had to be able to handle the currency aspect in full.[12]

It is no longer easy to categorise different financial actors. Because of deregulation and market dynamics, the conventional, previously state-administered categories tend to be blurred. At least four major tendencies

---

of creditor nations and impose other measures to ensure that payment imbalances would be corrected both in surplus countries and in deficit countries (Ikenberry 1992: 314–15).

The main US negotiator, Harry Dexter White, devised a much more modest plan, proposing fairly small resources for correcting imbalances and severely limiting the obligations of creditor nations to contribute to the relief fund. This became the basis for a new system. The role of a monetary stabiliser was given to the IMF. The International Trade Organisation (ITO) was never realised, because of opposition in the US Congress. The International Bank for Reconstruction and Development assumed the task of helping to finance post-war reconstruction.

Later in the 1940s, Harry Dexter White stood trial for his alleged connection to anti-American (communist) activities. Eventually, also, the Bretton Woods system came to work very differently from how it had been planned. By the 1970s, the IMF became active in making stabilisation loans conditional on deflationary policies. The burden of adjustments was transferred totally to the deficit countries (with the exception of the US, which remained outside obligations). In other words, the post-Bretton Woods IMF is imposing exactly the policies that Keynes warned about.

can be distinguished. First is the disappearance of non-commercial financial actors such as co-operatives, savings banks, and state banks, or their transformation into universal commercial banks, and the creation of new private funds to replace public arrangements (private pension funds in particular).[13] Second is the concentration of the resources. Due to the boom of mergers and acquisitions, there tend to be fewer and bigger actors than before in the markets. In 1987–97, nearly US$1,400 billion-worth of mergers swept through the financial industry; in the late 1990s, the value of the annual deals exceeded US$250 billion.[14]

The third tendency is towards the universalisation of financial actors. The actors reorganised through mergers, acquisitions and other arrangements assume an increasing variety of activities, many of which used to be the exclusive sphere of particular actors (also because of the strict regulations of the Bretton Woods era). Big banks, with multiple activities and links to a number of institutional investors, and insurance companies merge, and create 'financial conglomerates'. As *The Economist* reports, 'almost weekly exotic new combinations of banks, fund managers and insurance companies are cooked up and served to the world's investors'.[15]

The fourth main tendency is the globalisation of actors and activities, facilitated not only by deregulation and technological innovations but also by the emergence of more than sixty offshore centres throughout the world. One indication of this transnationalisation is the huge growth of cross-border transactions in bonds and equities, as depicted in Table 1.3 of Chapter 1. Although the share of foreign holdings and investments may not yet have risen above 5–35 per cent, the trend towards globalisation of activities has been clear.[16]

Major private actors Despite difficulties in categorising financial actors, Tables 2.1 and 2.2 attempt to set forth a rough outline of the major private actors at the turn of the century. The point of these tables is to facilitate an understanding of the market actors and their resources; the point is not to give a full list of actors and their complex, interdependent activities.

Table 2.1 describes the principal actors of the wholesale financial markets: the ones who have direct access to these markets, and the ones specialising in these activities only, many of them being market leaders. The first major group is banks. Deregulation and neoliberalisation have meant that the non-commercial banks have all but disappeared or been turned into *commercial banks* (at least in the OECD area). In many countries, regulations used to separate commercial and investment banks. The continental European tradition of 'universal banks', combining commercial and investment banking, has become the mainstream, although in the US and Japan they are still kept at least partially separate. In the US, most banks – with a few very notable exceptions such as the Citibank and Chase Manhattan, the world's biggest forex traders – are still small and confined to the state level, due to regulations. Commercial banks take deposits, lend money, and create credit, as far as their liquidity and capital ratios allow. Also, they have been usually responsible for forex trading.

Investment banks (previously called merchant banks in the UK) facilitate international payments, manage new issues of equities/bonds and rights issues, give advice and help in privatisation as well as in mergers and acquisitions in all industries, and engage in securities and forex trading, to the extent that regulations in their countries allow them to. Following London's Big Bang in October 1986, investment banks have increasingly gained full access to bond and equity markets, and, recently, to forex markets as well. Many traders of banks have specialised in particular kinds of derivative products, also in forex markets.

Brokers (broker houses) have traditionally handled the bulk of stock exchange transactions and a major part of the forex transactions. Following deregulation, banks have begun to own brokers or set up their own operations. The development of over-the-counter (OTC) markets and electronic brokerage, as well as new financial innovations, has further diminished the role of independent broker houses. Nevertheless, at the turn of the century, an important part of financial transactions is still conducted through broker houses. For instance, the 1995 Bank of England survey showed that brokers were used in 35 per cent of forex deals by value; in 1998, the share was 27 per cent. The OTC-markets and the new electronic systems have been diminishing, particularly the share of traditional voice brokers, who quote prices over telephone lines to dealing rooms.[17]

Financial markets are becoming thoroughly computerised. As will be argued later, the risks of the unregulated OTC-markets and computerisation have stimulated the rise of new centralised and formalised net settlement systems. These systems reduce the underlying risk of forex dealing and, as will be discussed later, also greatly facilitate the identification of transactions for taxation purposes.

Mutual funds are pools of shares run by professional investment managers. For any actor willing and able to invest in financial assets, mutual funds give an alternative to taking the risk of devising an independent investment strategy on one's own. In principle, participants such as wealthy individuals, banks, pension funds, insurance companies or multinational corporations should own the mutual funds, in accordance with their shares. In practice, at least in Europe, banks own many of the mutual funds and try to attract others to invest in them. The activities of mutual funds are, at least in the OECD countries, strictly regulated. For instance, they are not allowed to engage in high leverage building or short selling; and usually

TABLE 2.1 Principal private actors of the global financial markets (2000)

Actor	Types	Main features	Resources
Banks	1. Non-commercial (savings banks, co-operatives, state banks)	1. Owned by the members, and often aiming to give low-cost loans to members and/or support social purposes or state industrial planning.	In 1996, the world's top 20 banks had assets worth more than US$8 trillion (one-fourth of world's GDP); and tier 1 capital worth more than US$300 billion. The biggest banks are European and Japanese; in the US, banking remains more regulated and consequently also more decentralised, with some crucial exceptions, most notably Citibank and Chase, the biggest forex traders.
	2. Commercial	2. Banks in the classit profit-maximising business of taking deposits and lending money; however, also services and securities and forex trade, depending on regulations.	
	3. Investment banks	3. Banks in the profit-maximising business of facilitating transactions and raising or investing funds; also trading in securities and forex.	
Brokers		In most countries, broker houses have traditionally had a near-monopoly of stock exchange transactions and a major part of the forex transactions. Due to deregulation and technical developments, banks have begun to own brokers or set up their own operations.	Small resources compared to the funds they assist to invest; but broker houses do engage in investment activities, often by reserving the (presumably) best deals for themselves.
Mutual funds	Unit trusts, investment companies, etc. engage	Collective investments in money market instruments, bonds or equities;	In 1996, the total assets of US mutual funds stood at US$3.4 trillion

in similar activities; terms and organisation vary with countries.	participants such as wealthy individuals, banks, pension funds, insurance companies or multinational corporations own the mutual funds; for practical purposes, however, a fund may be controlled by one actor, such as a bank (by organising also the participation of others).	(more than one-tenth of world's GDP); Fidelity alone controls more than 10% of this. In Europe and Japan, there are also significant mutual funds, although the top fund managers are banks and insurance companies.
Hedge funds	Like mutual funds, but much less restriction on their investment activities and techniques (registered in the US or in the offshore centres); tend to take significant speculative positions.	In the late 1990s, funds under management amounted at least to US$200 billion. Due to high leverage, investment volumes are at least ten times more, that is, US$2–3 trillion, and probably much more. Many hedge funds are also socially constructed as market leaders; some, like Soros's Quantum Fund, have had a guru-like status.
1. Macro hedge funds	1. Speculate on expected future changes in macroeconomic conditions (like exchange or interest rates); 65% of hedge funds.	
2. Relative value or arbitrage-type hedge funds	2. Exploit arbitrage opportunities embedded in the relative prices of related securities; 30% of hedge funds.	

Sources include 'Top 1000 World Banks', *The Banker* (July 1996); Edwards 1999; K. Singh 1999: 25–9; Useem 1989: 250; Valdez 1997: 30–4, *et passim*.

they also have other restrictions on taking excessive risks or building highly speculative positions, such as those regulating the composition of their investment portfolio.

The term *hedge fund* was apparently first used in a 1966 *Fortune* magazine article to describe the activities of investment funds based on limited liabilities and a small number of partners which emerged in the 1950s. Hedge funds are mostly unregulated. In US law, they are exempt from the 1940 Investment Company Act if they have fewer than 100 investors or partners (or if all their partners meet other eligibility criteria for exemption) and they do not make public security offerings. In Europe, with the strength of the UCITS Directive of the EEC, hedge funds are not classified as regulated undertakings as long as they do not promote the sale of their units to the public. As if to emphasise the blurred line between hedging and speculation, the hedge funds typically do just the opposite of what their name implies: they speculate. They may try to eliminate excessive risks by finding novel, complex investment strategies; and they may fail in that.

Most hedge funds are registered either in the US or in the offshore centres and tax havens such as the British Virgin Islands, the Bahamas, Bermuda, the Cayman Islands, Dublin and Luxembourg. As speculative vehicles for 'high net-worth individuals' and powerful institutional investors, hedge funds are free to hold whatever financial instruments they wish and to pursue whatever investment or trading strategies they choose. Quantum, Quasar and Quota Funds managed by George Soros, and Tiger and Jaguar Funds managed by Julian Robertson are among the most important, globally operative hedge funds that can be classified as macro hedge funds.[18] They are also examples of financial actors that are socially constructed as market leaders or financial gurus.[19] Most hedge funds, however, have a short life-span, about three years. Hedge funds offer both extremely high incentives to their managers and, on average, higher yields than other funds. Yet, for instance, in 1994, following a collapse in bond markets, many of them suffered severe losses. Indeed, there is no systematic empirical evidence that their managers would be particularly skilful or that they would give excess *risk-adjusted* returns to their investors.[20]

Other private actors Other private actors in the global financial markets are listed and described in Table 2.2. *Very wealthy individuals* are an important source of funds. The assets of the top three billionaires are more than the combined GDP of all least developed countries and their 600 million people. The income gap between the fifth of the world's people living in the richest countries and the fifth in the poorest was 74 to 1 in 1997, up from 60 to 1 in 1990 and 30 to 1 in 1960. Income inequalities have also risen sharply within the rich countries – particularly in the US and the UK – and the global poor are now as, or more, poor than they were in 1820.[21]

An increasing number of the well-off are persuaded to invest their liquid funds in financial markets. The world's 200 richest people more than doubled their net worth in the four years to 1998, to more than US$1 trillion. There are perhaps6 million dollar-millionaires in the world, holding some US$17 trillion in assets. A lot of this concentrated individual wealth is invested in financial markets or, more precisely, in different kinds of investment funds. For instance, about 80 per cent of hedge fund investors are 'high net-worth individuals'. It seems to be no coincidence that many hedge funds are registered in tax havens and offshores. Tax havens have helped to avoid capital and income taxation; some US$5 trillion-worth of assets is parked in offshores and tax havens. But it is equally noteworthy that financial markets have been instrumental in creating new 'high net-worth individuals'; many of the richest people of the late 1990s are fund managers or, in some cases, petty investors turned millionaires.

Private pension funds have become more prominent as well, particularly as fund-providers, but also as independent investors. Pension funds are pools of funds stemming from collecting regular payments *now* for *future* pensions. Pension funds will invest, or, more typically, let investment banks, mutual funds or hedge funds invest, the available funds in assets in global financial markets (perhaps 80–90 per cent of funds are invested in other investment funds, which in turn invest them in other assets, including each other's shares and assets). Private pension funds used to be common only in the Anglo-American systems and Japan. In Japan, however, strict regulations have limited their room for manoeuvre in financial markets. In the context of an ageing population in the OECD countries, cuts in the welfare state have also favoured turning state-based systems at least partially private and funded; and then increasing their further privatisation and deregulation. These have been highly contested issues, particularly in the EU, but thus far the trend has been clear: more funds are created and released for the further expansion of global financial markets.

Insurance companies organise the sharing of risk by selling protection against 'accidental' incidences or death. They have to manage funds with varying liquidities. The insurance companies try to improve their returns by investing these funds in as profitable a manner as possible. Participation in mutual funds – or increasingly also in hedge funds – is a common way to improve the return on the funds. Moreover, savings schemes linked to life insurance in particular intentionally create additional funds. Some of the life insurance schemes are represented explicitly as investments in financial markets. Some companies specialise in sophisticated financial

TABLE 2.2 Other major private actors in global financial markets (2000)

Actor	Types	Main features	Resources
Wealthy individuals	1. Authoritarian rulers. 2. Established high-society families. 3. Gurus, leaders and winners of new industries (Bill Gates). 4. Gurus, leaders and winners of financial markets (George Soros) 5. Drug-trafficking bosses, etc., criminals	Tax havens have helped to avoid income taxation; some US$5 trillion-worth of assets is parked in offshores and tax havens. Financial markets have also been instrumental in creating new 'high net-worth' individuals; many of the richest people are fund managers or petty investors turned millionaires.	The world's 200 richest people more than doubled their net worth in the four years to 1998, to more than US$1 trillion. There are perhaps 6 million dollar-millionaires in the world, holding some US$17 trillion in assets. A lot of this wealth is invested in financial markets (funds).
Private pension funds	An alternative or a complement to public arrangements, where pensions are paid from payments and taxes collected simultaneously (but there are also public pension funds).	Pools of funds stemming from collecting regular payments now for future pensions. Pension funds will invest, or, increasingly, let investment banks, mutual funds or hedge funds invest, these in global financial markets (perhaps 80–90% of funds invested in other investment funds).	In 1996, the ten biggest managed, private pension funds control assets worth US$1.5 trillion. Altogether, pension funds have assets worth perhaps US$8 trillion, or more. They actively lobby for further privatisation of social security and pensions, also to get more resources.
Insurance companies	Insurance companies often work together with a bank, or may even be merged with	Insurance companies organise the sharing of risk by selling protection against accidental incidences or death.	In 1993, the premiums in the US, Japan and Europe were some US$1.6 trillion. These premiums will

	They have to manage funds with varying liquidities, and savings schemes linked to life insurance in particular create additional funds; some are explicit investments in financial markets.	be invested prior to any money being paid out. Participation in mutual funds is a common way to improve the return on the funds. Some companies specialise in sophisticated financial investment.
a bank. Some are forming banks themselves.		
Multinational corporations (MNCs)	MNCs produce and sell goods and services in many countries. Thus, they have to deal with the volatility of exchange rates; they may also be listed in more than one stock exchange. They may have financial departments, seeking the best ways to raise and transfer funds across borders. Some big corporations also have in-house corporate 'banks', some of which also do retail banking, although wholesale banking remains a priority.	Waves of mergers and acquisitions are further concentrating industrial power in mega-corporations. The biggest 100 of these corporations, with the average high transnationality index of 54 (of max. 100) control assets worth more than US$4 trillion and account for 4–7% of the world GDP; and the 300–400 biggest MNCs conduct two-thirds of world trade, a large part of which is intra-firm.
In terms of numbers, most enterprises are local or national; and also for the big multinational corporations, their globalness varies. Due to deregulation, banks can now also own non-financial companies more extensively; some MNCs have been taken over by small investment companies raising huge sums with bonds.		

Sources include McLean 1998; Palan 1999a: 43; UNCTAD 1999: 77–84; UNDP 1999: 3; Valdez 1997.

investment. A space for the further expansion of these insurance markets is created by: (i) marketing attempts to create new, individual insurance needs, and the coupling of special insurances with the purchase of goods; (ii) the emergence of a *risk society* with increasingly individualised socio-economic insecurities and threats, including growing risks of unemployment and criminal offences, and mounting risks and hazards caused by scientific and industrial development;[22] and (iii) the neoliberal tendency to commodify and privatise likewise the common, redefined and emergent insecurities, risks and hazards.[23]

Under these circumstances, rational and sufficiently wealthy individuals (or, still in the majority of cases, nuclear families) insure all aspects of their rather atomised everyday lives, including life/death, health, employment, education, loans, car, home, and a number of other consumer durable goods. Thereby they take part in creating new funds, which will be at least partially released for the further expansion of global financial markets. On the other hand, the emergence of unpredictable, large-scale technological risks and catastrophes has, in turn, encouraged the development of *financial reinsurance*, which, among other things, is also devised to yield benefits from the possibilities for higher revenues in tax havens.[24]

The last category of Table 2.2 is *multinational corporations* (MNCs). MNCs are organisations that produce and sell goods and services in a number of countries. Consequently, they have to deal with the uncertainty of exchange rates. They may also be listed in more than one stock exchange. Many of them have established financial departments, seeking the best ways to raise and transfer funds across borders, and administering the transfer prices of international trade conducted within the corporation. Some big corporations also have in-house corporate 'banks', some of which also do retail banking (consumer loans, credit cards, etc.), although they mostly concentrate on wholesale banking. Waves of mergers and acquisitions are further concentrating industrial power in mega-corporations. The biggest MNCs produce at least a third of the world's industrial product, and conduct two-thirds of world trade, a large part of which is intra-firm. Despite their prominence in production and exchange of goods and non-financial services, at least some of them are claimed to make, in the 1990s and early 2000s, the major part of their profits in financial markets.[25]

On the other hand, due to deregulation, banks can now also possess non-financial companies more extensively than before. Some MNCs have been taken over by small investment companies raising huge sums with bonds (this was particularly common in the US in the 1980s). An increasing number of others have started to maximise shareholder values, in accordance with ideas of financial actors, instead of other possible objectives. As a consequence of all these developments, the distinction between financial and non-financial firms has been obscured. The world's biggest MNCs are now tightly entangled in the global financial system.

The Extraction of Further Resources to Financial Markets

In the first chapter, 'The Economics of Financial Instability', I argued that the financial actors and their powers are based on a complicated *process of multiplication* of loans, assets and transactions. Now we can see how this is just one side of the story. The re-emergence of 'high finance' is in fact connected to a multitude of interconnected social processes which tend to draw more and more economic resources to financial markets.

On the basis of the above analysis of the actors and their resources, it appears that a number of processes create further input to finance. Global wealth is increasingly concentrated in the hands of a few very rich individuals, leading to a greater propensity to invest the surplus in the financial markets. Moreover, an increasing number of well-off middle-class people are persuaded to invest in financial markets. Even more importantly, there is an on-going struggle to privatise and fund pensions, which will relieve further resources for financial activities. In the context of growing insecurities and risks, partially caused by neoliberalism, private insurance companies attempt to make well-off people cover every aspect of their lives with insurance premiums, some of which have become explicit investment in the financial markets. New, 'emerging markets' are created and opened, with fresh resources and investment opportunities. And because of the power of finance, there has also emerged a drive to make non-financial corporations concentrate on maximising short-term share-holder values, and thereby accelerate financial multiplication.

From this point of view, even financial *crises can be functional* to the growth of the system. The IMF, and ultimately the states in trouble, tend to bail out the actors that have got into trouble. In effect, this means that the financial crises bring new and fresh resources to global financial markets. Also, the monetary reserves of states have been increased rapidly. A large part of these reserves is invested in financial markets, particularly in the dollar-valued US Treasury bonds in the Wall Street. This helps, in its part, to keep up the process of financial multiplication.

Although a systematic study of this (hypo)thesis is beyond the scope of this book, we may assume that financial multiplication would be much more meagre and fragile without the continuous input of further resources into the system. There is also at least tentative quantitative empirical evidence for this claim. According to Felix's calculations of G-7 data, the ratio of gross value added of finance, insurance and real estate activities (FIRE) to gross domestic product (GDP) remained constant until the mid-

1970s, after which it has continued to rise in every country while non-financial output growth slackened.[26] According to Felix, this post-Bretton Woods trend suggests that 'forces endogenous to the FIRE activities keep them expanding at the expense of the non-financial sector's growth'. He continues:

This non-linear pattern fits Hyman Minsky's financial fragility model, an extension of Keynesian analysis, rather nicely. Driven by its endogenous dynamics, the financial system, according to that model, moves gradually from stable financing to rising debt leveraging and volatile and inflated asset prices that makes it less able to handle exogenous shocks without falling into systemic crises. The trajectory of FIRE/GDP appears to be capturing the prolonged cycle in G-7. However, it has not been a closed economy dynamic. The OECD reports that since 1975 the fastest growing component in the rise of international service trade has been financial services, which have been growing at 13 per cent year, and that foreign direct investment (FDI) in financial facilities led the upsurge of FDI in services during the 1980s.[27]

I have suggested in this chapter that there is a complex socio-economic dynamic behind this trend. A number of interconnected processes have contributed to the growth of the financial sector at the expense of the rest of the economy. Once set in motion, this dynamic tends to be self-reinforcing. Moreover, it is by no means restricted to the G-7 countries. Knowing this, we may also assume that the associations of global finance lobby for policies that will ensure the continuous flow of further resources and investment opportunities to global financial markets.

Positioning of the Individual Agents

Banks, broker houses, mutual funds, hedge funds, pension funds, insurance companies and multinational corporations are *collective actors*. They are dependent on the co-ordinated and regulated actions of a number of individual agents. Collective actors are a rule-based, organised system of relational practices of *individual agents*. Indeed, all investment decisions must be made by individual managers or dealers, or, in a collegial manner, by a group of them. In addition to their individual competencies (acquired through long and often expensive training), their transformative capabilities are based on the facilities and resources of the collective actor they represent, reproduce and are entitled to make decisions for.

Now, if we are interested in the way the financial markets function, we should be able to analyse the positioning of these individual agents in terms of:

- The practical and discursive rules they follow, or are supposed to follow but may fail to do so.
- The regime of accountability and incentives they are committed to.

These rules and procedures constitute their everyday practices and, consequently, structure their actions.

Knowledge of 'how things are to be done': the role of orthodox economics Where, and how, are the individual agents of financial markets socialised and educated prior to entering the business? In the City of London, for instance, despite tendencies towards pluralisation of the social basis of recruits, the majority of traders, dealers and bankers are still men who come from upper-(middle)-class families (quite a few of them are aristocrats); they received their basic education in private schools; and about half of them have an Oxbridge university degree.[28] In a 1999 issue of *Investors Chronicle*, brief profiles of 'top 20 fund managers' are drawn.[29] Most fund managers seem to have degrees in economics or business; the more 'exotic' degrees such as physics, mathematics or international relations are usually from an Oxbridge college. Particularly in the 1980s, when the financial markets exploded in size, most investment banks and funds started to prefer to hire economists, with big salaries and huge incentives, despite the often-repeated claim that economic theory 'serves almost no practical function in an investment bank'.[30]

The typical background of these agents indicates two considerations of great importance. First, many of them have gone through highly elitist institutions in their formation and education. The rest, with a more pluralist background, are likely to think about their positioning in terms of 'having made it'. Second, and even more importantly, their education has been about familiarising themselves with the discourses of business studies and economics. Although business studies are more practical, dealing mostly with the know-how of the rules and practices of different markets, particularly from the point of the appropriate techniques of firms, they typically presuppose essential elements of the *worldview of orthodox economics*.

As explained in more detail in Appendix 1, most variations of orthodox economic theory are based on an non-realist philosophy, which denies the existence of social beings and relations,[31] and instead asserts a set of mostly – and in many cases explicitly – untrue or very partial assumptions. These assumptions are justified by their instrumental value for enabling simple and parsimonious models that are able to predict certain allegedly important things.[32] They are typically tailored for the building of mathematical and statistical models and using certain areas of mathematics for analysing the properties of these models. This gives economics an exact and scientific appearance. But it is only an appearance. Economics can explain little[33] and predict hardly anything at all.[34] The optimisation techniques may be, to an extent, useful as what they essentially are, namely *techniques*, for calculating the likely consequences of complex investment strategies in markets, where measures are already quantified and conventions and agreements determine the formula of payments. However, in general, economics tends to misunderstand even the role and nature of mathematical functions. Mathematical functions such as $y = f(x)$ say nothing about what makes y or x, only that quantitative variations in y are formally (or by convention), not substantially, related in some way to quantitative variation in x. Moreover, the sign '=' says nothing about causality. Qualitative analysis of these objects is required to disclose real social and causal relations.[35]

Instead, economists have concentrated on refining the ever more complex mathematical tools at their disposal. They think that better formal tools help to achieve what economics strives for: ability to predict and control certain things such as amount of production, prices and inflation and employment and income of different 'factors or production'. But the apparently sophisticated tools do not help: economists cannot predict, except in the very short run, usually by assuming 'business as usual' continuity. Outside the public sphere, they are often aware of this themselves, and it is a source of a number of private jokes and anecdotes among qualified economists.[36]

Yet, they are misled by the non-realist philosophy about the sources of this inability. Instead of tackling the consequences of dealing with open systems, relational, contextual social entities, and complex, reflexive reasoning of actors, they continue to refine their formal tools in the vain hope of finally arriving at truly predictive models. The fact that they are able to fit a mathematical/statistical model to a set of *ex post* empirical data – quantified traces of *past* events and processes – brings some comfort, even if they know that many others can do the same, but with different models. Indeed, it is much harder to predict the future than the past! And it should be alarming that even the past can be 'predicted' in so many ways with economists' tools.

There is one thing that economists can do, however. They can draw *ideological and political conclusions* from their models. Equally well, they can interpret the prospects of assets, firms and countries in the terms of these ideologial models. The ideological conclusions follow logically from the assumptions about the nature of the world. Since mathematical analysis does not add anything to the substantial assumptions, the principle must be: 'garbage in, garbage out'. That is, the conclusions are already built into the assumptions, which are, in the orthodox economic theory, unrealistic and often widely inaccurate accounts of reality.

Typically, and in most cases with only minor modifications, the models of orthodox economics support the thesis of optimal efficiency of free market capitalism,[37] quite independently of the specific context under discussion. Obviously, the suspicion is that this ideology is, indeed, the reason for the hegemony of economics. Typically, and at least individually and in the short run, the free market ideology of orthodox economics runs in accordance with *the interests of those entitled to make investment decisions* in capitalist market economy or, at least, have a lot of individual resources at their disposal.[38]

Essentially, the so-called Washington consensus is nothing but a restatement of the orthodox economics. Since the 1980s, the apparent economic policy requirements of most countries have been spelled out in the Washington consensus. This is, roughly speaking, the consensus between the White House (and, of course, the British government), the IMF, the World Bank, the *Washington Post*, the *Wall Street Journal* and the *International Herald Tribune*. According to this consensus, growth can best be achieved via 'free' international trade, sound budgets – which usually means fiscal austerity, which translates into cuts in welfare spending – low inflation, privatisation, economisation of social life, and deregulated markets, including financial markets.

The fact that the education of financial actors has entangled them with the Washington consensus has far-reaching consequences. Before even entering the financial markets, they are supposed to have internalised the assumptions, logic and conclusions of the Washington consensus. Furthermore, sociologically-oriented studies indicate that the cultures of the collective actors, which these individual agents enter, place a high premium on conformity in everything from dress and discourse to management strategies. And, indeed, there seems also to be a willingness to accept inherited structures and strategies without question.[39] Any lack of accord with the worldview embedded in the institutional cultures is soon swept away.[40] You have to be a George Soros to be critical-minded and confident enough to criticise the way the financial markets function, or question the orthodoxy.

Once within the financial organisations, these individual agents start to socialise with other managers, dealers and brokers (also from other firms), and build networks and discursive communities, which constantly mediate interpretations of available profit-opportunities, trends, techniques and threats – besides insider gossip and rumours. Moreover, in the stories circulated within these networks, anticipatory judgements are made about the future losers and winners, including companies and countries; and the

market leaders and 'gurus' are socially defined and constructed. These on-
going discourses provide ideas for investment strategies. Technical analysis
is subordinate to these general ideas. Many ideas, techniques and investment strategies come and go like clothing fads in London, Paris and Rome.
However, what happens tacitly at the level of 'it-goes-without-saying' is
even more important; the basic assumptions of the orthodoxy are reproduced and, inevitably, naturalised and reified.

**The regime of accountability and incentives: the rise of short-
termism** What, then, is the regime of accountability and incentives to
which the individual financial decision-makers are committed? What kinds
of effects does this regime have? Traditionally, in the US-based mutual
funds, for instance, the incentive structure has been regulated; it may still

---

Box 5 The power of George Soros

George Soros was born in Budapest, Hungary in 1930. In 1947 he
emigrated to England, where he graduated from the London School of
Economics. In 1956 he moved to the United States. In 1969, he began
to accumulate a large fortune through an international investment fund
he founded and managed, namely the Quantum Fund NV. This
coincided with the transition to the post-Bretton Woods era. Soon he
became rich and famous. Already by the late 1970s he was affluent
enough to start his philanthropic activities.

In his books, Soros has outlined his principles of devising investment
strategies. First, he looks for *flaws* in every situation and tries to benefit
from them (Soros 1998: 21). Second, he acknowledges that 'financial
markets attempt to predict a future that is contingent on the decisions
people make in the present' (p. xxiii). Markets are based on complex
reflexivity; there is no 'equilibrium'. Third, he says from this it follows
that rational participants try both to create a picture of the situation
and 'to make an impact, to mold reality to their desires' (p. 7). That is,
market participants can also have direct intentional power over market
developments, because of their superior resources, or because they make
others anticipate changes, and/or because others tend to follow the
market leaders and gurus.

Two well-known examples from the early 1990s illustrate the power
of Soros and the like. His 1992 attack on British sterling was perhaps
more ideologically than financially motivated, but it brought him more
than US$1 billion in profits. In 1990, the UK had joined the European

be prohibited to tie incentives directly to profits. The regulators in the 1940s assumed that profit-based incentives encourage *excessive risk-taking and shorter time horizons*. By the 1990s, due to deregulation and the rise of offshore centres, the situation had mostly changed.

For instance, it seems that in the top banks of the deregulated London, fully qualified dealers can expect a basic salary of between £50,000 and £60,000, in addition to which, if they reach the profit target (typically £1 million a year), they receive a bonus of 7.5–10 per cent of this sum. Any additional profits produce larger bonuses; the larger the profits the higher the bonus. In other words, the bonus derived from profits is usually *much bigger* than the basic salary. Senior dealers receive between £80,000 and £100,000, plus a bonus between 10–15 per cent of the annual profit they achieve. In 1996 at NatWest, for instance, dealers typically handled

---

Exchange Rate Mechanism (ERM). By 1992, the Major government was increasingly unhappy with the situation: subordination to the policy of the Bundesbank, overvalued sterling and the recession caused growing popular dissatisfaction. Soros decided to bet on a crisis *and* to do everything possible to provoke it. Quantum Fund quietly established credit lines that would allow it to borrow about US$15 billion-worth of British pounds and to convert that sum into dollars at will. Once already long in dollars and short in pounds, Soros turned the attack noisy. He publicised his short-selling, and made statements in newspapers declaring that the pound would soon be devalued. It worked. The attack began in August; in late September Britain dropped out of the ERM, and the pound was set floating (see Krugman 1999a: 121–2).

In 1993, Soros' Quantum Fund purchased between two and three million ounces of gold at US$345 per ounce as well as ten million shares in Newmont Mining. When Soros' purchases became known, speculation increased markedly, to the extent that the price of gold rose to over US$350 an ounce; thus, Soros made profits (Harmes 1998: 103).

Unlike most investors, Soros has a public identity as a *political citizen*, too. He argues that both the global financial markets and the market fundamentalism justifying them are fundamentally flawed. The rules have to be changed by collective decisions. Even his powers over markets are limited: 'If I impose the rules on myself but not on others, it would affect my own performance in the market but it would have no effect on what happens in the markets because no single participant is supposed to be able to influence the outcome' (Soros 1998: xxv).

sums between £100 and £500 million, that is, from US$150 million up to almost US$1 billion.[41] Possibly, these incentive structures have been created to tackle the problem of high incentives provided by the hedge funds. A story from the late 1980s illustrates this: 'In the UK, for instance, Crispin Odey moved from Barings, where he was highly acclaimed as a conventional fund manager. He set up his own hedge fund, and in his first year, his earnings soared from over £100,000 to some £19 million. After one good year, he hit a disastrous path.'[42]

Who would care about the risks if there were a fair chance of multiplying your already-abundant incomes by the factor of 190? In the early 2000s, it is not only banks in the offshore centres – including Wall Street and the City of London – but also hedge funds and even pension funds that push their managers to maximise absolute short-term yields. The prevalence of this incentive structure is reinforced by the fact that individual investors to these funds seem to be interested only in the absolute yields, not in the risk-adjusted yields. The more liquid their investments are, the more easily they increase or take away their shares on the basis of short-term performance.[43] Likewise, the above-mentioned banks in London pay bonuses on the basis of absolute profits, not on the basis of risk-adjusted yields.

At least as importantly, high *leverage* also encourages short-termism. When borrowing cash or securities to implement their trades, institutional investors must pay their creditors (usually banks) monthly or quarterly fees which can become prohibitive if carried over the long-term. Accordingly, the structure of transactions cost thus induces a strong bias towards short horizons.[44] Last but not least, the rules of accountability for dealers and fund managers can encourage excessive risk-taking and short-termism as well. Their performance is scrutinised all the time:

> Fund management these days is a very competitive business! Independent organisations provide regular statistics on fund performance and, if the manager has performed less well than comparable funds, they may find themselves being dismissed. This has led to charges of 'short-termism' in their investment decisions. However, as a director of one major fund commented to the author: 'The long run is the sum of short runs. If we get them right, the long run will be right too.'[45]

It has also been claimed that computerisation has additionally promoted short-termism. In the past, it was costly and time-consuming to find out the prices in exchanges and markets in other countries and continents. Now everything can be seen on-line on the screen; the cost of this information is fairly low. More sophisticated arbitrage opportunities than ever before are being spotted due to the use of computers, often linked to constant feeds of live prices and using 'expert systems' techniques. Some of these techniques constitute automated feedback loops. For instance, many of the electronic broker programmes will automatically sell off securities if their values drop below a pre-determined floor. Under these circumstances, it is, in principle, easy to trigger a chain-reaction. But, perhaps more crucially, computerisation also implies that a dealer has to be quicker than ever to take advantage of an arbitrage opportunity, because everyone else is using computers, too.[46] Again, short-termism is strongly encouraged.

There are thus compelling, structural reasons for the hectic, impatient discourse, which takes (very) short time-horizons for granted. 'The long run is the sum of short runs. If we get them right, the long run will be right too.' This is a dangerous fallacy – but not uncommon in economics, which tends to atomise time into an aggregate of separate short-runs.[47] In any case, it is clear that not only in offshore banks and hedge funds but even in mainstream banks and pension funds, 'short-term rhetoric has crowded out alternatives'.[48]

Collective Associations of Financial Actors

The individual and collective financial actors are not just market players. They have also created collective associations to pursue issues of common concern and interest, such as the International Organization of Securities Commissions (IOSCO), the Joint Forum on Financial Conglomerates, and the International Swaps and Derivatives Association (ISDA).

In the following, I will discuss three associations in some detail.[49] The first is the British Bankers' Association (BBA). It was formed in 1919, but its current role and structure date from 1972 when membership was extended to foreign banks in London.[50] Until then, membership had been restricted to British commercial banks in Great Britain and the Commonwealth. These changes created a broadly based banking association, representative of all banks in the UK and able, as such, to participate in the European Bankers' Federation. Based in Brussels, the Federation is recognised by the EC Commission, the Council and the European Parliament as the representative body for the community's commercial banking sector.

The BBA is the trade association for the banking industry in the UK. The membership currently includes all major banks and numbers some 330. Well over three-quarters of them are foreign-owned or foreign-controlled although, in local asset terms, British-owned banks predominate.

As a trade association the BBA is the forum in which the banks in the UK seek common ground to enable the banking industry as a whole to speak collectively on matters of common interest and of public policy. Being the voice of the banks in the UK the British Bankers' Association communicates the industry's views to the British government, to the Bank of England and City regulators, to the press, to opinion formers, to the institutions of the EC and to governments and regulators around the world.[51]

The second is the London Investment Banking Association (LIBA). LIBA is the principal trade association in the UK for firms active in the investment banking and securities industry. It works like the BBA, but with a more clearly articulated programme. The LIBA seems to be particularly active in the EU, advising on policy and taking part in discussions about financial markets regulations. It is concerned with fairness of practices and the rules of competition. But it is also interested in making European finance competitive by means of ensuring that the EU will not regulate more than other financial centres. However, it is also concerned that the increased number of acquisitions and mergers within the industry will lead to institutions, supported by their home governments, which will attempt to dominate the global financial markets. LIBA is warning about the concentration of power, particularly in the hands of the biggest US players; and it is also acting against the dominance of the US markets and actors.

The third collective association worth mentioning is the Institute of International Finance, Inc. (IIF). It is the world's only global association of financial institutions. The IIF was created in 1983 in response to the international debt crisis by thirty-eight banks of the leading industrialised countries. In the year 2000, members include most of the world's largest commercial banks and investment banks, as well as a growing number of insurance companies, investment management firms, multinational companies, trading companies, export credit agencies, and multilateral agencies. Over half of its members are European-based financial institutions, and representation from the leading financial institutions in emerging market countries is also increasing steadily. The Institute has more than 300 members, based in more than fifty countries.[52]

The IIF has three explicit, primary goals:

- First, to support members' risk management, asset allocation and business development in emerging markets. To this end, the IIF provides members with the reporting, data and analysis of economic and financial developments and prospects in emerging market economies.
- Second, to serve as a forum for engaging the private financial community in discussions with finance ministers; central bank governors; and the IMF, the World Bank, and other multilateral agencies designed to enhance private sector–public sector co-operation. These discussions

focus on issues such as preventing financial crises in emerging market economies and mitigating political risks for private sector infrastructure projects.

• Third, to provide a vehicle for exchanging views on global financial supervision issues and to advance the common views of its members with key regulatory authorities.

According to the IIF itself, its 'frequent missions to emerging market economies allow IIF economists to discuss policies directly with top government officials and representatives of private financial institutions and the business community'.[53] Furthermore, 'the Institute has unique access in these countries as an association representing the world's leading financial organisations'; and 'its location in Washington, DC, also allows for close contacts with the IMF, World Bank, and other official agencies'.[54]

What, then, are the views and opinions championed by the IIF? They are known as being advocates of the 'hands-off' approach by governments and, even, the IMF. 'The IIF was particularly hostile to the suggestion that the IMF might "lend into arrears" during a crisis, that is, offer support to governments that had not resolved disputes over payments to their private creditors.'[55] This suggestion was brought up in the 1996 G-10 report and would have favoured governments in debt negotiations.

Also, after the Asian and Russian crises, they have been constantly signalling their support 'for case-by-case, market-oriented approaches to crisis resolution'. IIF managing director Charles Dallara has said, 'a goal of the official sector should be to strengthen the framework for sustainable flows of capital to emerging markets and to ensure that policies are not initiated that could have the opposite effect'.[56] The IIF takes this to mean that some of the measures taken after the 1997–98 crises have already gone too far. These measures include: (i) strict application of the Paris Club principle of 'comparable treatment'; (ii) the requirement that countries should include 'collective action' clauses in their international bond covenants, as distinct from voluntary inclusion of such clauses; (iii) the permission for IMF lending to countries that are in arrears to private creditors; and (iv) support for the IMF approval of stays of litigation. The idea seems to be that the freedoms and rights of the private players in the global financial markets should be defended against the regulatory attempts of the IMF.

In sum, the IIF seems to be championing *radical free-market policies* also in the financial markets. It is defending the freedom and power of the private financial actors against the interventions of governments and multilateral agents such as the IMF. There is very little in the programmes of BBA and LIBA that would go against the orthodoxy of economic liberalism. However, LIBA seems to be alarmed by the concentration of power in the business, particularly in the hands of the biggest American players, and is thus championing fair rules of competition. In any case, we may conclude that the discourse of the collective associations of finance stems from the *pure form of the orthodoxy of economics.* As we remember, the Washington consensus is concomitant with the orthodoxy of (neo)classical economics. It dictates that growth can best be achieved by neoliberal means. The associations and lobbying organisations representing the interests of finance are also known to advocate, directly, further privatisation of pensions and social security and opening up of new markets. All this is highly consistent with the hypothesis that the associations of global finance lobby for policies that will ensure the continuous flow of further resources and investment opportunities to global financial markets.

Conclusion: The Direct Power of Financial Actors

The social relations of the system of globalising financial markets are causally powerful: they empower actors positioned in these structures with transformative capacity, that is, power. But what exactly is it that these actors can transform? What kind of power do they have?

First, a distinction has to be made between intended and unintended effects. Financial actors are trying to make short-term profits. If they have sufficient resources – possibly by building up high leverage and by selling short assets they do not have – they may be able to influence prices of securities or currencies by their sheer weight in the markets. The more the financial resources will be *concentrated* and the more the financial conglomerates rule the increasingly *deregulated* markets, the more feasible it is to manipulate prices this way. Manipulation is also possible because the financial markets are *socially structured.* Market leaders and financial gurus are socially constructed – and followed. The heavyweights and the market leaders thus dominate the business. An obvious consequence of this is that there is a strong tendency for further concentration of resources.

Sometimes, however, the sheer weight may work against the manipulators and create vicious feedback-loops with a strong susceptibility to a major crisis. It is crucial to acknowledge also that the heavyweights and market leaders are themselves products of the rules, options and interdependencies of the financial markets and the consequent process of *financial multiplication.* It is worth quoting Paul Krugman on the developments leading to the Russian crisis of 1998 at some length:

What nobody realized until it happened was that the competition among hedge funds to exploit ever narrower profit opportunities had created a sort of financial doomsday machine. Here's how it worked. Suppose that some hedge fund – call it Relativity Fund – has taken a big bet in Russian government debt. Then Russia defaults, and it loses a billion dollars or so. This makes the investors who are the counterparts of its short positions – the people who have lent it stocks and bonds, to be returned in the future – nervous, so they demand their assets back. However, Relativity doesn't actually have those assets on hand; it must buy them back, which means that it must sell other assets to get the necessary cash. And since it is such a big player in the markets, when it starts selling the prices of the thing it has invested in go down. Meanwhile, Relativity's rival, the Pussycat Fund, has also invested in many of the same things. So when Relativity is forced into sudden large sales, this means big losses for Pussycat as well; it too finds itself forced to 'cover its shorts' by selling, driving the prices of other assets down. In so doing, it created a problem for the Elizabethan Fund ... and so on down the line. If all this reminds you of the story of Asia's financial meltdown, it should: at a fundamental level, it was the same kind of a process, involving a vicious circle of plunging prices and imploding balance sheets.[57]

The financial actors have the power to influence financial markets for both their own benefit and, sometimes, demise, with indirect consequences to non-financial actors such as firms or states. Consider the two examples of speculations by Soros (discussed in Box 5, above). Both episodes are examples of games that are basically zero-sum, at least in the short-run. Nothing new was produced; no new values created. The profits of the Quantum Fund were taken out of the pockets of other actors. In the 1992 sterling speculation, the profits came from the state of the United Kingdom (and in particular, from the Bank of England). In the 1993 gold speculation, the profits came from other investors in gold and gold business.

Markets based only on zero-sum games could not grow very much. In this chapter, we have come to the conclusion that the financial multiplication process would be rather impotent without the *continuous extraction of further resources* into the system. Hence, given the way practices of governance of the global political economy have been organised in the 1980s and 1990s, the financial system tends to feed itself by drawing more resources from other sectors of the economy. Indeed, it grows rapidly in terms of the resources of its most powerful actors – and crisis-propensity.

In the next chapter, I shall argue that the power of financial markets has to do with the wider global dynamics as well. Finance is part of the game of global power politics and struggle for dominance. Moreover, states are competing for the location of financial assets and activities. Partially for these reasons, a structure has emerged that allocates capital on the basis of particular priorities, and quickly punishes any actor – including a state – trying to deviate from the norms that have been thus created. In other words, the dominant position of the US, the hegemony of neo-liberalism and the power of global financial markets are closely linked. Also the lobbying activities of the financial players are backed up by this structural power.

Notes

1. Henwood 1997: 13.

2. Valdez 1997: 188.

3. See de Goede 1999.

4. Holesovsky 1977: 329. Earlier forms of 'joint stock companies' worked in a more restrictive manner: participants invested their share in the enterprise, and received a share of possible profits accordingly. In these earlier forms, the commitment was not usually liquid for participants; and they may have been, at least partially, personally responsible for the possible debts of these companies. But the rise of the secondary markets started to change these practices.

5. See the addendum in Marx 1980/1894: 894–6.

6. In Chapter 27 of *Capital 3*, Marx analyses the rise of joint stock companies and the role of finance. According to Marx, stock exchange and finance constitute 'private production without private accountability' (p. 435). By taking loans and investing the borrowed funds, these new capitalists do not risk the capital they have acquired with their own work, or by hiring others to work for them, but 'social property' (p. 436). This also enables the development of 'a system of cheating and deception', as trust on promises must be based on speculation on uncertain future developments (p. 435). Moreover, the system enables a few opportunists and fortune-hunters to expropriate the property of the traditional capitalists. However, Marx never developed these insights at any depth. In fact, the crux of Marx's argument is based on his deterministic philosophy of history. He maintains that this is the final stage towards transformation to a system based on 'immediate social/socialised property' (p. 434; see also p. 438).

7. Polanyi 1957/1944: 14.

8. Ibid., pp. 15–20.

9. Ibid., p. 21.

10. Gill 1997a: 7.

11. The latter aspect has been emphasised by Gill 1997a; see also Gill 1997b: 215.

12. *Financial Times*, 23 January 1998, p. xvi.

13. Valdez 1997: 13–19, 52–90.

14. See K. Singh 1999: 27–9; and in particular, *The Economist*, 16 August 1997, pp. 67–9.

15. Ibid., p. 67. The claim of the article is, however, that this trend may not be viable. Specialisation is needed. As long as stock markets continue to soar, 'investors may choose to ignore such problems; but when the markets turn, budding financial conglomerates could find themselves with more awkward questions to answer'.

16. Hirst and Thompson (1999: 42–61) are right, however, to emphasise the national differences between countries, and the importance of policy choices. Some of the biggest countries, including the US, are relatively independent also in this respect. Globalisation remains partial, asymmetrical, unequal and dependent on policy choices.

17. Valdez 1997: 165; BIS 1999a: 15.

18. In March 2000 it was reported that Tiger, a group of hedge funds run by Julian Robertson, was to close Jaguar, its flagship fund, after running up big losses over the past two years. This only serves to prove the point that the life-span of hedge funds is usually short.

19. Harmes 1998: 103.

20. This is the conclusion of Edwards (1999: 196–7), who assesses available evidence and studies.

21. UNDP 1999: particularly 'Overview', 1–13 and 38–9.

22. See Beck 1992.

23. This corresponds also to the perspective of the new, mobile elites on freedom and security, perhaps their prime values. As Bauman (1997: 14) aptly puts it: 'These de-regulated, privatized, diffuse concerns with guarding the purity of consumerist life also come together in two contradictory, yet mutually reinforcing political demands directed towards the state. One is the demand to further enhance consumer freedoms of free consumers: to privatize the use of resources by "rolling back" all collective intervention in private affairs, dismantling politically imposed constraints, cutting taxes and public expenditure. Another demand is to deal more energetically with the consequences of the first demand: surfacing in the public discourse in the name of "law and order", this second demand is about the prevention of the equally deregulated and privatized protest of the victims of deregulation and privatization.' These elites are willing and ready to complement 'law and order' with the feeling of safety achieved by a full-blown private insurance and security system, however expensive.

24. About financial reinsurance, see Valdez 1997: 283–4.

25. Chavagneux 1999: 12.

26. Felix 1995b: 23–30.

27. Ibid., p. 31.

28. See Leyshon and Thrift 1997: 146, 314–20.

29. *Investors Chronicle* 1999: 14–32.

30. Ormerod 1994: 6.

31. For a thorough exposition and critical analysis of the consequences of these moves, see Bhaskar (1986: 224–308) who concludes by arguing that this kind of science 'at once naturalises and normalises things and reflects in an endless hall of mirrors the self-image of Bourgeois Man'.

32. This is the standard interpretation of Milton Friedman's position, widely shared by many economists. For more details, see Appendix 1. Hodgson (1988: 48–50) has shown, however, that Friedman is quick to change his position in one and the same text: what begins as an instrumentalist assumption is soon represented as a certain theory about the world. More generally, by changing the status of their fundamental assumptions in this manner, depending on the context and audience, economists are easily able to avoid all criticism (for the true believers and unthinking followers, the assumptions form a theory beyond doubt; for other, more suspicious and thoughtful interrogators, they can be represented simply as useful – and hypothetical – assumptions).

33. What can it explain, then? Well, for instance, the demand/supply theory of prices seems to be in some respects a better explanation of price-formation than the ancient, clumsy labour theory of value, although even the demand/supply theory falls short of being a real explanation (what are the elements in social, causally efficacious complexes that bring about and constitute 'demand' and 'supply', and what are the social rules and resources that constitute the conditions for exchange, supply and demand?). Similarly, game theory, which can be counted as a strand of economics, can also be helpful in explaining the typical herd behaviour in financial markets: under the conditions of radical uncertainty and fear of sudden losses, every single actor faces a Prisoner's Dilemma (PD) kind of a situation; for everybody, it is rational to take their money away from X, but thereby the value of X collapses, and everybody is much worse off than they would have been had they kept their money in X. One crucial difference to the real world story is, of course, the fact that usually the players in the PD-game of the world financial markets are bailed out, while it is the outsiders who bear the main burden of the consequences of these losses.

34. In his systematic and critical study of the background assumptions of economics, (Lawson 1997: 14) states bluntly that economics 'fares poorly in its own terms; it neither provides particularly accurate forecasts of events nor illustrates the world in which we live. But of equal significance, the whole project is riddled with confusion and incoherence. [...] the failure of the contemporary project to explain, predict or otherwise illuminate is met only with a restricted set of responses: with continuous revisions to certain parts of theories, the collection of ever more data, the development of increasingly sophisticated forms of computer software, and so forth.'

35. See Sayer 1992: 178–80.

36. For details and systematic analysis of the rhetoric of economics, see McCloskey 1986.

37. There are some economists and rational choice theorists who have relaxed the property-, ownership- and control-assumptions implicit in neoclassical economics, thereby going beyond just studying capitalist market economies (see Elster and Moene 1989; cf. also Bowles and Gintis 1998). But these exceptions have been and remain rare.

38. Of course further distinctions should be made. Thus, Robert Cox (1987: 358 *et passim*) distinguishes between the interests and ideas of: (i) those who control the big corporations and banks operating on a world scale; (ii) those who control big nation-based enterprises and industrial groups; and (iii) locally-based petty capitalists. Monetarism and globalising neoliberalism are conceptions that are most closely associated with (i), although they can be made consonant with (iii), too (e.g. through privatised pension systems, which might be alluring also to better-off public sector employees, etc.).

39. Harmes 1998: 104.

40. In personal communication, Anna Leander has insisted that although there may be more divergence than I indicate here, it may not be so important since as market actors (which is what matters) they will act on: (i) the financial interests they defend which are favoured by orthodox policies; (ii) the signals governments send to them regarding their commitment to defending these interests where again orthodox policies play a positive role; and (iii) the expectation that everyone else in the market will react in a similar way to deviations from the orthodox path. So, independently of their private evaluation of these policies they will (have to) react so as to reinforce the Washington consensus.

41. Hayward 1999, mimeo: 12–13.

42. Hills 1996: 20.

43. See also Edwards 1999: 191.

44. Harmes 1998: 106.

45. Valdez 1997: 86.

46. Ibid., p. 168.

47. In economics, atomistic instants of time constitute a statistical time-series or are connected, at best, through simplistic, Pavlov-dog-type learning processes of separate, individual actors.

48. O'Barr and Conley, as quoted in Harmes 1998: 106.

49. The importance of the first two stems from the fact that they represent the interests of the actors in the biggest financial centre, London, and also their role in the UK and EU politics. The IIF, in turn, is the only truly global association of financial actors and interests.

50. The following information is taken from http://www.bankfacts.org.uk/

51. Ibid.

52. See the website of the IIF at http://www.iif.com/about.htm

53. See http://www.iif.com/intro.htm

54. Ibid.

55. Kahler 1998: 17–18.

56. See http://www.iif.com/intro.htm

57. Krugman 1999a: 133.

3

Geoeconomics and Beyond: The Structural Power of Global Finance

The geopolitical space of the planet is organised into territorial states.[1] By diplomatic and administrative means, the sovereign states have governed production, exchange and finance in the expanding capitalist world economy. In the nineteenth and early twentieth centuries, the orthodoxy of *laissez-faire* liberalism prevailed. However, within the Bretton Woods world order, at first devised bilaterally by the US and the Great Britain in 1943–44, the participating states were given the responsibility to regulate and confine global finance in a non-orthodox, Keynesian manner. Most states outside the Soviet and Chinese sphere of influence joined this system.

In the re-emergence of global finance, the same two states – the US and the UK – have played a key role. The development of eurodollar markets in London was a conscious strategy by the British to remake London as the financial centre. In the 1960s, the London eurodollar markets began to prosper. The first offshore facilities were established in the Caribbean islands and elsewhere. The US banks and other financial actors dominated the business, with the consent of the US government. At the turn of the 1970s, the Nixon regime attempted to resolve the perceived decline of the hegemony of the US – and the 'instability' of the global economic order – by changing unilaterally the rules and principles of the Bretton Woods monetary system.

It is the argument of this chapter that, ever since these developments, the resuscitated global financial markets have played an important role in the transformations of interstate relations and systems of regional and global governance. Moreover, the competition between sovereign, territorial states for the location of financial activities and capital have pushed many states to introduce offshore facilities and major tax concessions, which in turn has conditioned the policies of other states. Moreover, financial (inter)-dependencies both condition and enable states in different ways. Therefore, states continue to struggle over the formation of these contexts.

Once created, the system of global financial markets has assumed emergent properties. The concept of *structural power* helps to explain more thoroughly the role of the financial markets in the complex nexus of global power relations.[2] Financial capital tends to be allocated collectively, in accordance with the expectations generated by the shared frameworks of interpretation.[3] Many of the financial actors are so positioned that they cannot avoid affecting the outcomes, independently of their will. The dealers and fund-managers make their far-reaching investment decisions on the basis of their largely shared discursive understandings of the world. As already argued in Chapter 2, the investment managers, brokers, dealers, etc., reproduce certain discourses in their daily activities. These discourses presuppose the essentials of orthodox economic theory and the Washington consensus.

Similarly, the credit-rating agencies – Moody's and Standard & Poor in particular – base their assessments on models that presuppose the validity of the basic tenets of orthodox economics. Because of the competition to attract investments, and the widespread fear of sudden financial capital flight, the discourses of financial actors have non-intentional power effects over both states and other economic actors.

The power of the financial markets tends to reinforce economic *neo-liberalism*. Moreover, whether intended or not, the development of various offshore centres and tax havens has encouraged both further globalisation of finance and practices of tax evasion and also criminal activities. In particular, the transnational option of tax evasion has been used as an argument against national taxes on capital. The burden of taxation has been transferred to work – i.e. to incomes of the ordinary wage-earners – and land, which are much less mobile than capital and cannot evade taxes as easily.

For many actors in the global political economy, it is quite reasonable to advocate liberalised financial markets not only for their own sake but also because they constitute a decisive element in the global context within which political agendas are set, discussed and fought over. They may or, sometimes, may not understand these links consciously; and typically they also tend to reify and naturalise them. These misrepresentations in fact help to reproduce the social relations of this global context. It is easier to advocate a contested political aim if the global context appears to deem that aim almost necessary or natural.

Globalising Capital and the Competition Between Territorial States

Although the power of finance appears to be non-territorial and seems to indicate a significant measure of dominance over most of the territorial

situation without any further ado. They turned inwards and concentrated on building the European Exchange Rate Mechanism (ERM) also to act as a buffer against the volatility and fluctuations of the dollar.

Nixon's unilateral move freed American hands from the ties and restrictions of the gold-based, collectively-managed system. It also had many other far-reaching effects, some of them intended, some not. The resulting post-Bretton Woods system gave leverage both to the US government and to Anglo-American financial markets and operators. The US government became *more sovereign* in its economic policy. It could continue financing its deficit with dollars and IOUs, and, alone among governments, could also move the exchange price of the dollar against other currencies without suffering the economic consequences that would face other states which attempted to do the same. It could dictate the level of interest rates on the basis of domestic considerations, whereas any change in the US interest rate would have wide repercussions all over the world through the dominance of dollar-nominated loans, bonds, reserves and contracts.[14]

This new 'Dollar–Wall Street (DWS) regime'[15] tended to loosen the control of central banks over international financial relations, centring the control instead upon private financial actors. The most prominent of them are registered in the US or the UK and located in Wall Street, New York, and the City of London, the two centres which together have amassed some 40 per cent of the volume of currency transactions. This does not mean that other centres and actors are unimportant. Many of the biggest banks in the world are Japanese, and Tokyo is the third major financial centre of the world. Also, Swiss actors and markets have traditionally been important, and many other Continental European financial actors are weighty as well. But the US financial institutions dominated the international business well into the 1980s, and they continue to benefit from the exceptional position of the US dollar and the US state; and typically they have had more legal room for manoeuvre than their Continental or Japanese counterparts. Indeed, in the late 1990s, the European financial institutions were concerned about the increasing centralisation of the markets in the hands of the dominant US actors.[16]

The US and British governments actively supported the rise of the new actors, practices and boundaries, such as eurodollar markets, offshore centres, growth of mutual and hedge funds, etc. The new system materialised from the day-to-day problem-solving of US foreign policy-making in the late 1960s and early 1970s. With far-reaching effects, the DWS regime shifted the basis of US hegemony towards the more indirect structural power of global financial markets. Soon this shift turned out to have *unintended, self-reinforcing consequences*. In particular, the system turned out to be more unstable and crisis-ridden than expected by its ideologues. Yet, as was also soon discovered, if managed well, the financial crises could further strengthen the DWS regime:

> Using its control over the IMF and the World Bank largely with the support of its European partners, Washington discovered that when its international financial operators reached the point of insolvency through their international activities, they could be bailed out by the populations of the borrower countries at almost no significant cost to the US economy. This solution was first hit upon during the Latin American international financial crisis at the start of the 1980s and it was a solution with really major economic and political significance.[17]

The territorial expansion of the DWS regime to 'the emerging markets' entails new resources and investment opportunities for the actors. The expansion thus also strengthens financial multiplication. But once a financial crisis hits a country outside the Anglo–American centres, funds will tend to flee into Wall Street and, also, the City of London. The collective mobilisation of resources by the IMF and other multilateral agencies tends to prevent the crisis from spreading to the main centres, and draws fresh resources to global financial markets. The position of the major centres and the main actors is thus strengthened; and new resources for issuing bank loans and bonds or investing in all kinds of assets are created. The costs of stabilisation are borne by the crisis–ridden countries.

One effect of all this is that after every crisis the outside areas become more dependent on these centres and the biggest private financial actors, which can continue to grow and increase their activities and, also, profits. And, of course, the stabilisation and adjustment programmes of the IMF and other multilateral agencies – mostly dominated by the US – are based on the idea of *restoring the confidence of the private investors*. According to the recipe, the confidence should always be restored by means of neoliberal austerity programmes, deregulation, opening up of markets to transnational actors and re-regulation in accordance with US interests and legislation. This serves to facilitate access to these markets and, most importantly, further the structural power of global finance.

In Peter Gowan's interpretation, despite the rise of the new growth motors in information technology and biotechnology, the US non-financial economic performance has been in decline since the late 1960s, as revealed by its chronic balance of payments deficit; involvement in mounting debt; declining real wages level; and tendency to substitute Southern markets for the more competitive markets in Europe and South-East Asia.[18] The US state has responded to these problems resolutely.[19]

In the language of the US foreign policy-makers of the 1990s, *geoeconomics* has on the whole replaced geopolitics in the global power game.

Geoeconomics is about domination of markets. Since Nixon and Reagan, the aim of the US state has been to preserve and, then, cultivate US leadership and economic power, also relative to others. The US has combined systematically enforced unilateral trade policies to maximise the market shares of US-based corporations,[20] with attempts to universalise US legislation[21] and punish a large number of reluctant countries by imposing economic sanctions on them.[22]

Although many of these policies have been successful, it is the global financial markets that seem to have assumed the key role. The indirect but decisive support of the DWS regime has also given encouragement to the project of locking-in the US as the powerful, unquestioned centre of the New World Order.[23] In particular, Gowan claims that the DWS regime became the core of foreign policy for the Clinton administration. Just after Clinton's inauguration, he created a National Economic Security Council (NESC), alongside the powerful Cold War body, the National Security Council. An experienced financial actor, Robert Rubin, became the head of the NESC. Previously, Rubin had been a former senior partner in Goldman Sachs, the well-known Wall Street-based investment bank engaging in hedge-fund-like activities. The new team also included Al Gore, Robert Reich and Larry Summers.[24]

Following the ideas of the National Economic Security Council, the Clinton administration has pushed countries further to open up their markets to US products, capital and services, not least financial services, on US terms. The American Open Door strategy has been meant to warrant that all the borders are open to US goods, capital and services, and that there would be 'no more free riders'.[25] The National Economic Security Council aims to strengthen the hegemonic stability of the world economy. The IMF, the World Bank, the OECD, the World Trade Organisation (WTO), and the failed proposal for the Multilateral Agreement on Investments (MAI), have all had a well-defined role in the 'new constitutional' project to lock in this version of economic liberalism. The actors and agreements of global governance have further subjected states to market discipline. As Stephen Gill summarises the outcome of the on-going project of the new constitutionalism:

> Indeed, public policy has been redefined in such a way that governments seek to prove their credibility, and of the consistency of their policies according to the degree to which they inspire the confidence of investors. In this way, new political and constitutional initiatives in the sphere of money and finance are linked to the imposition of macro-economic and micro-economic discipline in ways that are intended to underpin the power of capital in the state and civil society.[26]

Gill continues to argue that the new constitutional project, advocated by the US state alongside many MNCs and financial actors, relies upon the market, especially the capital market, to *discipline* economic agents. The three Cs – Credibility, Consistency and Confidence of investors – summarise the norms laid on most states. In this sense, the global financial markets have assumed a pivotal role in the reproduction of the dominance of the US in the post-Cold War world.

Although the US has learnt, over time, to use the globalising financial markets to pursue its own particular purposes, there are definite *limits* to the freedom of action and power of the US government. First of all, from the US government's point of view, the DWS regime stemmed from a series of responses to the problems caused by its *declining* position in the global political economy. In that sense, the episodes leading to the rise of the global financial markets have been a sign of weakness rather than strength. Secondly, a major financial crisis in the US – or a major crisis spreading to the US – would threaten its position. The euro or yen might emerge as an alternative, more credible vehicle for world trade and finance. Should Wall Street and the dollar decline rapidly in importance, the US would quickly face: (i) the consequences of the difficulties of continuing to roll over the accumulated IOUs; and (ii) the spectre of the return of the dollar stock from all over the world, which could cause a major currency crisis and/or inflation.[27]

Last but not least, the global financial markets not only facilitate but also constrain the actions of the US state. A 1992 *Wall Street Journal* analysis of the perimeters of the US economic policies is revealing. US federal debt, the *Journal* reported, stood around US$3 trillion, with interest costs approximately US$200 billion a year. Any attempt to pursue expansionary or inflationary fiscal policy would be disciplined by the financial markets. The reaction is likely to be 'swift and painful'. If Clinton ignores the market, the *Journal* asserted, he will find out very quickly who is in the 'driver's seat'.[28]

The decline of Britain and the rise of offshore facilities and tax havens   As we recall, Polanyi, among others, has claimed that in the late nineteenth and early twentieth centuries, 'gold standard and constitutionalism were the instruments which made the voice of the City of London heard in many smaller countries which had adopted these symbols of adherence to the new international order'. The Pax Britannica was maintained partially by force, 'but more frequently it prevailed by the timely pull of a thread in the international monetary network'. The financial system centring on the City of London had become an essential part of the power of London, well beyond the formal boundaries of the British Empire.

After World War II, the era of formal empires was coming to an end and, also because of the war, Britain was almost bankrupt. Yet the British were keen to restore as much of their previous global dominance as they could. Harold Wilson of the first post-war Labour government decided to reopen the City of London as an international financial marketplace.[29] Well into the 1950s, London's international financial position was ensured because the city served as the financial centre for the closed sterling bloc of the Empire/Commonwealth. However, as the long-term viability of this bloc came increasingly into question in the late 1950s and early 1960s, British financial authorities concluded that London's international position might be better preserved if it were to act as a financial centre for *offshore dollar transactions*.

The term 'offshore' was not, however, first used to designate the euro-dollar market of the City of London. According to Ronen Palan, the term was probably coined in the 1960s in reference to those 'offshore' radio stations such as Radio Caroline in the UK or the Peace station in Israel, which evaded national broadcasting restrictions by being located on vessels situated just outside the territorial waters of their respective countries.[30] The metaphor of offshore seems to have been so successful because it captures well the idea that individuals and companies are making use of some new types of boundaries, or 'shores', and in doing so are able to escape containment within a territorial sovereign state and thereby its control.[31]

The idea of switching location to avoid taxes or regulations is older than the term 'offshore'. Its origin lies in the introduction and rising levels of income taxes by the territorial states, in the context of a world economy in which economic transactions and relations are not tied to any given territory. In the 1920s, the British Treasury struggled with tax evasion by companies which were nominally directed from the Channel Islands. The US state had similar problems with the Bahamas, Panama, Newfoundland and other low-tax jurisdictions. Also, complicated transnational legal arrangements were invented to avoid taxation. In the late 1930s, new powers were given to authorities in the US, the UK and other countries to prevent tax evasion by nominal relocation. Despite the resistance of the House of Lords and other pro-wealthy political forces, these new powers mostly worked.[32]

As direct foreign (particularly US) investment started to grow again in the 1950s, some new jurisdictions began to offer 'convenient facilities'. In particular, small English-speaking statelets, often islands, which generally had been (and sometimes still remained) colonial dependencies of the British Empire, could offer numerous advantages for MNCs. They had a modern-style legal system, the currency of the mother country and in many cases they benefited from the tax treaties that had been extended to them. Since their own tax-base was poor, an appealing alternative was to charge a small fee on company registrations. Guarantees of secrecy, exemptions from taxes and – from the 1960s onwards – specially tailored laxity of regulations made this option attractive to companies. These facilities were discreetly publicised in the small community of international tax specialists, who were giving advice to the rich and re-emerging transnational business.[33] Since the late 1980s, they have been more and more openly advertised in the fancy financial and travel magazines that the big airlines, for example, distribute for free.

Step by step, British governments structured the City of London on the model of the offshore centres of many of its (former) dependencies. In the beginning, this may have evolved as a response to day-to-day problem-solving of a number of political and balance-of-payments crises, but gradually it emerged as a conscious strategy. The euromarket is believed to have emerged in 1958. During the Suez Canal crisis and the ensuing run on British sterling, the British government imposed restraints on sterling credits to countries engaging in third-party transactions within the sterling area and, in addition, raised the bank rate to 7 per cent. In response, British banks began actively to seek dollar deposits to use in trade credits. These transactions in dollars were then not considered to be taking place under the exchange rate regulation, reserve regulation or any other regulations of the British state.[34]

The late 1950s was also the time of the growth of transnational firms. Capital controls were relaxed and the convertibility of currencies for non-residents was introduced. Hence, the supply and demand for the new extra-territorial financial services emerged simultaneously. They were encouraged to meet in London, in the new juridical space opened up by the dollar markets of deposits and loans. The eurodollar market developed rapidly. In 1963, the eurodollar loan market was supplemented by the eurobond market, which consists of bonds underwritten by international banking syndicates and not subject to any country's securities laws.

The US took measures to protect its low domestic interest rates by blocking access to US capital markets and encouraging the US multinationals to fund expansion abroad from their foreign earnings. The US banks were likewise encouraged to set up branches abroad to service the growth of the US MNCs. To attract these activities, the Bank of England exempted foreign banks from all credit and interest rate requirements, except in sterling transactions with residents.[35] 'The license so nonchalantly granted them by the US and British governments to operate in London in dollars, not sterling, made this foreign business much more profitable than their [US banks'] taxed and regulated business at home.'[36] Ultimately, the role of the City as an offshore centre was itself largely dependent upon US government policy, which allowed US banks to operate free of domestic US banking regulation by establishing operations in London.

It is important to note that, since the early 1960s, the City of London has also benefited from the exploitation of the facilities of the related offshore centres within the sterling area. Secrecy and freedom from exchange controls and bank reserve requirements made the tax havens particularly attractive. Both banks and non-bank investors began to locate their assets in these tax havens, closely connected to the City of London.[37]

In these ways, the British authorities supported the eurodollar market and related offshore facilities in the 1960s, and more broadly the globalisation process in the 1970s and 1980s.[38] Strange summarises the consequences of these moves: 'All subsequent history of the management (and mismanagement) of international finance showed the importance to the United States of having London as partner to New York in developing a lively and innovative system for the transnational creation of and trade in credit.'[39]

By the time of the unilateral 1971 decision by the Nixon regime to end the convertibility of dollar to gold, London had re-emerged as the biggest and most important financial centre of the world. However, in the mid-1970s, there was an attempt by the Labour government to introduce capital controls. The speculators demonstrated their strength. Soon they forced – eventually with the support of the IMF conditionality – the British government away from their attempt to follow Keynesian economic policies.[40] Hence, the process of making London an offshore centre could continue. It culminated in the 1979 UK Banking Act, the first Act of the Thatcher government, which removed all distinction between offshore and onshore markets. Since then, the City of London has been considered a full-fledged offshore financial market.[41] In 1981, in the US, the newly elected Reagan administration followed suit and enacted a law allowing so-called 'International Banking Facilities' in the US, thus giving Wall Street the same offshore status as the City.[42]

The welfare states relying upon tax-and-transfer policies for redistribution and fiscal policy appear to have been vulnerable to the mobility of capital. In contrast to the immobility of the separate, territorial nation-states, the mobility of capital was speeded up by the new facilities of communication and transportation and the post-war liberalisation.

However, it was the creation of eurodollar markets and offshore facilities that made possible a more radical escape for capital. Well before the ascendance of Reagan and Thatcher, at least some wealthy individuals and firms (including financial actors) could go back in time to the days of nineteenth-century *laissez-faire* capitalism by switching their nominal or legal location to an offshore registration. At first, this was illegitimate, bad for reputation, risky and potentially costly for most actors. However, for various reasons, some of the national authorities allowed this to happen, most notably the US and the UK, even when they could have stopped it. Elsewhere, the tacit consent to migrate offshore may have been a compromise between contradictory demands of labour/electorate and capital (against the democratic demands for better welfare services and higher taxes, the offshore facilities offered an easy way to give tacit concessions to capital). Later, the process became increasingly difficult to reverse.[43]

Once established, both the City of London and the new offshore centres in the Channel Islands, Caribbean and elsewhere were open to anybody who was allowed access by their national authorities, whether from the English-speaking world or not. There had also been offshore facilities in the French- and German-speaking Continental Europe. Since the 1920s, the anachronistic mini-states, Andorra, Liechtenstein, Luxembourg and Monaco, have provided tax exemptions and regulatory laxity. Since 1934, Switzerland has provided banking secrecy and new residence for wealthy individuals and families. Except Switzerland, these Continental European tax and regulatory havens are small, anachronistic jurisdictions, which generally failed to 'move with the times'.

It is often argued that European tax havens did not set themselves deliberately on a path that distinguished them for tax and regulatory laxity, but rather it was the other way around. From the early 1920s, the world around them was launched on a course to develop welfare states. This led to an unprecedented rise in taxation and socially oriented regulation; in contrast to *laissez-faire* regulations of the nineteenth century, these states remained tied to the nineteenth-century practices.[44] Thus they provided 'natural' tax havens to the wealthiest class. Their importance has started to rise since the 1960s, along with the establishment of offshore facilities in the former British Empire.

For the mini-states and some developing countries, the temptation to build offshore facilities to attract financial activities is obvious. Even a very small slice of the assets and flows involved may appear irresistible. At the turn of the century, perhaps half of the world's stock of money resides in or flows through tax havens. Offshore financial assets stand currently at US$5–8 trillion-worth of deposits and investment funds, of which perhaps 30 per cent is located in the Caribbean.[45] The English-speaking offshore centres of the Caribbean are relatively wealthy, mainly due to their offshore status. The Cayman Islands, with a population of under 30,000 people, is said to be the world's fifth largest banking centre in terms of deposits. Although over 500 banks were licensed in the Cayman Islands, only seventy had any physical presence there other than a nameplate. And although only eight carried out local business, financial business is estimated to account for one-third of total employment and has made these islands appear modern and rich.[46]

Andorra, Liechtenstein, Luxembourg and Monaco in Europe, however, are even richer, on top of which is added the glamour of being meeting places for the rich and famous. The tax-evaders are the real winners, but the indigenous population of these mini-states can become rich with the negligible slice of the taxes and income that the bigger states lose because of them.

Once the dynamics of this process of escape, evasion and deregulation gained strength, and extra opportunities for both economic actors and states were opened up, a tendency towards a new competitive game of regulatory laxity has surfaced. MNCs can use the financial services of the City of London and offshore centres and thereby undermine the position of national banks and taxation authorities. Traditional commercial banks face increasing international competition from the new financial actors and centres, endowed seemingly with abundant resources and not restricted by cumbersome rules and regulations. Investors see new options for non-

---

Box 6 Offshore facilities, tax havens and transnational crime

For good reasons, offshore centres and tax havens have been associated with the rise of transnational crime. Susan Strange (1998: 123) claims that it is common knowledge that 'the business of money laundering could not have so prospered and grown without the facilities for swift and relatively invisible transnational movements of money'. The value of laundered money – from the trafficking of drugs, arms, nuclear material, human body parts, etc. – is thought to amount to US$400 billion a year, which is 5–10 per cent of the money parked in or going through the offshore centres and tax havens.

The key offshore facility is *secrecy*. When no questions are asked, and very few know the identity of the account-holder, money laundering is easy. In Switzerland or the Bahamas, for instance, this secrecy has been backed up by criminal law. In many other places, there is, in practice, a very high level of bank 'confidentiality'. A few transfers between bank accounts, owned by artificial persons or firms, and the money can be returned as apparently legal to any use in the country where the criminals are based or operate.

Despite the huge sums involved in drug trafficking, etc., Strange

regulated, risky but high-profit activities rising. The double temptation of tax evasion and fast financial expansion persuades many of the wealthiest to transfer their assets, incomes and, even, residence offshore. And of course, where else would all the money from the criminal activities go? Despite these 'market pressures', the 1996 OECD Report claims that in only one case out of seven categories of regulatory measures were the subsequent rounds of OECD deregulation of the 1980s and 1990s carried out because of the direct pressure stemming from the offshore centres.[47] The one case in which market pressures from the offshore centres explain deregulation directly is the relaxation of mandatory reserve requirements. In the cases of interest rate controls, quantitative investment restrictions, capital controls, securities market regulations, restrictions on line-of-business and ownership linkages, and restrictions on foreign bank entry, deregulation has been realised by explicit political decisions, mostly in the context of multilateral diplomacy. Although the cases of France and Sweden in the early 1980s illustrate that these decisions were often made after painful failures to continue Keynesian and/or to implement democratic socialist or social-democratic policies,[48] any simple story about the in-

---

claims that tax evasion, private fraud, financial crime and public embezzlement are in fact bigger problems. The richest people of the world do not have to pay taxes. Many of them have made their fortune by crime, fraud, embezzlement or, more straightforwardly, by robbing their countries.

Indeed, why should any money be lodged with any offshore centre or tax haven? The possible reasons are limited: criminality and money laundering on the one hand, and tax avoidance, tax deferral or transfer pricing, on the other hand. If money laundering accounts for at most 10 per cent of the offshore-based money, a large portion of the rest must stem from tax avoidance. Thus, roughly, some US$5 trillion is hiding from the tax authorities in the offshore centres and tax havens. The offshore havens facilitate trafficking of all kinds, financial crime, embezzlement by dictators and corrupt politicians, as well as systematic tax avoidance by the richest people of the world.

Under international pressure, the Swiss government passed, in March 1990, a bill that outlawed the laundering of funds from criminal activities and required financiers to check the identity of account-holders. Meanwhile, many other centres have created even more water-tight systems of secrecy.

evitability of 'place competition' is bound to be misleading. MNCs and investors have to trust the place where they relocate, and the establishment of trust – and the related process of reputation-building – is complicated and fragile. In some contexts, significant territorial actors can also initiate, unilaterally, an upward spiral of regulation (if they want).[49]

Finally, two important factors of the wholesale financial markets have to be highlighted. First, the Anglo–American system of ownership, stock markets, banking, taxation, pension funding, etc., has been particularly prone to the development of what Strange calls 'casino capitalism'.[50] The post-World War II Nordic, Continental European, Japanese or Asian model used to be more productivist in orientation. In the social-democratic and corporatist models, control over major corporations has *not* been for sale in the stock exchanges; in many cases, the state has played a role in industrial planning; pensions have been public and usually not funded; taxation has been higher and more strictly implemented; and the activities of banks and investment funds have been national and confined to strictly defined tasks.

The US and the UK have led the way in deregulation, and in the process they have been transformed, too. Yet, in a sense it is not wrong to say that financial deregulation has amounted to Anglo-Americanisation of practices, particularly in the OECD area, but increasingly everywhere. This has also had far-reaching effects on the restructuring of relations of production, exchange and accountability.[51] Moreover, deregulation has meant more room for manoeuvre, new open markets for financial actors, and the migration of money offshore. The ones most familiar with, and capable of, these kinds of operations have been Anglo–American. This has given them a competitive edge. Deregulation has also meant that more resources are drawn to the increasingly global financial markets; and that the economic policies of states have been directed towards serving, first and foremost, the rentier interests.

Second, it is equally noteworthy that 'the bulk of "offshore" financial transactions are plotted and arranged in world cities like New York, London and Tokyo'.[52] Since arguably a considerable portion of the world economy has already migrated, or is in the process of migrating towards offshore,[53] it may appear that the bulk of economic activity is now located in the exotic offshore centres in the Caribbean, anachronistic European principalities or occasional developing countries. In fact, this is not at all the case. In practice, the traditional financial centres – London and New York – remain the most important sites of financial *activities*, alongside new centres such as Tokyo and Singapore. It is rather that these major centres themselves are now based on the newly built offshore facilities, and that the rest of the offshore centres are merely used for evading the eyes of the police, regulators and tax departments.

The role of Japan in the process of de/re-regulation The multi-lateral Bretton Woods system was transformed by the unilateral actions of the US and the UK (with the background support of small statelets offering strategic offshore facilities). Countries such as Canada, Germany and Switzerland soon followed suit. As argued above, the US has been able to exploit the DWS regime to particular ends, including resolving acute economic problems and the restoration of its hegemonic position in global politics. Similarly, the City of London has reinforced London as one of the major cities of the world, despite the collapse of the Empire and the manifold economic difficulties of Britain. Emulating London, New York soon formed its own offshore facilities.

Tokyo, Singapore and some other South-East Asian cities have sub-sequently followed the examples of London and New York in establishing offshore facilities. Although Japan did not play any important role in initiating the process of deregulation, it has indirectly contributed to reinforcing the process. In the subsequent rounds of multilateral re-regulation of the 1980s and 1990s (a selective return to Polanyi), Japan has been a much more central player. Tokyo is also the third biggest financial centre, and Japanese banks are among the biggest in the world. On the other hand, there is at least circumstantial evidence to show that the US government has also tried to exploit the DWS regime and the power of hedge funds to gain *relative advantage* over its main economic competitors in Asia, namely Japan and the Asian tigers. Hence, to get a more com-prehensive picture of the geoeconomics revolving round global finance, it is essential to discuss briefly the positioning of Japan in the global political economy.

After World War II, Japan's economy was reorganised by the US author-ities. The responsibility for governance was, finally, ceded back to the Japanese in the 1950s. Within protectionist barriers, but with full access to the world markets, Japanese firms became highly competitive by the 1960s. Corporatist industrial planning helped Japanese firms to achieve leadership in many markets. The US started to have an increasing deficit in its balance of payments with the Japanese. The 1971 'deliberate act of sabotage' of the US government also aimed at correcting this imbalance with the Japanese. It did not help. But a new kind of tie of interdependence developed, and the Japanese started to finance the US deficit by investing the surplus in the US government securities, thus in effect funding the military-Keynesianism of the Reagan era.

Until the 1980s, the Japanese financial system was based on state control. The state was in charge of the creation and price of credit. The rate of savings was high and Japanese banks became among the biggest in the world. The Ministry of Finance, the Bank of Japan, the Ministry of Trade and Industry, the Longterm Credit Bank and other state agencies kept interest rates low and helped to direct credit to export industries. However, after the oil crisis, and at the latest by 1983, the increasingly indebted Japanese state started to loosen control over the trade of public bonds and other securities. New laws were enacted, and markets deregulated. The consequences of these developments were far-reaching. Again, Strange's summary of the developments is apt:

> The high savings and low interest rates in Japan combined with low savings and relatively high interest rates in America increasingly tempted the big Japanese banks to go abroad to London and New York in search of profitable arbitrage, especially in the bond markets. By 1986, Japanese banks were the biggest lenders in the international financial markets. In going abroad, they weakened the control of the government over the financial system, escaped the 'Chinese walls' compartmentalising financial dealings and possibly added to the volatility of exchange rates.[54]

It is also important to note that by the mid-1980s the Japanese surplus was increasingly invested in the US financial markets, particularly in the US

Box 7 The Bank for International Settlements (BIS) regime

The BIS was set up by US and European, private and central bankers in the 1930s to help reduce financial instability. It provided a forum for the leading central bankers, who started to meet monthly. However, it failed to prevent the 1931 financial crisis, which, eventually, made the 1930s depression 'Great'.

The Bretton Woods negotiators associated the BIS with the pre-1931 liberal era and with the bankers' vision. They passed a motion at the conference calling for the institution's abolition 'at the earliest possible moment'. That moment has not arrived yet.

The BIS re-emerged from the ashes of the Bretton Woods system. Since the 1970s, it has acted as a meeting place for central bankers. In the wake of each crisis, from the bank failures of 1974 (which came about through currency speculation), to the debt crises of the 1980s and Black Monday in 1987, central bankers met within the BIS to construct an increasingly complicated set of norms, rules and decision-making procedures for handling and preventing future crises. From the Basle Concordat of 1975 to the Basle Accord of 1988 and beyond, these rules have regulated financial markets; instigated new forms of

Treasury bills, but also in stock markets and real estate. Japan, and in particular the financial markets of Tokyo, became dependent on developments in London and New York – and also more vulnerable to sudden fluctuations in their bond and stock markets. In the wake of deregulation, unsustainable bubbles emerged in the US, in the Nordic countries, and elsewhere. Japan got more than a fair share of this 'global epidemic of moral hazard'.[55] Both land and stock prices tripled in the late 1980s and banks appeared skilful in hiding their bad loans.

First came Black Monday in October 1987. It started in London and New York, but spread to Tokyo. 'Had it not been for imposed circuit breakers suspending dealing in shares that fell in one day more than 15 per cent, the panic in Tokyo would have been unstoppable.'[56] Globally, the immediate and spontaneous intervention of the state of Japan was decisive. The Ministry of Finance orchestrated a big buying campaign by the biggest Japanese securities firms. Besides halting the crisis, this intervention also stimulated a new round of OECD re-regulation.

However, the 1988 Basle capital–assets ratios aggravated the problems of Japanese banks. The Basle Accord forced the Japanese to follow the

---

supervision; and allocated responsibilities for multilateral lender-of-last-resort actions (Helleiner 1994: 17).

The *laissez-faire*-minded bankers, economists and politicians were always suspicious about the Bretton Woods institutions, including the IMF; but they did have faith in the BIS.

The times they were achanging. Since the early 1970s, the IMF has become a flagship for the orthodoxy and, simultaneously, the BIS has gained in new importance. Helleiner (p. 191) describes the results of the BIS regime as 'pro-market type of regulation designed to prevent financial crises'. Yet, in contrast to the most pure form of neoliberalism, the BIS ideology does not assume that markets would operate smoothly without any regulation.

Gowan's (1999: 28) criticism that the BIS provides only vague, non-legal guidelines is thus somewhat off the mark. Rather than the legal form, the problem lies with the underlying ideology. In the world of financial innovations, emergent markets, banks' 'off-balance-sheet' activities, and offshore facilities, the BIS has been too weak, for instance, to adhere consistently to the capital–assets ratios. But the BIS has not only been weak and West-centric, it has also been supporting the further expansion of financial markets – at the expense of production and the welfare of people.

standards based on Western practices and conceptions of adequacy: the banks could not continue to hide bad, unpayable loans, at least not as easily as before. The banks had to sell some of their hidden assets and at the same time issue more shares to raise capital to back their loan portfolios. This triggered the fall in Tokyo share prices. Given that the Japanese banks were fully backed up by the state, it is no wonder that 'many Japanese thought the 1988 Accord was little more than a clever American ploy to get their own back on Japanese banks for the success of Japanese export industries in world markets'.[57]

The December 1989 downturn in the Tokyo stock market marked the beginning of a long series of crises and stagnation. The Bank of Japan raised its interest rates in 1990 to stabilise the situation, but, unintentionally, in 1991 land and stock prices began a steep decline. Within a few years, the prices were 60 per cent below their peak of 1989–90. During the 1990s, Japan has been locked into a long and stubborn depression, a deflationary liquidity trap in which people want to hold money (cash) instead of investing or consuming.[58]

In the 1990s, in the midst of the recession, the Japanese were oscillating between Keynesianism and fiscal orthodoxy, as well as between a nationalist and a US-centric view. Politically, for some the crisis implied a quest for a more autonomous stand; others have concluded, as the Washington consensus dictates, that the US model is the best option for restoring growth and prosperity.

The crisis-ridden years since the late 1980s have also coincided with the rise of unilateralism and economic nationalism by the US. The concept of 'managed trade', systematically pursued by the US towards Japan, involves replacing a rule-based trade regime with a results-based regime. In other words, Japan has accepted quantitative targets for its imports and exports with the US. Moreover, the US interprets unilaterally what it considers as fair trade and thereby uses the powers given by Super-301 (Section 301 of the Trade Act of 1974), anti-dumping laws and other legal means to restrict and direct trade, as well as to impose its norms on Japan and other countries.[59] The US has acted as a judge, jury and executioner in deciding unfair trade practices. Because of the recession at home and difficulties with the US markets, many Japanese firms started to invest in, and move to, China, Malaysia, Thailand and South Korea. This has encouraged new Asian regionalism.

By the 1980s, the ASEAN region, with Japan as its economic centre, was identified as the main rival of the US. Also in the 1990s, the US trade deficit with this region, including in particular Japan, persisted. The new US doctrine that full economic access to other countries is a *national security issue* was meant first and foremost to facilitate opening up the economies of East and South-East Asia.[60] The new programmes and rules of the IMF and the WTO, pushed by the US, aimed specifically at opening the financial markets and at giving complete freedom for financial operators to enter every financial system with the same rights as local operators. At stake are control and dependency. Global financial markets create new relations of dependency and undermine national planning capacities and control. The superior resources, also stemming from the global financial multiplication process, of the US (and British and European) financial actors entitle them to dominate the ensuing game. Financial markets, which have been liberalised by means of US-style re-regulation, also imply the opening up of possibilities for buy-outs, acquisitions and mergers.

However, as so often in the dialectics of domination, the developments have not been unidirectional. The Japanese savings rate continues to be very high compared to that of the US; and US growth has been debt- and deficit-driven. But because of the economic problems in Japan, the Bank of Japan (instead of Japanese private banks) has become the largest single lender to the US government. Moreover, Japanese institutions have started to prefer short-term US Treasury bills instead of long-term securities. Consequently, the US government has become increasingly vulnerable to Japanese decisions, also to those of public authorities. A major crisis has almost always been anticipated by a shift of foreign funds from long-term assets into more liquid, shorter-term ones.[61]

The Indirect Power of Finance: Directing Financial Flows

As a reflective collective actor and a complex organisation, a modern state can assume a hegemonic project. The US interest in promoting what became known as the 'globalisation' process from the 1960s onwards has stemmed, step by step, from the understanding that the emerging open global financial order feeds into its action-possibilities and resources. Despite the dangers posed by the recurring crises, the financial markets have indeed helped the US to reproduce its position as a world leader *vis-à-vis* other states.[62] However, any hegemonic project of a state must have ethico-political content. Most recently, since the Reagan–Thatcher era, the content of the US (and UK) hegemonic project has been that of neoliberalism, known also as the Washington 'consensus'.[63]

Once created, the global financial markets have assumed emergent properties. The concept of *structural power* helps us to understand more thoroughly the role of the financial markets in the complex nexus of global power relations. Many of the financial actors are so positioned that they cannot avoid affecting the outcomes, independently of their will. The understandings and discourses of financial actors have non-intentional power effects over states and economic actors. In effect, the indirect power of the financial markets tends to reinforce economic *neoliberalism*.

As a hegemonic discursive formation, neoliberalism does not have to be associated with any state (indeed there is no non-contingent reason why neoliberalism should be hegemonic in the US).[64] Hegemony also refers to discursive formations that achieve, first, rhetorical *leadership* and then, once established, self-evidence as *common sense* about 'normal' and 'appropriate' forms of subjectivity, practices and conduct. However, in a world of sovereign states, a particular state and domestic society tends to provide a model, and this is also promoted by the state machinery itself. Hence the two meanings of 'hegemony' tend to overlap. Also the hegemony as ideational leadership – or as a normalised common sense – can be partially maintained by force or by systematic exclusions of contradictory voices from the public sphere. Yet, force and exclusions work only up to the limited extent that they go mostly unacknowledged. The less contested and visible the force and exclusions, the better they are at maintaining and developing hegemony (in the sense of legitimacy and voluntary consent to a model).[65]

Hegemony in this more impersonal sense refers to power and leadership in the public space of ideas. It is advocated and reproduced but also resisted by a multiplicity of actors, with asymmetric transformative capacities. Resistance and alternatives pose a challenge. Hegemony is based on particular ways of constructing the *plausibility* of claims and interpretations in contextual fields of communication. It is not primarily a property of actors but of relational, discursive practices reproduced by positioned actors in a concrete world historical context.

In the following, I will focus on how the hegemony of neoliberalism in the 1980s and 1990s has been backed up by the power of global financial markets. The global capital allocation process is socially structured and ideological, and tends to condition economic policies of states. This is often also what is at stake in the geoeconomics revolving round global finance, even when it is not clearly spelt out.[66] Regarding (lack of) freedom in the economic policy of states, it is crucial that the collective allocation of financial investment decisions can occur without any centralisation of decision-making. This is warranted, among other things, by the shared frameworks of analysis of financial prospects, also circulated in the media of the global elites; the tendency to follow gurus and heavyweights in the marketplace; and the role of credit-rating agencies. In various ways, the rapid reactions of financial flows seem to strengthen the plausibility of the there-is-no-alternative claims and interpretations of the advocates of neoliberalism.

The role of credit rating Debt is a commitment and implies various forms of dependency. A voluntarily taken one-off loan may appear inconsequential. If there are no difficulties in paying it back as agreed, the relationship between the debtor and the creditor may not alter the course of action of the debtor in any significant way. But assume that A has many loans, some shorter, some longer, and that together they constitute a substantial amount of A's annual income – or may even exceed them. Assume further that, given A's other commitments, it is not realistic to expect that many of the existing loans can be paid off within their agreed time-span. A is thus dependent on creditors' willingness to grant new loans, or to roll over the remaining loans. Moreover, loans cost money. Interest is the price the debtor is paying for getting money and only paying it back later. Thus A is also dependent on those deciding or influencing the interest rates.

Assume that A is a state that has become indebted in the global financial markets. The private market creditors may, first of all, refuse to roll over the existing loans of state A or grant new loans to it. The country in crisis may turn to the IMF and ask for a loan designed for these kinds of purposes. The IMF can, and does, lend money only on the condition that A follows the economic policy it deems the most conducive towards repayment and economic recovery. Without exception, this is in accordance with the dictates of the orthodox economic theory.[67] Other loans – by other states, multilateral agencies or commercial banks – may in turn be conditioned on the orthodox economic policy programme imposed by the IMF. A state may become entangled in conditionality for a considerable time. Governments come and go and constituencies and political systems change, yet the dependency tends to remain.

All this is well known. In the early 2000s, the IMF controls the economic policy of perhaps every third 'sovereign' state on the planet. But there are also much more subtle mechanisms at work, stemming from the determination of interest rates. Since most international loans are dollar-nominated, the US interest rate decides their price. Whether the US government and the Board of the Federal Reserve acknowledge it or not, and whether the interest rate is used for explicitly political purposes or not, they have structural power over a number of other countries.

Moreover, given the post-Bretton Woods tendency towards financial disintermediation – that is, instead of banks mediating between depositors and lenders, securities are issued and later exchanged again and again in the secondary markets – a significant power mechanism has emerged. The rating of debt securities influences their price. New institutions have been developed to provide *judgements on the creditworthiness* of security issuers. The two major agencies are Moody's Investors Service (Moody's) and

Standard & Poor's Ratings Services. Both are headquartered in New York and have branches in the world's major financial centres. There are a few others, too, two other American, a British and a Japanese. But Moody's and Standard & Poor dominate the business.[68] The credit-rating agencies assess firms, municipalities and states. They make judgements on the 'future ability and willingness of an issuer to make timely payments of principal and interest on a security over the life of the interest'.[69] The more they appear capable of repaying, the higher the rating. The higher the rating, the easier it is to sell the securities; their price (interest) is also lower. The credit-rating agencies use both quantitative and qualitative information. The latter includes news and interviews. A collegial body, often resorting to a formal vote in the absence of consensus, makes the final judgement. The practices of credit rating have two far-reaching consequences:

1. Funds are more readily and cheaply available to those who are assessed to be willing and able to make timely payments. Assuming object-ive rating, *this system favours those who are already strong and punishes the weak*. To the extent that the assessments have a real effect on the financial flows and conditions, self-fulfilling prophecies may also be at play.

2. The assessments are made on the basis of particular models and interpretations of reality and a selected set of data. What is characteristic of this framework is the domination of narrow assumptions about market efficiency, in which 'undistorted' price signals are the objective and state intervention is generally considered unhealthy.[70] In other words, the stand-ard financial orthodoxy reigns. Hence, *this system rewards those compliant with neoliberal ideals and rentier interests, and punishes those attempting to deviate from 'the right path'.*

In anticipation of these consequences, actors seek to discuss their situ-ation with the credit-rating agencies. At the extreme, the rating agencies may thus be able to dictate the policy of a corporation, municipality or state.

Obviously, this aspect of the structural power of finance depends on the incurred debts of actors. Credit rating – or, for that matter, US interest rates and the value of dollar – would be of much less concern if states had taken no international loans or issued any international bonds. For instance, Will Kymlicka has argued that 'the dependence on international financial markets is not an inherent feature of globalization, but rather a contingent result of international indebtness'.[71] Yet, this point downplays two im-portant considerations. Historically, the financial markets developed in conjunction with the modern state and its new instruments of taxation and raising funds now against future revenues. Also, normatively, the idea that states should be free of debt is problematical. Indeed, the principle of balanced (or surplus) budget can be highly restrictive and, under certain circumstances, counter-productive.

The social allocation of capital In addition to the dependency on loans and their cost, financial liberalisation has also created other kinds of *relations of dependency*. In particular, the *non-intentional power* of financial market actors has increased. These market actors, too, are so positioned that they cannot avoid affecting outcomes, independently of their will. To the extent that governments are trying to (i) preserve the relative stability of exchange rates and (ii) avoid sudden outflows of portfolio investments, they must be concerned, even anxious, about the reactions of the financial markets to their decisions and the ensuing economic conditions.

In Chapter 1, we have already seen that (the disappearance of) trust and confidence (is) are at the heart of financial (in)stability. Stability is about smooth financial multiplication; instability is about sudden turns of values and flows, with far-reaching consequences. It was argued that financial decisions must be understood in terms of sensitive trust or confidence in developments and related highly reflexive strategic considerations. The beauty contest metaphor helps to understand why this trust and confidence may have very little to do with the real beauty/economic capabilities. The dynamics of reflexive confidence on particular assets is coupled with attempts to exploit potential weaknesses.

The point of Chapter 2 about the social allocation of portfolio capital (including liquid loans) is very also important from the point of view of structural power analysis. Three main points were:

1. There is a shared framework of analysis of investments prospects. The prevalent discourse stems from the basics of orthodox economics and thus implies the Washington consensus. It also entails a rather consequential real tendency: firms and countries are *rewarded if they are compliant with neoliberal ideals and rentier interests, and punished if they attempt to deviate from the 'right path'*.
2. The incentives of dealers and managers and the situation of investment decisions have strongly encouraged short-termism, which has, in effect, ruled out alternative orientations. This actually reinforces (1), for a long-term analysis is replaced by a hectic, short-term attempt to read signs and indications of X being 'on the right path' and 'investment friendly'. And what matters, eventually, is not whether the prospects of development and growth are really there, but whether a dealer or a manager thinks that other investors think they should be there (and there are also higher forms of reflection on the strategic situation). In this process, the always-fragile confidence of investors is socially constructed.

3. The heavyweights and market leaders can also manipulate prices and orchestrate attacks that are intended to kick off a chain reaction leading to a drastic change in the price of an asset. The bigger, better known and more leveraged they are, the easier price manipulation and orchestration of attacks are (which does not always guarantee success).

The point is that there are shared rules and principles of what rational housekeeping should be like, yet nobody is ever safe. Rather, as in Bentham's Panopticon – famously taken by Michel Foucault as a metaphor for modern systems of surveillance[72] – everybody must know that they are being watched by the investors and that any real or imagined deviation from the path towards realising the orthodoxy of economic liberalism may entail immediate punishment.[73]

By way of a feedback loop, this system also has real effects on economic developments. There are self-fulfilling expectations, to the extent that the inflows of financial capital (and also direct investments) have an impact. Directing official development aid and other forms of support to those countries most compliant with the Western norms and rules has also supported the hegemonic functioning of global financial markets.[74]

Under constant surveillance by the actors of the financial markets and also the multilateral agencies controlled by the West, firms and states have to fulfil the investors' (and Washington's) requirements of rational housekeeping. In the case of firms, these rules and principles amount to constant rationalisation by means of sacking people, minimising social and pensions costs, and closing down factories. These measures are meant, in particular, to maximise 'the shareholder value'. In the case of states, the requirements are always the same: privatise, open up to world markets, save in social expenditure, cut taxes, minimise state intervention and deregulate first, then re-regulate in accordance with the American model (or the wishes of Washington and London).

Thus, the structural power of finance bolsters the Washington consensus and the neoliberal project of reorganising social relations of production, exchange and accountability. The neoliberal transformation also involves a further shift in the social relationships in favour of creditor and rentier interests, thus reinforcing and strengthening its own power to transform. Financial problems and crises tend to deepen the relations of dependency. Indeed, the instability of prices associated with institutional investors' collective and short-term allocation of capital seems to have increased the investors' structural power and, in turn, their ability coercively to reproduce neoliberalism among borrowers.

Chossudovsky summarises insightfully the developments related to the Asian crisis. The world's largest banks and brokerage houses are both creditors and institutional speculators. They have contributed (through their speculative actions) to destabilising national currencies, thereby boosting the volume of dollar-denominated debts. They then reappear as creditors with a view to collecting these debts. Finally, they are called in as 'policy advisers' or consultants in the IMF- and World Bank-sponsored 'bankruptcy programmes' of which they are the ultimate beneficiaries. In Indonesia, for instance, amid street rioting and in the wake of Suharto's resignation, the privatisation of key sectors of the Indonesian economy ordered by the IMF was entrusted to eight of the world's largest investment banks, including Lehman Brothers, Crédit Suisse-First Boston, Goldman Sachs and UBS/SBC Warburg Dillon Read. The world's largest money managers set countries on fire and are then called in as firemen (under the IMF 'rescue plan') to extinguish the blaze. They ultimately decide which enterprises are to be closed down and which are to be auctioned off to foreign investors at bargain prices.[75]

The role of globalising media Given the global context in which most states are or have recently become liberal-democratic in the 'three waves of democratisation', public opinion has to, at the minimum, give passive consent to what is going on. For a large part of the population in most countries, public opinion is constructed, first and foremost, in and via the mass media. For many, the media are simply TV and tabloids, although there are countries and social groups in which reading newspapers and magazines is (still) common.

Now, the increased privatisation, commercialisation and Americanisation of media are part of the global programme of neoliberal restructuring.[76] Commercial media seem to operate outside the scientific principles of source criticism and public verifiability, and the democratic principles of account- ability. Rather, accountability is defined in terms of money, and the money for the media is mostly drawn from advertisers. The advertisers may have a direct or indirect say on the content and style of stories or programmes; the distinction between non-advertisements and advertisements is becoming increasingly blurred. Consequently, it has been argued that with the increased privatisation and commercialisation of the globalising media, there is a real tendency for info-tainment and titty-tainment to substitute for in- depth public affairs analyses, debates and documentaries.[77] It appears that almost everything comes to be reduced to entertaining simulation (of simulation). It is in this social context that comments like that of Jean Baudrillard can be taken – paradoxically – seriously:

> So there is something more than that which is peculiar to our modern media images: if they fascinate us so much it is not because they are sites of the

production of meaning and representation – this would not be new – it is on the contrary because they are sites of the disappearance of meaning and representation, sites in which we are caught quite apart from any judgement of reality, thus sites of a fatal strategy of denegation of the real and the reality principle.[78]

Baudrillard claims that all sense of truth and origin is lost in the play of endlessly replicating systems of commodified signs and images. However, following Nigel Thrift, it is more helpful to analyse the resulting unknowing as a dynamic ideology – as systematic absences that make something essential unknown, not understood, hidden, distorted or simply undiscussed.[79] The role of the globalising media in reproducing neo-liberalism and reinforcing the power of global finance is a case in point: the silences and absences in media representations are as noteworthy as the systematic biases and distortions.

The media's role in reproducing the power of global finance is important. First of all there is the remarkable absence of history, wider contexts and wholes, and a silence about power and media's own role in reproducing the global relations of domination. What is being represented is a set of unconnected, atomistic events, which, if contextualised at all, are given meaning by the 'experts', that is, by people who are themselves deeply involved in the functioning of global financial markets. Moreover, these experts typically rely on a social ontology of atomistic events and their relations as constant conjunctions (see Appendix 1 for an analysis and criticism), and thereby tend to reinforce the atomism of the media. The orthodoxy of economics presupposes this social ontology.

It has become commonplace to report the immediate reactions of financial markets to any political discussion or decision. The assumption must be that governments and multilateral agencies should be accountable to financial markets. However, typically, the market reactions are represented as an external, nature-like reality, which is beyond the reach of politics (or human influence). This practice of reporting the reactions of finance to political developments is an essential part of the power of global financial markets.

Outside these reports – or business sections or programmes meant for specialised audiences of the already converted – the global financial markets hit the mainstream only when something exceptional and dramatic happens. Indeed, the commercial media seem to be most interested in short-term sensations and spectacles, for they are the best-selling. The outcome of the interaction of these social forces in producing the news and stories is always the same:

Since 1980, serious financial crises have been happening in one country after another, seriatim and affecting two thirds of the members of the IMF at least once. Each time, the Anglo-American media of the Dollar–Wall Street regime try to entertain us with juicy stories, full of local colour and details of local incompetence, corruption or whatever that just happened to cause each individual one of over half the countries of the world to turn out to be a basket case.[80]

Moreover, in the absence of any proper long-term analysis of global financial markets, what emerges is a series of hectic, short-term attempts to read signs and indications of X being 'on the right path to restore the confidence of the investors' and 'investment friendly'. Media practices are an essential element in the process whereby public policy has been re-defined: governments must now seek to prove their credibility, and the consistency of their policies according to the degree to which they inspire the confidence of investors. The globalising media are both a central watchtower of the Panopticon in its own right and an element in a complex process that mediates, filters and channels interpretations between the investors and the objects of their gaze. What is also remarkable is that Moody's and Standard & Poor's credit raters use news and media stories as their qualitative data in making assessments.

The globalising and Americanising media have thus an essential role in the functioning of the global financial Panopticon: everybody must know that they are being watched by the investors and that any real or imagined deviation from the path towards realising the orthodoxy of economic liberalism may entail immediate punishment. But it is much better to be as silent as possible about the power relations this vision entails.

Conclusion: Socio-economic Effects of the Power of Finance

By way of conclusion to the descriptive and explanatory part of the book, I shall now try to summarise the real socio-economic effects of the growing power of global finance. A systematic empirical analysis of these socio-economic effects is beyond the scope of this book. Instead, I shall draw some tentative conclusions from the discussions of Chapters 1 to 3. I shall also take up some plausible hypothesis from the existing literature and attempt to make a *prima facie* case for the view that the power of financial markets has had adverse effects on the long-term development of the world economy as a whole (the major differences between countries and regions are now bracketed; the debt problem is also not given its due). Finally, to conclude this chapter, I shall make a suggestion that there might be a connection between the lack of research on these matters and ideology as unknowing – as absences and silences.

Chapter 1 discussed the socio-economic consequences of financial crises. The total cumulative loss for a combined banking and currency crisis has been, on average, 14.4 per cent, for the countries concerned. The Asian crisis and its global repercussions cut *global* output by US$2 trillion in 1998–2000. This is perhaps 6 per cent of the global GDP; by far the worst crisis thus far. Given the frequency of the crises, the total loss since the late 1970s is substantial. Given, also, the current global financial system and the principles of governing it, those who suffer the most have typically had the least to do with producing the crisis. There is no mechanism that would compensate for the lost growth and its socio-economic consequences.

To contextualise the impacts of global finance, it is worth repeating the UNDP statistics about growing disparities. In 1998–99, with the world gross output per capita growing at the rate of 1.5–1.8 per cent, more than eighty countries have lower per capita incomes than a decade or more ago, and at least fifty-five countries have consistently declining per capita incomes. The income gap between the fifth of the world's people living in the richest countries and the fifth in the poorest was 74 to 1 in 1997, up from 60 to 1 in 1990 and 30 to 1 in 1960. The income inequalities have risen sharply also within the rich countries – particularly in the US and the UK – and the global poor are now as or more poor than they were in 1820.[81]

What has been the role of global financial markets in these developments? Already on the basis of the analysis of Chapter 1, it seems that global financial markets have aggravated global disparities. Those who suffer the most because of the crises are the weakest and poorest sectors of population. The absorption of wealth into the hands of the few was discussed more in depth in Chapter 2. The financial multiplication process, boosted by the processes of extraction of resources from the non-financial sphere to the financial markets, has amplified the concentration of resources in the hands of a relatively small number of collective and individual actors.

I also argued that financial markets have been instrumental in creating new 'high net worth individuals'. Many of the richest people of the late 1990s are fund managers or, in some cases, petty investors turned millionaires. The role of tax havens and offshore facilities in making the rich richer and undermining the taxation capabilities of states was also mentioned. The financial actors have used their direct power to push for neoliberal reforms – in particular privatisation of pensions and social security – conducive to further expansion of financial markets. Although the push for neoliberal reforms from the financial actors is obviously not the only explanation for growing inequalities, we may safely assume that the direct power of finance has had a significant effect on these developments in the 1980s and 1990s.

This chapter has focused on the structural power of finance. I have also discussed the role of offshore facilities and tax havens more thoroughly than in Chapter 2. Since the 1950s, the creation of eurodollar markets and offshore facilities – safeguarded by the institution of state sovereignty – has made it increasingly easy to escape from the rules and regulations of twentieth-century welfare states. Offshore facilities and tax havens have enabled a partial return to the nineteenth-century practices of *laissez-faire* capitalism. Following Strange, I have also argued that despite the huge sums involved in drug trafficking, etc., tax evasion, private fraud, financial crime and public embezzlement are in fact bigger problems. Again, we can safely assume that these phenomena too have also rather aggravated than reduced global disparities.

Furthermore, I have argued in this chapter that credit rating, social allocation of capital and globalising media form a Panopticon system of power and surveillance that promotes and maintains the hegemony of neoliberalism. The geoeconomic gamble of the US – loyally supported by the UK, which is dependent on the position of the City of London and offshore financial markets; and more ambivalently accepted by Japan, which has been squeezed between the US unilateralism and a liquidity trap caused by a financial crisis – is based on this Panopticon system of power. The socio-economic effects of the structurally backed hegemony of neoliberalism are sweeping. The demands and claims to privatise, save in social expenditure, cut down taxes, minimise state intervention and deregulate first, then re-regulate in accordance with the American model (or the wishes of Washington and London) have had effects on the welfare of perhaps most people on the planet.

There have been winners. The US has been able to re-establish its central position in international politics; London has regained its position as the biggest financial centre. The major banks, investment funds and many MNCs have benefited, as have their managers and the related legion of dependent politicians, consultants, economists and journalists. Also, the providers of casinos and tax havens (many of them mere statelets), and the lucky and skilful gamblers in the casino, and, in particular, their rich friends who are now able to avoid taxes, belong to the group of winners. Some other countries may have benefited, at least in the short run.

However, it can be argued that the increased power of global finance has meant absolute or relative worsening of life conditions for most people. It seems that all traditional measures – output growth, unemployment, interest rates, etc. – indicate slackening, if not worsening, global conditions. There are indications that, decade after decade, there has been, globally, less growth and more un- and under-employment of industrial and human capacities.[82] Even where there is growth, there seems to be less welfare than before: crime, insecurity and social disintegration tend to absorb most of the apparent growth, except for the very richest.[83]

The standard justification for global 'free market' financial markets is that they allow for more efficient allocation of capital. Yet it seems that the global financial markets are not primarily about funding long-term investments in production; rather they are about hedging and finding financial gains in forex and bond and equities markets. More implicitly, financial markets are also about power and discipline.

Although financial liberalisation has swept an increasing number of Southern countries, still only some twenty developing countries have regular access to global, private capital. The so-called 'emerging economies' have been able to finance only 10 per cent of their real investment with foreign capital during the 1990s. Even in the OECD countries, most saving and investment are still done domestically, and firms tend to invest, first and foremost, their own incomes or traditional loans from the banks – although bonds have clearly grown in importance since the early 1980s. In particular, the role of equities as a source of finance remains negligible. It is also noteworthy that despite relative financial integration, prices of apparently 'equivalent' assets remain different in different parts of the world. This indicates lack of integration in the capital markets for long-term investments.[84] As far as investment in production is concerned, global financial markets appear rather insignificant.

Yet global financial markets are powerful and consequential. David Felix has argued that the slackening global conditions are at least partially due to the re-emergence of global financial markets. He maintains that there are three main reasons for this. First, the resulting higher real interest rates – concordant with the system serving first and foremost rentier interests – have tilted investment decision towards lower fixed cost and shorter-term projects. Exchange rate volatility and fluctuations have had a similar effect by making future revenues more uncertain and/or by raising the costs of hedging against uncertainty.[85] Second, once 'liberated', the financial system moves gradually from stable financing to rising debt leveraging and volatile and inflated asset prices. Hence it becomes more prone to falling into systemic crises. Once the pivotal point is reached, the expansion of financial markets will be hampering non-financial economic development. According to Felix, the available figures suggest that the growing absorption of resources in financial services have, since the mid-1970s, been at the expense of the non-financial sector's growth.[86]

Third, Felix argues that financial globalisation has had an impact on macroeconomic policy. At first, despite weakened unions, slackening real wages and the new technologies, there was persistent inflation:

Fiscal authorities have felt impelled to respond sympathetically to business demands for administrative protection against foreign competition, thereby raising the lid on oligopoly markups. Inflation has thereby been reducing slowly and unevenly at needlessly high social cost. The current monetary policy leaves productive capacity and labour underutilized that a more stimulative aggregate demand strategy could exploit without raising the inflation rate, provided the current dominance of wayward financial market expectations over policy could be weakened.[87]

However, in the longer run – by the 1990s – the orthodoxy was able to tame inflation. Even under the new circumstances, the neoliberal hegemony continues to demand policies of austerity and a strong anti-inflation stand, despite the socio-economic costs. Consequently, states have been following increasingly *deflationary economic policies*.[88] Simultaneously, the hegemony of neoliberalism has also induced growing global disparities. We know that:

- Public expenditure by states constitutes a significant portion of global demand.
- The high social costs of neoliberalism and slackening real wages translate into less demand.
- The propensity to consume goods and services (other than financial) is (much) higher in the lower income groups.

Given these tendencies, the power of financial markets seems to imply a declining global demand for goods and non-financial services. As said, a systematic empirical study of the overall impact of different tendencies in the global political economy is beyond the reach of this study. In open systems, different tendencies – including conscious attempts to resolve economic problems – can counteract each other, and different spatio-temporal processes may overlap, intersect, interlope, and/or clash and no constant regularities occur. Yet, it can be plausibly suggested that there is a real tendency for a *declining* aggregate, *global demand*, also because of the power of global finance. This may also explain why even the most conventional figures indicate slackening, if not worsening, global conditions.[89]

Perhaps the lack of research on the connections between the dominance of finance and global economic conditions[90] has something to do with ideology as unknowing – as absences and silences? At least we can be certain that the remarkable absence of depth, history and wider contexts both in mainstream economics and commercialised journalism has been propitious for this unknowing.

Notes

1. By the turn of the twentieth century, the notorious science of geopolitics emerged with the exhaustion of the geographical space for the Western colonialists and explorers. It aimed at viewing the world as a whole and stipulating scientific laws about the state/imperial governance of the limited global space (see Tuathail 1996). More critically, here I merely refer to the way the global political space has been socio-historically constructed as territorial, i.e. how it has been organised, first and foremost, in terms of sovereign, territorial states. However, in their own existence, the traditional international institutions such as diplomacy, international law, great powerness and power-balancing have always been non-territorial (as practices and relations, not locatable to any exclusive territorial space), despite essential references to territorial states and attempts to make them appear as territorial as possible; and the expansion of the capitalist world economy has been based on globally universalised property rights and freedoms to move people (at least traders and investors), information, goods, money and capital across the borders. Since the 1960s, the territorial organisation of global political space has been exploited, e.g. by various legal arrangements that have created offshore facilities, which are, in fact, mostly just fictitious territories, not sites of practices.

2. For the lack of a better term, I shall stick to the term 'structural power' to refer to the intentional or non-intentional formation of the contexts for social action that are always presupposed at any particular moment of interaction. Guzzini (1993) is the best available analysis of the dimensions of structural power; I rely upon his distinctions. All aspects of 'structural power' actually refer to the positioning of actors in the relational and positioned discursive practices, some of which have become institutionalised in the *longue durée* of historical time. 'Structural power' should not therefore be seen as a different kind of power. The term only helps to draw our attention to the formation of the contexts of social action that always presuppose and imply power. For details of the concepts of action, structure and power, see Patomäki 1991.

3. Of course, the more specific models and the data used may not be shared by all; neither are the strategic plans and plots to influence prices. The point is that at the more abstract level, the basic assumptions of the conceptual framework underlying these models are mostly shared.

4. Strange 1986: 6–7.

5. Walter 1993: 166–8.

6. See Strange 1986: 6; Helleiner 1994: 13–14.

7. See Strange 1986: 31, 186; Strange 1998: 5–6. Note that Strange presupposes the US government's point of view about the necessity of the armament race with the Soviet Union, and defining the 'public good'; but independently of this presupposition, the point about the conflict over the distribution of financial responsibilities is pertinent.

8. Walter 1993: 168.

9. For seminal statements of this theory, see Gilpin 1981; Keohane 1980; and Kindleberger 1981. For important 1980s critiques, see Ashley 1984; and Strange 1987.

10. These discussions presuppose the basic tenets of neorealism, which, like orthodox economics, abstract away from social meanings, practices and relations. In addition to this economism, Grunberg (1990) has shown that the appeal of the theory stemmed from its mythic structure. The basic elements of American ethnocentrism gave rise to a story that was told in terms of ancient mythical narrative structures. Although false, it was thus a rhetorically powerful story.

11. Strange 1998: 6.

12. Had it done so, there may have emerged a shortage of global liquidity. In general, the Bretton Woods system was flawed because the system was built upon a currency of a particular state, instead of an independent, global currency.

13. Strange 1998: 6; Strange 1986: 41–3; Gowan 1999: 20.

14. Gowan 1999: 28–30. It should be remarked, however, that although I find Gowan's interpretations highly suggestive and original, his book does not offer systematic evidence for his claims. On the contrary, many of Gowan's arguments – and the footnotes allegedly backing them up – appear rather careless, and the evidence somewhat circumstantial and casual. On the other hand, his arguments also appear plausible because they accord with what I know about both global financial markets and US foreign policy, and are able to articulate, in an original manner, likely links between them.

15. As it is called by Gowan 1999.

16. See Chapter 2, section 'Collective associations of financial actors'.

17. Gowan 1999: 29.

18. See ibid., pp. 70–2.

19. Yet, although the growth rates of the US, too, have been constantly below those of the Bretton Woods era, the relative competitiveness of US firms, services and products has risen. There are a number of possible explanations: (i) technological breakthroughs and emergence of new markets (see Castells 1996; but compare with explanations of transformation to Post-Fordism in Ash Amin 1994); (ii) increased competitiveness may be due to lower real wage levels. The real incomes of the majority of Americans have been on the decline for nearly three decades (see Brenner 1998: 235–62); (iii) exploitation of the unique privileges and power of the US dollar as the main currency, which enables 'costless' devaluations and gives free credit to the US state; liberalisation and privatisation create a competitive edge for the US firms whose know-how is based on the functioning of that kind of system; global socialisation of risk of the US actors in the global financial markets allows them to benefit from the volatile system with little risk (as discussed in the main text).

20. The unilateralism and aggressive reciprocity of the US trade policy is discussed in Martin 1994.

21. A case in point is the infamous Helms–Burton law of 1996, which implies that the US is entitled to severe punitive actions against non-US states and corporations not following its policies of exclusion of what Washington deems pariah states. Later that year, the Iran–Libya Sanctions Act further extended Washington's extra-territorial reach.

22. In the 1990s, the US intervened militarily dozens of times in different countries in all continents, and imposed new unilateral economic sanctions, or threatened legislation to do so, sixty times on thirty-five countries that represent 40 per cent of the world's population; Maynes 1999: 517.

23. Reaffirming the US position as the dominant world hegemon has been the openly declared goal of the two US administrations since the end of the Cold War. The February 1992 document 'Defense Planning Guidance for the Fiscal Year 1994–1999' described the post-communist, post-Gulf period as a unique opportunity for global empire-building. Later in the 1990s, Secretary of State Madeleine Albright is quoted as saying, in defence of the widely divergent US opinion on the Iraq crisis, that the US does not need agreement with others 'because we are America, we are the indispensable nation, we stand tall – we see further into future'. More sensibly, the National Security Council Advisor Anthony Lake has argued that 'only one overriding factor can determine whether

the US should act multilaterally or unilaterally, and that is America's interests'. In the discourse of the US foreign policy elite, there seems to be also a rather arrogant tendency to identify other Western countries as 'vassals'. See Maynes 1999: 517; and Petras and Morley 2000.

Among the Continental European allies and major international civil servants, however, complaints about the imperial arrogance of the US of the 1990s have become more and more abundant. The French in particular have been blunt. At the time of the 1997 G-7 Summit, President Jacques Chirac stated: 'We're wasting our time here. We're nothing but extras in Clinton's marketing plan. [The Americans] have already decided to do everything without us.' In 1998, prior to his major visit to Latin America, Chirac stated: 'The United States has the pretension to want to direct everything, it wants to rule the whole world.' (Quoted in Petras and Morley 2000: 55 and 66.)

In his memoirs about his five-year term as United Nations Secretary-General (1992–96), Boutros-Ghali is equally outspoken: 'It would be some time before I fully realized that the United States sees little need for diplomacy; power is enough. Only the weak rely on diplomacy. [...] But the Roman Empire had no need for diplomacy. Nor does the United States. Diplomacy is perceived by an *imperial power* as a waste of time and prestige and sign of weakness' Boutros-Ghali 1999: 198 [italics HP]). Again, this seems a slight overstatement: the US does need multilateral diplomacy whenever it suits its interests, but avoids any commitment to multilateralism that would constrain it in the future.

24. Gowan 1999: 77–8.

25. Ibid., p. 78.

26. Gill 1999: 3.

27. Cf. Gowan 1999: 73–4.

28. Sinclair 1994: 142.

29. Strange 1986: 47–8; Strange 1998: 6.

30. Palan 1998: 626.

31. Palan forthcoming: Introduction.

32. Picciotto 1999: 51–2.

33. Ibid., p. 53.

34. Palan 1999b.

35. Picciotto 1999: 57–8; also Helleiner 1994: 83–91.

36. Strange 1998: 155.

37. Picciotto 1999: 58.

38. Helleiner 1994: 14.

39. Strange 1998: 6.

40. See Helleiner 1994.

41. Palan 1998: 33.

42. E.g. Gowan 1999: 26.

43. See Picciotto 1999.

44. See Palan forthcoming: Chapter 4.

45. These are very rough estimates, based on figures depicted in the journals *The Diamonds* and *The Euromoney*, as well as on the calculations of the UN Commission for Social Development. See Hampton and Abbott 1999: 1; Hayward 2000b (mimeo) and Palan 1999b and forthcoming.

46. Picciotto 1999: 59.

47. OECD 1996: 5–7.

48. See, e.g., Hayat 1999.

49. See Hudson 1998.

50. It is worth mentioning that Minsky (1982) explains the US economic cycles in terms of financial instability. He argues that over an extended period of prosperity, money-market innovations will take place, which will increase velocity and decrease collective *de facto* liquidity. As a result, the decrease in liquidity is compounded. In time, these compounded changes will result in an inherently unstable money market so that a slight reversal of prosperity can trigger a financial crisis. Already by the early 1960s, cumulative changes in US financial relations were taking place so that the susceptibility of the economy to a financial crisis was increasing. Since then, Minsky argues, it has been possible to explain the economic cycles of the US in terms of recurring financial crises.

51. See Chapter 2 and the section 'US power and its limits' of this chapter for details of these changes.

52. Palan 1999a: 28.

53. This is the starting point of Palan forthcoming.

54. Strange 1998: 148.

55. Krugman 1999a: 68.

56. Strange 1998: 46.

57. Ibid., p. 161.

58. Krugman 1999a: 64–74.

59. Gowan 1999: 84–9.

60. For a full story, see ibid., pp. 78–100.

61. Cf. Strange 1998: 48–57.

62. Helleiner 1994: 13–14.

63. Although an important and relevant question, I have to leave aside discussions on how the US and the UK came to adopt the neoliberal project.

64. Even nationalism as a widespread ideological discourse is non-national in this sense.

65. Ashley 1989: 268–85.

66. Famously, Michel Foucault is quoted as saying that 'actors more or less know what they are doing when they do it and can often be quite clear in articulating it. But it does not follow that the broader consequences of these local actions are coordinated, for actors don't know what they do does' (Dreyfus and Rabinow 1982: 187). We might add that sometimes it is simply better to not talk too openly about these broader consequences of actions; and that the systematic silencing of certain effects plays the role of a negative ideology (that is, the role of an ideology as absence).

67. For a brilliant historical and discursive analysis, see Teivainen 1995.

68. See Sinclair 1994.

69. Ibid., p. 138. Quoted from Moody's official publication, *Moody's Investors Service: Consistency, Reliability, Integrity*.

70. Ibid., p. 143.

71. Kymlicka 1999: 113.

72. 'The panoptic mechanism arranges spatial unities that make it possible to see

constantly and to recognize immediately. [...] Each individual, in his place, is securely confined to a cell from which he is seen from the front by the supervisor; but the side walls prevent him from coming into contact with his companions' (Foucault 1979: 200). For an application of this metaphor to the analysis of late-twentieth-century global political economy, see Gill 1995b.

73. Obviously, countries that are joining the game might have been successful capitalist economies under a social-democratic, corporatist and/or Asian or even communist rule (China), possibly precisely because they have followed principles of governance other than economic liberalism. At the outset, these differences may be partially tolerated by the investors and these countries might in fact emerge as particularly tempting locations of investment. But once the game is opened, there seems to be no way back: there is a constant pressure to liberalise more and indicate that 'you are on the right path'. Under the present system of global governance, a financial crisis might be a particularly useful device for making countries even more dependent on global finance (and the US and the IMF), and thereby forcing them to liberalise and Americanise more.

74. See Patomäki 1999b.

75. See Chossudovsky 1998.

76. See Herman and McChesney 1997.

77. About 'info-tainments', see ibid., pp. 153–4; about 'titty-tainment' (a term introduced originally by Zbigniew Brzenski), see Martin and Schumann 1997: 12 and 52.

78. Baudrillard 1993: 194.

79. Thrift 1983: 45.

80. Gowan 1999: 50.

81. UNDP 1999: particularly 1–13, and 38–9.

82. However, there are no consistent and commensurable figures for the world as a whole. During the Cold War, the state socialist part of the world was partially excluded from the calculations and estimations. Yet there are some indications. Felix (1995b) looks at the figures of G-7 countries and compares periods 1946–58, 1959–70, and 1974–89; and then also takes a sample of fifty-four countries and compares periods 1960–71, 1972–81 and 1982–91. For instance, for the G-7 countries, GDP/capita growth was both more stable and much higher (4.5 per cent) until the early 1970s; even since it has been much lower (c. 2 per cent) and more unstable. Since the early 1970s, real interest rates have been higher. There was also a general decline in the investment/GDP ratio, with the significant exception of East/South-East Asia and the oil-producing countries. According to IMF's *World Economic Outlook* October 1999, in the 1980s 'advanced economies' grew at the annual rate of 3.1 per cent (of which Japan's share was considerable), whereas in the 1990s the growth rate has been only 2.4 per cent. The developing countries as a group have been growing faster (as has their population!), but in fact that economic growth has occurred mainly in Asia, in particular in China and the Asian tigers. After the Asian crises, the previous growth rates of the Asian tigers haven't (yet?) recovered. In the late 1990s, more than eighty countries have lower per capita incomes than a decade or more ago, and at least fifty-five countries have consistently declining per capita incomes.

83. It has been emphasised by the so-called 'new economics' that adequate growth in welfare measures should not take GDP figures at face value, but should rather extract market transactions generating social bads from it. For instance, 'an Index of Sustainable Economic Welfare for the UK shows [...] that although GDP per capita has increased by about a third since 1979, sustainable economic welfare has fallen by a fifth during the

same period' (Robertson 1999: 132). In this measure, the UK has been doing worse than most OECD countries.

84. These claims are made, e.g., by Beddoes (1999: 16–17). About the role of equities as a source of finance, see, e.g., Stiglitz (1992: 280).

85. Felix 1995b: 20–2.

86. Ibid., pp. 23–31.

87. Ibid., p. 32.

88. See, for instance, Krugman (1999b), who argues that there is a 'growing number of observers who now regard deflation as a serious risk for the world's major economies'; and concludes: 'Conservative monetary policy may seem prudent and responsible to the European Central Bank today, just as it did to the Bank of Japan not long ago, but in retrospect that supposed prudence may look like disastrous folly.' However, despite his accurate observations, Krugman remains tied to the standard methodology of economics and remains unable to see the structuration of power relations as a source of these conservative monetary policies, not only in the EU and Japan but almost everywhere.

89. See note 82, above.

90. For a research project taking up some of the relevant issues, see Baker et al. 1998.

4

The Case for the Tobin Tax and Global Re-regulation

A number of reforms have been proposed to cure the ills caused by the global financial markets. The Tobin tax, a small tax on all currency transactions, is perhaps the most far-reaching of them. It would be the first global tax ever. The Tobin tax is addressed particularly against the power of speculative financial markets, in the name of the socio-economic consequences of this over-efficient system of financial flows. The shorter the time horizon of the investments, the stronger the impact of the tax. The favourite phrase of James Tobin to describe the impact of this tax is 'throwing sand in the wheels of the financial markets'. Tobin's 1978 article 'A Proposal for International Monetary Reform' is reprinted in Appendix 2.[1]

Tobin's two-fold argument follows Keynesian economic theory (in fact, Tobin seems to have merely internationalised Keynes's suggestion for a domestic financial transactions tax).[2] National economies and governments are *not* capable of adjusting to massive movements of funds across foreign exchanges, without real hardship and without significant sacrifice of the objectives of national economic policy. A tax would curb the excessive intercurrency mobility of private financial capital. Tobin's main concern seems to be *stability*. Simultaneously, though, he is also defending the *autonomy* of national policy-makers. Finally, although Tobin has been less explicit about the efficiency aspect, he has also argued that the dominance of financial markets tends to cause misallocation of resources.

However, there are reasons other than efficiency, stability and autonomy of national economic policy for reforming the global financial system. One is *justice as fairness*. Because of global interdependencies, financial fluctuations have far-reaching consequences to the lives of those who neither benefit from financial activities nor have any say in the decisions and developments suddenly hampering their lives. In other words, the millions bearing the consequences of recurring financial crises seem to get a punishment without committing a crime. Many (or even most) of those few causally responsible are rescued or bailed out; that is, they do not seem to get a punishment even when they fail. On the contrary, they can continue to enjoy their privileges. The principle of 'individual profits, socialised risks' is not fair in the sense of equal treatment. From this perspective, a tax would weaken these dependencies and reduce the risks of crises. Moreover, incomes could be transferred from the 'speculators' to improving the conditions of those actually or potentially afflicted by the global casino.

A more general argument from justice would start from the claim that global financial markets are co-responsible for widening global disparities. This is as unnecessary as it is unjustified. On the basis of real and causally efficacious (inter)dependencies, it is also possible to posit generalised – even if contested – guidelines of *distributive justice* on a global scale. There must be also a commitment to transform the characters and powers of agents, and the structure of institutions, in order to *reduce powerlessness* and vulnerability. From this perspective, the Tobin tax is an important step towards more just practices of global governance. The Tobin tax would yield revenues from the financial actors operating in the forex markets and generate public funds, which can be used to benefit also the less well-off.

Alternatively, an argument for the Tobin tax may also start from the shared ideal of *democracy*. In fact, some of the above arguments can be easily translated into an argument for democracy. For instance, Tobin's defence of the autonomy of national economic policies is an argument for democratic self-determination of economic policies (within the confines of a nation-state). Similarly, if the main worry is that those whose lives are transformed by the consequences of financial outcomes do not have a say in financial developments, the argument is really about democratic self-determination of citizens in an interdependent world. Democratisation also concerns empowerment of the powerless, to realise equal, practically effective – although not necessarily actualised – rights of every person to take part in collective self-determination. Attempts to tackle global power relations give rise to novel questions about democracy. Whether acknowledged or not, the Tobin tax seems to open up a discussion about *global democracy*, too.

Perhaps most generally, the case for the Tobin tax can also be made in terms of *human emancipation*. The doctrines claiming that current institutional arrangements in global finance are natural and 'optimally efficient' are false. Yet these misconceptions are necessary for the reproduction of the financial practices and related power relations. Because of their false underpinnings, these practices and relations should be changed. The Tobin tax would bring about some of the desired or needed outcomes. Hence, the Tobin tax can be said to constitute a step of emancipation in the sense of 'the transition from an unwanted, unnecessary and oppressive situation to a wanted and/or needed and empowering or more flourishing situation'.[3]

Economic Stability and Efficiency: The Need to 'Throw Sand in the Wheels' of Global Financial Markets

The series of financial crises of the late 1990s questioned and problematised the global institutional arrangements of 'global free market finance'. Despite assurances to the contrary, doubts emerged: perhaps the deregulated and freely convertible financial markets have not been collectively beneficial. There seems to be less stability; and most states appear to lack the autonomy to determine their own economic policies. Even if some states may have benefited from these arrangements, perhaps their citizens have not? What was usually represented as necessary, technically efficient and commonsensical, in any case non-political, became suddenly *politicised* all over the world. Some states such as Malaysia reacted strongly, and new, electronically networked political movements were formed to advocate changes and reforms such as the Tobin tax. The financial crises constituted a global crisis of meaning and legitimation. Also from the heart of the Washington consensus, many voices thus raised the demand: 'Something has to be done to reform the financial markets.'

In the following chapter I shall first discuss the official top-down response. There have been sincere attempts to move towards a 'post-Washington consensus', most notably by the chief economist of the World Bank, Joseph Stiglitz. It is telling, however, that in November 1999 he decided to resign. He said that in the capacity of chief economist his freedom of speech is restricted. Indeed, mostly the G-7/Washington/London calls for reforms have amounted to efforts to disguise further neoliberal disciplining of states as 'reforms', combined with an attempt to improve the rules of the BIS-centred regime (a further move from Friedman to a liberal version of Polanyi). After any financial crisis, the stabilisation of the situation is usually relatively quick, and, after a few years, there will be a (partial) recovery. This happened also after the Asian crisis. Thus, for the purpose of managing this particular crisis of meaning and legitimacy, the Washington consensus approach *may appear* to have been sufficient – at least until the next crisis.

There is an alternative approach: the currency transaction tax. Although the Tobin tax has been discussed widely after many of the crises since the late 1980s, the economic reasons for the Tobin tax are at odds with the underpinnings of the orthodoxy of the Washington consensus. It is thus not surprising that it was ignored by the official top-down voices (with the partial exception of Stiglitz). Yet, already on the grounds of economic stability and efficiency, there is a strong case for the currency transactions tax. However, the emancipatory potential of the Tobin tax depends on the form in which it will be materialised. This in turn also depends on considerations other than stability and efficiency. There is no reason to assume that stability and efficiency are the only values.

Towards a post-Washington consensus? In 1998–99, there were various calls for a new Bretton Woods conference and/or for restructuring the existing Bretton Woods institutions. The French leaders proposed an idea of a new founding conference, 'Bretton Woods II'. Germany's new Prime Minister Gerhard Schroeder, who endorsed 'placing greater controls on international capital and restructuring the global financial system', backed the proposal of the French leaders.[4] However, very few details of these proposals have been revealed – if, indeed, there are any. Among the European governments, there seems to be no well-articulated vision deviating from the Washington consensus. The main initiatives have come from Washington and London.

New codes, reinforcing orthodoxy Prime Minister Tony Blair and Gordon Brown, Chancellor of the Exchequer of the UK, have emphasised that, if left intact and unco-ordinated, the international financial institutions – the IMF, the World Bank – will be insufficient to prevent future international crisis. They propose not only more co-ordination between the institutions but also a 'code of conduct' for states, a 'code of transparency' and new standards for the corporations, and even a 'new global regulator'.[5] On the whole, the substance of these codes, standards and regulations seems to imply further reinforcement of the Washington consensus. Gordon Brown's explanation of the crisis[6] seems to indicate that, mostly, reforms are needed *within* the states suffering from a crisis for, ultimately, they are also to blame for the crisis:

> The current financial crisis originated in national economic policy mistakes in Asia and a destabilising lack of transparency. It grew because of their poorly regulated and often distorted financial sectors. It became global because of insufficient supervision and ineffective risk management in the developed country financial markets. It became a crisis because the initial policy responses were more appropriate to over-extended public sectors whereas the problem was over-exposed private investors. And it has become a human tragedy affecting millions because our social policy approach is still deficient.

In the chain of this reasoning, the ultimate cause of the crisis lies with national policy mistakes and the peculiarities of Asian capitalism. However,

Gordon Brown also calls for better supervision and risk management, that is, a modification of the BIS-centred regime, as well as more powers to the IMF. He even admits that the 'initial policy response' by the IMF and Washington was wrong, and he would also like to see a better approach to social policy (whatever that is taken to mean). In his conclusion, however, Brown makes it clear that he would like to see more of the same instead of any changes in the principles of governance:

> The key challenge is to devise new international rules of the game that, by boosting credibility and investor confidence, help deliver stability and prosperity. Our task is not to weaken support for the IMF and World Bank at a time when the need for surveillance and coordination across the world is more pressing, but to strengthen them by building the operational rules and architecture for the new global financial system.

Brown supports furthering the neoliberal project of the new constitutionalism. Governments must seek, first and foremost, to prove their *credibility*, and of the *consistency* of their policies according to the degree to which they inspire the *confidence* of investors. Given that Brown is often considered to be on the left in the orthodoxy of the new 'centre' of the Washington consensus, this demonstrates the limits of the top-down reforms.

Wider participation, more legitimacy? In the wake of the Asian crisis, the second immediate top-down response to the global crisis of meaning and legitimisation was to encourage wider participation in governance. Rather than democratisation *per se*, the hope seems to have been that by getting more actors involved in discussions and, in a more limited way, in agenda-setting, the outcomes of the Washington-led governance would become more legitimate. In his opening speech to the IMF 1998 annual meeting, President Bill Clinton made a gesture towards this direction by arguing that even 'the best designed international economic system will fail if it does not give a stake and voice to ordinary citizens'.[7] He went on to point out that there is a need to 'encourage democratic participation in international organisations'.

However, Clinton also made it clear in his speech that the reason for these initiatives and gestures is the fear that countries may increasingly start to close markets and turn away from globalisation:

> Unless the citizens of each nation feel they have a stake in their economy they will resist reforms necessary for recovery. Unless they feel empowered with the tools to master economic change, they will feel the strong temptation to turn inward, to close off their economies to the world. Now, more

than ever, that would be a grave mistake. At a moment of financial crisis, a natural inclination is to close borders and retreat behind walls of protectionism. [...] The world economy today needs more trade and more activity of all kinds, not less. That is why when the leaders of APEC meet next month, we must press forward to tear down barriers and liberalise.

The overall political direction is thus already set: further neoliberal reforms. Clinton urges governments to 'hold fast to policies that are sound and attuned to the realities of the international market place', and endorses support to 'the fundamental approach of the IMF'. The logic is clear: wider participation may be valued as an aim in itself, but is needed, first and foremost, for legitimisation purposes. There seems to be no intention to open up the current institutional arrangements to democratic politics.

The Financial Stability Forum Despite attempts to curtail the political significance and consequences of the Asian crisis, the problem of financial instability has been taken seriously by Western leaders. In April 1999, following the calls by Brown, Clinton and others, and in particular in response to the Tietmeyer Report, the G-7 set up the Financial Stability Forum (FSF). It is based in Basel, Switzerland, under the auspices of the BIS. Andrew Crockett, general manager of the Bank for International Settlements (BIS), was appointed chairman of the FSF in his personal capacity for a term of three years. The Forum is supported by a small secretariat located at the BIS,[8] and is concerned with two major issues:

1. Universal implementation of the already existing national standards of the major Western countries (usually including Japan). The task is to enforce these standards also outside the core Western group.
2. Improving existing regulations to deal with the new problems posed by highly-leveraged institutions; offshore centres; and transnational capital flows. This has been done in response to panic invoked by the LTCM débâcle (see Box 3) and the angry reaction by some of the countries affected by the Asian crisis.

What this amounts to is a recognition of the dangerousness of the crisis of meaning and legitimisation; and of the need to make the system more *stable* by reforming aspects of it. The reforms are conducted in accordance with traditional BIS and IMF approaches, namely by means of sophisticated re-regulation. The problem is that (1) presupposes the false 'blame-the-victim' interpretation of the Asian and other financial crises and simultaneously reinforces the G-7 countries, and the US in particular, as the commonsensical, normal and appropriate model of national subjectivity, practices and conduct. The problem with (2) is that it is concerned only with stability – but does not go far enough, not even in that regard.

Since the late 1970s, more than 100 countries, including the US and the members of the EU, have experienced currency or banking crises or both and must have 'deviated' from the 'normal' and 'appropriate' rules. The crises have been systematic. Although the lack of regulation and transparency did play a role in generating the Asian crisis, the 'blame-the-victim' interpretation is also false in this case, particularly when represented as the only, main or ultimate explanation. The Asian tigers were pressed into financial liberalisation. The pressure put on them was also a move in the global power game of geoeconomics and has tended to undermine state capabilities. Thailand, for instance, used to have restrictions on bank lending to real estate. In the process of liberalisation it abandoned these restrictions without establishing a more sophisticated risk-based regulatory regime. The result was a bubble.[9] Moreover, as was argued in Chapter 1, the characteristic, endogenous functioning of a *laissez-faire* financial system,[10] including the tendency for rapid and exponential financial multiplication, was also a crucial cause of the Asian crisis. Western banks and funds played a major role in generating the Asian bubble, and, as the LTCM débâcle (at the time the crisis spread to Russia) demonstrated, the major financial centres also seemed to have their fair share of 'crony capitalism'.

By (2), however, the Western central bankers and regulators seem to acknowledge, quite correctly, the systemic nature of the crises. They even identify some of the most important systemic problems of global financial markets. The highly leveraged hedge funds have to be monitored and regulated; the offshore centres have to be made to co-operate and re-regulate; and the risk exposures of short-term capital flows have to be managed prudently. In line with the orthodoxy, however, the idea of the Forum is that only such policies and regulations are in order which help to facilitate the self-regulation of the market and enable further, unrestricted growth of finance and its power. It is assumed that, under 'normal' conditions,[11] markets are price-clearing and tend to lead to optimal outcomes by allocating resources efficiently. Thus, the more transactions there are the better. The core problem of the US$1.6 trillion that are converted freely every day is not touched. By 2010, the amount will be perhaps US$6 trillion, and growing (in the absence of a major crisis or other overriding forces and tendencies). There is no clear attempt to tackle the power and dominance of finance or its political and socio-economic consequences.[12]

Joseph Stiglitz Almost the only critical voice from the heart of the Washington consensus has been that of Joseph Stiglitz. He joined the World

Bank in February 1997 after serving as chairman of President Clinton's Council of Economic Advisers. Until January 2000, Stiglitz was the senior vice president and chief economist of the World Bank.

Since the 1970s, he has been publishing on different aspects of financial markets in a rather unorthodox manner. Stiglitz grounds his analyses on a set of more realistic assumptions than economists usually do.[13] In particular, he has promoted incorporating time, imperfect information, the problems of moral hazard and adverse selection, and the costs of acquiring information to economic theory. In a 1981 article, which provides 'the first theoretical justification for credit rationing', Stiglitz, with Andrew Weiss, argued that 'the usual result of economic theorizing that prices clear markets is model specific and is not a general property of markets'.[14] Ten years later, he suggested that since this 'new' microeconomics is already well established, it should be applied also to macroeconomics of economic fluctuations. He went on: 'Capital is at the heart of capitalism; it is, accordingly, not surprising that we should look for failures in capital markets to account for one of the most important failures of capitalism, the market fluctuations in output and employment which have characterized capitalism throughout its history.'[15] Stiglitz acknowledges that the resulting model 'bears a close resemblance to traditional Keynesian models'.[16]

As the chief economist of the World Bank, one of his first papers was entitled 'Moving Toward the Post-Washington Consensus'.[17] According to Stiglitz, the Washington consensus used to hold that good economic performance requires liberalised trade, macroeconomic stability and getting prices right. Once a government has dealt with these issues – essentially, once a government has 'got out of the way' – private markets would allocate resources efficiently and generate robust growth. In the mid-1990s, there were critical discussions in the World Bank about the wisdom of this 'consensus', particularly in the light of the East Asian miracle: 'Here was a regional cluster of countries that had not closely followed the Washington consensus prescriptions but had somehow managed the most successful development in history.'

In the immediate aftermath of the Asian crisis, Stiglitz took issue with those 'ideologues that have taken advantage of the current problems in East Asia to suggest that the system of active state intervention is the root of the problem'. He suggested, quite correctly, that 'the heart of the current problem in most cases is not that government has done too much in every area but that it has done too little in some areas'. The dogmatic versions of the Washington consensus fail to provide the right framework for understanding either the success of the East Asian economies or their current troubles. Moreover, the one and only goal of the Washington consensus – towards which its policy recommendations may have been

argues that it is usually considered unfair if someone accepts the benefits of a practice but refuses to do his part in maintaining it.[44] This also applies to the gamble 'heads I win, tails the taxpayer loses'; and to the currently established principle of 'individual profits, socialised risks'. From this perspective, the bailouts and socialisation of risk make the game unfair, and thus the current financial practices unjust.

In the moment of a crisis, a refusal to guarantee bad loans and risky exposures is likely to make things worse. There are good reasons for not letting banks, for instance, collapse like they did after 1929. But in the long run, the financial actors can be made to pay for the socialisation of risk. Indeed, the Tobin tax can be a way of doing this, particularly if the revenues are used to build a fund to intervene in crises. David Woodward's suggestion for a Global Intervention Fund is a possibility:[45]

- The present system of loans to governments could be replaced by a Global Intervention Fund, which would support exchange rates against speculative pressures, in much the same way that Central Banks defend the exchange rate (i.e. by using foreign currencies to buy local currency).
- Intervention could be triggered automatically when the reserves reach a certain level (say three months of imports); and the only condition required would be an acceleration of the rate of depreciation of the exchange rate in a crawling-peg system.

As will be explained later in Chapter 5, this system can easily be combined with a two-tier Spahn model of currency transactions tax, consisting of a low tax rate for normal transactions and an exchange surcharge on profits from very short-term transactions deemed to be speculative attacks on currencies.[46] In addition to being economically sound, this system would also seem to be more just than the present one: those accepting the benefits of a practice will be obliged to do their fair part in maintaining it.

However, there is also a further problem of justice as fairness. Those hundreds of millions of ordinary citizens in different countries, who have suffered from various financial crises since the 1970s, have in no way decided – voluntarily – to take part in the practices of global financial markets, or to accept the consequences of the financial risks taken by others. At the minimum, justice as fairness would seem to imply some compensation for these past and present injustices.

Moreover, the spectre of further financial crises clearly points to the need for a global social policy; it must be made sure that the innocent will not suffer in the future in the same way.[47] Hence, given the nature of interdependencies in the global financial system, justice as fairness seems to indicate the need for a tax-and-transfer system on a global scale.

Obviously, the Tobin tax would serve that purpose well. It would be able to transfer incomes from the 'speculators' to improving the conditions of those actually or potentially afflicted by the global casino.

Justice as a commitment to reduce powerlessness and vulnerability Rawls claimed that if actors are engaged in a just, or fair, practice they can face one another openly and support their respective positions, should they appear questionable, by reference to principles which it is reasonable to expect each to accept. This dialogical and voluntary aspect of justice should have wide transcultural appeal in the late-modern world, although its plausibility can be tested, circularly, only in a sustained dialogue with a plurality of concrete others. Similarly, Onora O'Neill argues that the first condition of justice is that actors do not coerce or deceive each other.[48] Coercion or deception would not be accepted as general principles in any context. Transactions and, more generally, participation in practices must be sufficiently voluntary and based on reliable and transparent knowledge about the consequences of the relevant transactions and practices.

O'Neill maintains that if policies, principles or practices appear, at any point in time, questionable, they must be *in fact* refusable or at least renegotiable. Just agents and institutions should and will allow others, including those most vulnerable to them, the space to refuse and renegotiate offers and arrangements. It is not reasonable to expect each to accept terms that are not refusable or at least renegotiable, should there be, for instance, good reasons to change the understandings on which the original commitments were based.[49] From this perspective, the IMF's 1999 decision to continue to respect, although with reservations, Article VI, Section 3, of its constitutive treaty, according to which 'members may exercise such controls as are necessary to regulate international capital movements', is to comply with the bare minimum of the requirements of justice.[50] If countries find out that financial liberalisation is detrimental, they may reintroduce capital controls. Also, the IMF has a duty to respect agreements and allow for renegotiations of any particular (neoliberal) arrangement.

But this kind of defence of state autonomy addresses only a very limited aspect of the problem of justice. A more comprehensive notion of justice points towards a more globalist response. According to O'Neill, a genuine action-guiding commitment to enacting principles of justice in a world of disparate agents, many of them vulnerable to others' powers, must also be a commitment to transform characters and powers of agents and the structure of institutions so as to reduce powerlessness and vulnerability.[51]

This has straightforward implications in the globalising world of the early 2000s. The first requirement is that globalising markets, transactions and relations should be adequately *regulated*, particularly if there are reasons to believe that actual markets magnify rather than minimise the implications of disparities in power and vulnerability. As was argued in Chapter 2, there are reasons to believe that global financial markets contribute to magnifying these disparities. Secondly, every sensible attempt must be made to *lessen both economic and political inequality*.[52] Hence, also from this perspective, there are good reasons for a tax-and-transfer system on a global scale. Although obviously not the only possible way to lessen inequalities, or a solution to all problems, the Tobin tax can serve this purpose well.

Justice as a commitment to reduce powerlessness and vulnerability also points towards a more democratic system of global governance than that of the Bretton Woods institutions (the IMF and the World Bank). Currently, they are based on the 'one dollar, one vote' system of voting and the almost unquestionable hegemony of orthodox economic theory. Empowerment of the weak and vulnerable must also mean democratisation.

The Emancipatory Potential of the Tobin tax

An argument for the Tobin tax may also start from the shared ideal of *democracy*. Outside China and a number of 'pariah states', nearly everyone today professes to be a democrat. Moreover, there are now fewer fundamental disagreements about the meaning of democracy than during the Cold War. There is even a tendency to attempt to make a particular liberalist conception of democracy the prerequisite for international legitimacy.

Many of the above arguments can be translated into the language of democracy. In particular, Tobin's defence of national autonomy for economic policies is, in fact, an argument for safeguarding democratic self-determination of economic policies within the confines of a nation-state. From where is the value of national autonomy derived in this argument? Since Tobin is arguing against nationalist economic policies, it must stem either from the need for different economic policies in different countries due to different conditions; or from the shared value of democratic self-determination. Indeed, Tobin argues that the conditions of states continue to differ, and so must their economic policies.

Although it is beyond what Tobin can say in his professional writings in economics, he also seems to value democracy as such. In a telling passage, he contends that 'to claim, as some right-wing ideologues did, that the victory of the West in the Cold War was the victory of economic liberalism was ridiculous: it was the victory of democracy and mixed economies'.[53] However, for him, it seems, democracy must be national. There are also more general limits as to how far Tobin's approach can lead in terms of transforming global power relations into a more democratic system of governance. These are the limits of the discourse of economics.

A critical, emancipatory argument for the Tobin tax The overly efficient and powerful financial markets tend to cause undesirable consequences. The basic idea about the Tobin tax is, thus, to curb the power of global financial markets. The concern about unnecessary and undesirable power relations and the consequent socio-economic outcomes can be generalised: the problem can be addressed in terms of emancipation from unwanted relations of domination. Emancipation is a transition from an unwanted, unnecessary and oppressive situation to a wanted and/or needed and empowering or more flourishing situation.[54]

The doctrines claiming that current institutional arrangements in global finance are natural, necessary and/or 'optimally efficient' are false. These arrangements are constructed on a basis of particular misconceptions, in the context of the late-twentieth-century struggles of global geoeconomics. As discussed in Chapters 1 to 3, these misconceptions include orthodox economics, which originates in nineteenth-century Britain, although its most prominent advocates since World War II have come from the United States (see also Appendix 1); and the hegemonic stability theory that was developed in the 1970s in the US (see in particular Chapter 3, the section 'The US power and its limits').

These misconceptions are necessary for the reproduction of financial practices and related power relations. Orthodox economics has justified the demolition of the Bretton Woods system and the move to freely floating exchange rates. The orthodox discourse has also grounded the subsequent rounds of financial liberalisation and, in an adjusted form, the BIS-centred re-regulation. The hegemonic stability theory has, in turn, justified unilateral US actions to transform the global, collective institutional arrangements in favour of its particular visions and interests, as well as its unilateral trade policies. Orthodox economics and US support have justified the British project of remaking London the financial centre of the world. Orthodox economics also constitutes the practices of investment, credit rating and media coverage, which collectively allocate capital flows, directly and indirectly. This collective allocation of capital is the basis of the global Panopticon system of surveillance and punishment. These institutional arrangements tend to reinforce economic neoliberalism, with far-reaching, mostly adverse consequences for the majority of people.

Now, truth is a positive value, without which no scientific or practical discourse would be possible. I cannot claim anything without claiming that my statement or interpretation or explanatory model is true, that the world really is like the interpretation or model says it is. All truth claims are, of

42. Rawls 1958: 178.

43. For a critical discussion on Rawls's rationalist and Kantian moral methodology, which presupposes abstract, non-historical and non-contextual individiduals as the starting point, while in fact making specific assumptions about what they *should* want and desire, see Patomäki 1992a: 66–73.

44. Rawls 1958: 180.

45. Woodward 1999.

46. See Spahn 1996; and Chapter 4 for an attempt to combine these models and develop Spahn's idea further.

47. See Deacon 1997; Deacon 1999.

48. O'Neill 1991: 300–1.

49. Ibid., pp. 301–2.

50. Articles of Agreement of the International Monetary Fund, Article VI, Section 3.

51. O'Neill 1991: 302–3.

52. Ibid.

53. Tobin 1999a: 43.

54. See Bhaskar 1986: 183–211; Bhaskar 1994: 141–60.

55. This example is taken from Collier 1994: 170.

56. Ibid., p. 172.

57. In Patomäki 1992c, I have stressed the importance of two obligations in particular: (i) constant openness for further dialogue and debate, and (ii) non-violence, which is in fact already implied by (i).

58. Kant 1983/1793.

59. That is, it remains as a *practical* problem. However, Kant was struggling also with the ontological dichotomy between moral reason and the empirical world. For a critical realist, who locates reasons in the causally efficacious world, this theoretical problem should not persist.

5

Feasibility? Overcoming the Technical Problems

It may well be that the Tobin tax would be difficult to establish and maintain. Perhaps a currency transactions tax would be unworkable because traders would find ways to evade it. And even if it were possible to establish the Tobin tax, would the tax really accomplish its main task; namely, to stabilise the markets and prevent speculation? According to some observers, the Tobin tax might even be counter-productive. All things considered, perhaps it would be best to be content with the more modest reform proposals, such as those of the Financial Stability Forum (FSF)?

The tax evasion problem is a serious one. There are two major concerns: financial substitutes for currency transactions, and locational substitutes for contemporary financial centres (or booking sites). The tax must cover all possible substitutes, and attempts at financial transactions through tax havens must be systematically penalised in one way or another. However, by going through the tax evasion problem in some detail, I will argue that it is in fact much less alarming than is sometimes feared.

It is important to recognise two crucial facts. First, many of these details are not only technical but also *political* and have implications for diverse interests. Accordingly, there should be room for negotiations and compromises among the actors establishing the Tobin tax regime. Second, it is not possible to decide all the details before experiencing the effects of the tax. Hence, the tax code and related institutional arrangements have to be revisable, based on an inbuilt learning process. There has to be a new international agency to perform this task comprised of states and other relevant actors (the proposal for a Tobin Tax Organisation will be discussed in more detail in Chapter 7).

Would the feasible Tobin tax, then, be efficient? It is true that a small currency transactions tax would not prevent all relevant speculation from taking place. If the expected profit margins were big enough, as with the emergence of anticipation of a major change in the exchange rate, the Tobin tax would play only a relatively small role. Perhaps this indicates that the Tobin tax would be inefficient when most needed? The standard

transactions and in fact are equivalent to forex trade, would be settled in a domestic currency.[20] If it becomes clear that the markets have found a substitute for forex transactions, the tax should be extended to cover the substitute. This would also mean more extensive taxation of transnational capital and more revenues to national and global purposes.[21] From the point of view of distributive justice and democratic powers to tax and transfer, the extension of the tax base may actually be a welcome movement.

To make sure that the currency transactions tax is comprehensive, there are basically two alternative approaches. The first is to extend the tax to cover substitutes, as suggested above. This is the market-based, *ex post* approach. Or, alternatively, the legitimate forms of transactions have to be regulated, by establishing an international system of licence for both financial actors and instruments. This is the *ex ante* administrative approach. As a consequence of the licence system, only transactions with legitimate counter-parties and instruments would be legal.

[...] complications may arise, particularly from cross-border transactions with non-bank institutions. It would thus become necessary to license all forex market participants at a supranational level, which would become the legal basis for their being subject to the tax. The licensing must be comprehensive and include banks, brokers, securities companies, fund managers, insurance companies, pension funds, leasing companies, and, eventually, larger commercial firms.[22]

Also, the transactions should be licensed and carefully regulated.[23] The market-based and administrative approaches are not mutually exclusive. Even in a system based on the administrative approach, existing instruments can become at least partial substitutes for each other.

Kenen argues that if the tax regime is universal and the tax rate is low, the incentive to develop substitutes is non-significant and hence the market-based *ex post* approach should work without excessive administrative costs. If necessary, 'governments could readily rule that the [financial instrument X] was designed expressly for tax avoidance and could thus treat [the instrument] as a taxable transaction'.[24] One implication of this position is that the context of neoliberal financial markets can be left intact in most respects. However, Kenen may underestimate the problems posed by non-regulated actors such as hedge funds or MNCs and non-regulated transactions such as OTC derivatives, and hence the *ex ante* administrative approach may, after all, be better even here. That is, even in the case of a low universal tax, it may turn out necessary to regulate the legitimate actors and transactions more strictly than is the case in 2000.

After the transactions covered by the tax have been defined, the Tobin tax regime must find rules and principles to:

- define in detail *how* the actual currency transactions should be subject to taxation
- determine *who will pay*, including whether it is the buyer or seller who should pay the tax;
- decide *whether it is the dealing or booking site* that determines to whom and how and when the tax should be paid; in other words, whether to adopt *a market-based or a national approach* to the taxation.

How should different types of currency transactions be subjected to tax? Spot transactions may be taxed on a simple *ad valorem* basis, that is as a percentage of the value being exchanged (like the value added tax, VAT, in the EU countries and elsewhere). Derivatives are more complicated. It is not immediately clear what the taxable amount of the currency transaction should be. For instance, Shome and Stotsky argue that 'a tax on the value of a futures contract would understate the value of the underlying assets on which the futures contract applies, but taxing the underlying value of the assets would be *onerous* unless the tax were levied at a much lower rate than on ordinary equity or debt'.[25]

However, as Kenen points out, various types of transactions are close substitutes and hence should be taxed (mostly) at the same rate.[26] For instance, a three days forward transaction is a very close substitute for a two days spot transaction, and so on. Therefore, a tax on spot transactions must be levied on all forward transactions, including standardised futures. The tax must also apply to swaps of spot and forward transactions; and consequently to all swaps. However, to avoid double taxation, swaps should be treated as a single transaction (not as a sum of the notional values of the underlying assets). According to Kenen, options are the most difficult case. Because an option may never be exercised, it is not reasonable to tax it at its notional value. One possibility would be to levy tax, at first, only on the premium and, then, on the notional amount if and when the option is exercised.[27]

In Kenen's opinion, banks should always pay the tax. He argues that, in the retail market, the banks should pay the whole amount (which they could at least partially transfer to their premiums). In the wholesale market, the payment of the tax should be split into two: the seller pays half, the buyer pays the other half. However, given the new developments and also the prominence of MNCs, hedge funds and the like in the forex markets, this does not sound reasonable. Rather, it seems that it is better that the seller pays half, the buyer pays the other half in the case of all transactions, wholesale or retail.

Book-keeping and reporting practices must be tailored to accord with the requirements of tax collection. However, it is possible to make a simple

as in Tobin's original proposals, or even more. As Felix and Sau argue, we should also consider taxation at a level that would have more significant macroeconomic and other global ethico-political objectives, by stabilising the financial markets more efficiently, and also by collecting more revenues for global purposes.[39]

What difference would a higher tax make? A higher tax would hit regularly occurring short-term movements much harder; it may also mean a drastic decline in derivatives trading (as far as swaps are concerned, first the underlying assets are taxed, and then the swap between them will also be taxed). By and large, however, this coincides with the aims of the Tobin tax. The Keynesian premise is that 'speculators have shorter horizons and holding periods than market participants engaged in long-term foreign investment and otherwise oriented towards fundamentals; speculators concentrate on how "the markets" will respond to news, not on basic economic meanings and portents'.[40] More generally, it can be argued, along Keynesian lines, that intensive speculative trading based on contradictory judgements (due to radical uncertainty) on what the yields will be, is at best needless, and at worst tends to aggravate volatility, fluctuations and uncertainty.[41] These, in turn, create other problems, including recurring financial crises; unjustified subordination of economic policies of states to the disciplinary power of finance; and tendencies towards deflationary economic policies and growing disparities. It is these short-term speculators that should be more deterred by the higher tax.

However, as a higher tax would curb global financial markets much more effectively, it would also take more *liquidity* out from the markets. For this reason, Spahn has argued that a high flat-rate tax may in fact be an impediment to smoothly functioning markets. This goes against Keynes's point that the essence of the problem is precisely over liquid investments and the resulting short-termism and speculation.[42] Spahn argues that besides short-term speculation and long-term investments, there is also 'liquidity trading', constantly recurring hedging or arbitrage for margins as little as 3 to 5 basis points. He presumes that this has a stabilising function:

> A Tobin tax has the enormous disadvantage that it cannot distinguish between liquidity trading and speculation. Sound interbank transactions would thus be affected indiscriminately by the tax although they are non-speculative in nature. This, according to some authors, must lead to thinner markets with less liquidity, which could even increase volatility. The introduction of a Tobin tax could also cause a severe liquidity shock with large disturbances on a global scale.[43]

The concepts of 'liquidity trading' and 'noise trading' are derived from the standard neoclassical equilibrium models.[44] Moreover, these categories are difficult to distinguish, conceptually and empirically.[45] Even if we deemed these categories as clear and existentially plausible, it would not be possible to calculate the ratio of 'stabilising liquidity trading' to 'noise trading'. Rather, in the Keynesian sense, even most forms of hedging and arbitrage are speculative, since they are based on anticipation of the reactions of others within financial markets, not on assessing long-term economic prospects. Nevertheless, cautiousness is in order. The introduction of a higher-rate tax may pose problems. To avoid triggering a sudden reversal of the financial multiplication process, with unpredictable consequences, it may be a good idea to introduce a tax *gradually*, that is, to start with a lower tax. To allow also for the possibility that decreasing liquidity would have 'disturbing effects', it is best to let *experience* decide. By raising the level of taxation step by step, the contingent real world effects can be taken into account when the tax regime is being developed further.

The second difference that a higher rate would make is in tax evasion. A higher tax would create, to use the terminology of economics, incentives to innovate substitutes for currency transactions. Consequently, the tax evasion problem would become more severe. Even costly and risky substitutes for forex transactions might become relatively attractive. Moreover, some sovereign states (or statelets) might be willing to let the banks and currency exchangers based in their territory get away with the tax, if not *de jure* then *de facto*, in order to create a competitive edge for them.

It is thus likely that a high tax will make the *ex ante* administrative approach necessary. There has to be a register of legitimate and standardised transactions. Any actor contemplating forex-related market innovations would have to apply for permission from the supranational body governing the Tobin tax regime to introduce the new instrument. If the body rules that the new financial instrument is a form of currency transaction, it should naturally be subject to the tax (or denied legitimacy). Any illegal transactions, and particularly attempts to innovate illegal substitutes for currency transactions, should be strongly penalised.

If necessary, new forms of capital controls must be introduced to back up the Tobin tax. The capital controls, too, should be governed globally. At the very least, banks could be required to report on the currency positions they hold both for their own and their clients' accounts, independently of where the deals are being made. Any activities within non-co-operative offshore centres should be prohibited. The sanction could be temporary or partial suspension of state guarantees or a highly punitive central bank interest rate for a sufficiently long time. These kinds of measures should also make the Tobin tax manageable at a higher rate of taxation.

A low, non-universal tax If most states and all major financial centres have to be in the system from the very beginning, the currency transactions tax may be ruled out on the grounds of political prudence. For instance, if the US and the UK refuse to join, the Tobin tax will remain a pipe dream. Would it, then, be possible to establish a non-universal tax regime, at least to start with? Tobin himself (followed by many other supporters of the idea) has assumed that the tax has to be more or less universal.[46] The sceptics are even stronger in their judgement: 'If any major financial centre does not comply with the regulations then unbalanced foreign exchange positions and foreign exchange transactions will be booked to offshore institutions in that centre.'[47] Garber and Taylor discuss the implications of a hypothetical unilateral French tax (which, in 2000, is already outdated by the EMU). They claim that even if the French regulators could impose the tax on French bank subsidies abroad, the tax nevertheless would not have the intended effects on the behaviour of the market actors. Moreover, the French authorities would also fall short of raising any substantial revenues.

As market participants seek to avoid the tax, its implementation will immediately push foreign exchange transactions out of Paris either to London or to New York, and the transactions will be booked in those centres. If the French regulators can impose the tax on French bank subsidies abroad, the French banks will be cut out of the foreign exchange business. This is the first main implication.[48]

Garber and Taylor make strong assumptions. First, they assume that even a slight increase in the transaction costs and premiums of the French banks would lead to customers – MNCs, various investments funds, etc. – immediately switching to non-French banks. In contrast, it can be (at least as plausibly) claimed that it is likely that a low tax (0.05 per cent) would not seriously threaten the profitability of currency transactions of the French banks. Half of the banks' ample profits come from forex dealing and they are unlikely to give up such a profitable business so easily. There are also institutional reasons why banks and their customers would continue business as usual, despite the small tax. It takes time and money to build a trust-based relationship between a customer and a bank. Although in the super-efficient forex markets, the basis for institutionalised, trust-based relations with customers may have been eroding rapidly, it remains a factor. Second, Garber and Taylor also assume that a small tax would be enough to deter the French banks from participating in the wholesale forex markets. Again, this is a very strong *a priori* assumption, and for the reasons specified above it is probably false as well. Under a low tax of

0.05 per cent, any transaction with a cover higher than mere 2.5 basis points would remain profitable. When the profit margin is high enough, even a 5–10 basis points additional cost should by no means be an insurmountable obstacle.

Garber and Taylor also maintain that the tax policy equals a depreciation of the taxable country's currency by the rate of the tax:

> Suppose that on a normal day, the franc foreign exchange market clears with no intervention by the Banque de France – that is, no one approaches the authorities to exchange francs for foreign currency at the lower end of the band, which is, say 3 francs per deutsche mark. Gross values of franc foreign exchange are then unaffected by the tax and no one pays the tax. On days that the Banque de France intervenes, however, some banks must engage in an explicit foreign exchange transaction with the Banque de France in Paris and pay the 1 per cent tax. [...] a transactions tax policy imposed at the national level is equivalent to nothing more than a widening of the band at the edge at which the domestic currency is weakest. This is the second main implication.[49]

They take for granted that the unilateral tax must be very high (1 per cent). Furthermore, they assume that the French banks would have to pay the tax only when they trade with the Banque de France. It is very hard to see why. A unilateral tax could be much lower, and every transaction by any actor is liable to tax at a gross value of each transaction (there are electronic means to gather the relevant information without excessive administrative costs; and the *ex ante* administrative approach would make it even easier to control and tax all currency transactions).

The real concern is whether the unilateral, low-level Tobin tax would just translate into currency depreciation. Their claim is that when the foreign actors have to turn to the French institutions to buy francs, they will face an *effective rate*, which is lowered by the rate of the tax. This would come down to the 'widening of the band at the edge at which the domestic currency is weak'. To the extent that this would also happen in practice in the world of open systems, not only in the non-realist economic theory, there would be a *partial* depreciation of the franc. However, a tendency towards a partial depreciation, where the absolute maximum is set by the low tax rate (0.05 per cent) – and only at a lower edge of the band – does not look like the most serious of problems, given the volatility and fluctuations of the current global forex markets.

Hence, the only really notable tax-avoidance option taken up by Garber and Taylor is the transferral of currency transactions to tax-free banks outside France. 'National efforts to stem such transactions will drive the forex component of these bank deposit transfers offshore; and the trans-

Box 10 Actions taken by the Western governments against the offshore centres

The G-7-based Financial Stability Forum (FSF), the OECD, and the EU all started to take actions against the offshore jurisdictions in 1999–2000. FSF's report was released in March 2000. It avoids criticising the institution of offshore facilities *per se*, yet it concludes that 'OFCs that are unable or unwilling to adhere to internationally accepted standards for supervision, co-operation, and information sharing create a potential *systemic threat to global financial stability*. Such OFCs constitute weak links in an increasingly integrated international financial system and hinder broader efforts to raise standards of soundness and transparency in the global financial system.' Moreover, their role in transnational criminal activities is also emphasised.

Based on the results of an FSF survey, the jurisdictions with financial offshore activities were grouped into three categories depending on the quality of supervision and perceived degree of co-operation. Group I has more or less adequate legal infrastructures and supervisory practices and tends to co-operate with the BIS authorities. Only Hong Kong SAR, Luxembourg, Singapore and Switzerland belong unconditionally to this category. Group II is a middle category, whereas Group III falls short of any adequate standards. Group III jurisdictions are Anguilla, Antigua and Barbuda, Aruba, the Bahamas, Belize, British Virgin Islands, Cayman Islands, Cook Islands, Costa Rica, Cyprus, Lebanon, Liechtenstein, Marshall Islands, Mauritius, Nauru, Netherlands Antilles, Niue, Panama, St Kitts and Nevis, St Lucia, St Vincent and the Grenadines, Samoa, Seychelles, Turks and Caicos, and Vanuatu (see the Report at http://www.fsforum.org/).

A key point is *information sharing*. To be co-operative, these jurisdictions will have to make information about ownership structures and financial activities accessible to outsiders. The jurisdictions willing to co-operate have to submit to consultations with the IMF and, after reforms, to a third-party assessment. The publication of the list is in itself already a sanction to the others. However, in June 2000, the OECD gave these sites a year to clean up their 'harmful practices' or face unspecified, co-ordinated 'defensive measures by member countries'. These measures could include economic sanctions, a ban on banking transactions and a cut-off of development aid (*International Herald Tribune*, 14 June 2000).

actions will appear on domestic balance sheets only as a domestic currency credit item.'[50] This is also the crux of Garber's argument, in another paper, against a non-universal Tobin tax. He argues that a new division of labour between banks would emerge: 'The role of banks in the taxed jurisdictions will be to provide cross-border credit to the untaxed banks.'[51] There is also the equally worrying spectre of foreign actors continuing to speculate with the French franc. Hence, a unilateral tax may appear rather ineffective.

But is it reasonable for the French banks to transfer their funds to foreign banks? At the margin, even with a very low tax, it is *possible* that the French banks could *sometimes* find it better to lend francs to non-French investors who would make the required forex deals and then return the francs (plus possible profits, minus a premium to the foreign bank or broker). Technically, in the OTC markets, this would be a standard operation.

Moreover, although the fund-transferral may seem a less severe problem with a very low tax rate, in a non-universal system nothing would prevent foreign actors from speculating with French francs. However, the francs have to come from somewhere:

> Currency traders wishing to bet against the French franc, to take a concrete example, must obtain francs in order to sell them short. Except for francs made available by the liquidation of existing offshore asset positions, which are by definition limited in amount, these can be obtained only by borrowing from French financial institutions. Hence, the idea of taxing or placing deposit requirement on loans in domestic currency to non-residents.[52]

We do not need to assume, as Garber and Taylor do, that 'measures are [only] aimed at forex transactions and positions [...] and not at cross-border credit'. To protect the non-universal Tobin tax regime from the transferral of funds and activities, we can make the banks residing in tax-free areas pay a higher tax on cross-border credit to non-residents of the Tobin tax zone (TTZ). If the basic rate of the Tobin tax is low, say, 0.05 per cent, or 0.1 per cent, the tax on loans to non-residents could well be twenty times higher, say 1 or 2 per cent. This should prevent banks from transferring funds to the rest of the world for forex purposes. If the TTZ is big enough, it may even encourage non-resident banks to be more favourable to the extension of the Tobin tax to their respective countries as well.[53]

Moreover, it should be easy to implement this tax. It can be administered, like the Tobin tax proper, 'by adding a few lines of code to banks' computerised trading programmes'; and 'compliance could be monitored by periodic inspection of banks' computer records'.[54] An additional problem may be that a government that wanted to provide a tax-free dealing site could adopt or invoke a legislation to confer confidentiality on individual foreign transactions. A possible response is to penalise all non-booked transactions, wherever they occur, and to raise the tax for cross-border inflows and outflows involving non-co-operative tax havens *much* higher. Hence, a low, non-universal Tobin tax is not only possible but quite feasible as well (all the technical considerations of a universal tax are obviously relevant in this context too). However, for reasons to be spelled out in the next section and discussed further in Chapter 6, it is best to make the TTZ as large as possible. It may be written into the Tobin tax agreement that it will not enter into force before, say, thirty countries have joined it and roughly 20 per cent or more of the global forex markets is covered by it. A non-universal Tobin tax has to be complemented with a somewhat high tax on domestic-currency lending to non-residents; and with a much higher punitive tax on any capital outflows and inflows to and from non-co-operative tax havens.

However, the punitive tax on capital outflows to and inflows from the blacklisted tax havens may give rise to a novel tax evasion problem. Since the punitive tax could be as high as 25 per cent, it is likely that attempts will be made to circulate money from these tax havens to the TTZ via the non-blacklisted jurisdictions outside the TTZ. The key to this problem is *global* co-operation on information sharing and enforcement of transparency of the offshore centres. These must be coupled with strict sanctions on those banks and other actors attempting tax evasion. As stated, if the risk is a temporal or partial suspension of state guarantees or a highly punitive central bank interest rate, say, for a year, the banks should think twice before engaging in such illegal activities. For other actors, an ultimate sanction might be dissolution of their corporate identity and reorganisation of their existing economic activities. Moreover, the relevant management should bear a personal responsibility for this kind of grave violation of tax laws.

In the first phase, the rule is that the actors based in the TTZ should pay the full amount if the counter-party is from the outside. However, when the tax is still non-universal, it might be a particularly attractive idea to impose tax in both 'places': first at the place where it is recorded and second also in the dealing sites, which are located within the TTZ if any of the parties is not from within the Tobin tax zone. This would maximise the tax coverage.

The two-phase model makes it possible for a grouping of countries to proceed quickly without the consent of every state. Yet it would not compromise the aim of a universal and uniform tax. There would be an open invitation for countries to join the system when they wish. There must also be a political build-up for outsiders to become more favourable to the idea of the Tobin tax. Besides the demonstration effect of a successful Tobin tax regime, and an explicit political campaign for it, the fact that banks are encouraged to trade with each other *within* the TTZ rather than with outsiders should also build pressure on others to join, particularly along the enlargement of the TTZ. The tax-imposing countries would also have the privilege of participating in deciding what to do with the revenues, in addition to keeping a portion of those revenues themselves. This should add to the political pressure for the remaining financial centres and other countries to join in.

A high, non-universal tax Would a high, non-universal transactions tax work? A lot depends on the overall, global context: economic developments, political struggles over the legitimacy of taxing global finance, innovations concerning forms of surveillance, taxation, and capital controls, etc. The

---

Box 11 The two-phase model of the Tobin tax (version A)

1. In its *first phase*, the system would consist of the EMU countries and a group of other countries, or a bigger group of other countries without the euro-EU. However constituted, this grouping should establish an open agreement – any state is invited to join at any time – and a supranational body orchestrating the tax and collecting the revenues along the lines proposed above:

- Small underlying transactions tax (10 basis points, at the most). If the counter-party is from outside the Tobin tax zone (TTZ), the bank within the TTZ would have to pay the full amount.

- A relatively high tax on domestic-currency lending to non-domiciled actors (actors based in a country which is not yet part of the tax regime); perhaps twenty times the transactions tax, that is, up to 2 per cent.

- A higher punitive tax on any capital outflows and inflows to and from non-co-operative tax havens, up to 25 per cent.

2. In its *second phase*, which should be carried out either when all major financial centres and most other countries have joined the first phase system, a universal and uniform Tobin tax at a higher rate would be applied. Although the cross-border credit tax can be abolished, it may be necessary, however, to preserve the punitive tax against tax havens.

future might well provide new coincidences and contingent episodes, with demonstrations of the power of hitherto repressed possibilities.

However, the historical experiences thus far suggest that unilateral attempts by an isolated country are not sustainable in the longer run. It does not seem to be possible to establish unilaterally a high and selective currency transactions tax – or one of its various equivalents – except as a *temporary* measure. This seems to show that a non-universal Tobin tax should not only be low, all-encompassing (cover all the substitutes) and systematic, but also based on as wide a global collaboration as possible.

A few countries have introduced something close to a unilateral currency transactions tax. The case of Italy has already been mentioned. For a while, Italy levied a tax on forward purchases or sales of foreign exchange. Traders quickly created a 'domestic' currency swap market on the interest rate differential between the lira and other currencies, to be settled in the lira. The selective and narrow duty was eventually abolished. Another, more recent, case is Malaysia. After the Asian crisis, in 1998, Malaysia reintroduced capital controls. Soon it replaced the strict capital controls with a unilateral tax on the outflows of capital. In effect, this is a variation of the unilateral Tobin tax.[55] At least in principle, this is not doomed to failure; other things being equal, it might even be possible to generalise this experiment to cover all emerging markets, with positive effects. However, there seems to be pressure on Malaysia from London and Washington, the lobby organisations of finance, and the globalising media. They are pressing Malaysia to abolish all 'costly and harmful' duties and measures.[56]

These examples indicate that there are two main considerations: tax evasion and mechanisms of domination in the global political economy. These tend to coincide. For instance, the original market-friendly, 'soft', selective tax or measure may turn out to be insufficient because financial actors will find ways to evade the taxes and regulations. Stronger and more comprehensive measures would seem to be necessary. However, attempts to make the measures more wide-ranging soon meet their limits on two fronts. On one side is the immediate reaction of 'the markets'. As Tobin et al. point out, 'in today's world of high capital mobility, even the minor exercise of policy autonomy can produce major exchange market pressures'.[57] Even mere minor changes in the tone of discourse on economic policy may provoke a reaction.

On the other side is the hegemonic project of the Washington consensus.[58] The IMF and the World Bank, and the governments of the US and the UK, are quick to react and put diplomatic pressure on the countries deviating from the 'right path'. The globalising Anglo-American media will produce and distribute juicy stories about the corruption and old-fashioned statism of these countries: 'Their policies are doomed to failure.'

Consequently, the New York-based credit-rating agencies may react as well; there are worrying signs... And all this will, naturally, influence the investors – and, it goes without saying, the actions of their lobbying organisations. The media will, of course, carefully comment on the reactions of the investors. There will be a number of local actors playing the same tune. A system of mutually reinforcing mechanisms is in place, and is causally efficacious.

The countries which have been drawn into this trap may be quick to announce that they never intended the taxes and measures to be there for good. Once the immediate troubles are over, they will return to the 'right path'. But this will only make things worse for them in the short run, and for others to come in the longer run. Speculators will smell blood:

> It can even be argued that such interventions, especially if temporary, could just as well encourage speculation to the extent that they send negative signals to financial markets, namely: distress and the lack of international coordination. This could provoke nervous reactions of market participants and drive even the sedate investor into speculation. Such measures also encourage 'moral hazard' to the extent they raise expectations of a bailout by central banks.[59]

There might also be indirect effects on the capability of these countries to form an integral part of the global economy. Under these circumstances, the more resistant governments may be drawn towards more and more nationalistic and autarchic solutions, possibly accompanied by authoritarian domestic measures (because of the need to silence the internal opposition, strongly supported from the outside). This is not only undemocratic: further economic problems will follow. And so it goes, until, perhaps, there is a return to the 'right path'. This will, of course, be celebrated in the globalising media, independently of the results of the new orthodox policies.

The above summary may exaggerate the power of the global mechanisms of domination. Nevertheless, it seems reasonable to expect that a high-level, unilateral Tobin tax (or any equivalent measure) may become too expensive, even if it was initially successful. First of all, it seems that a non-universal tax has to be low. Moreover, as Spahn puts it, 'fiscal policy measures could eventually become more propitious for market [and political] developments if adopted *multilaterally*'.[60] The power to transform is dependent on collective action by many actors. Multilateral co-operation is essential for achieving any real change in the global political economy dominated by the Washington consensus and financial capital.

Making the Tobin Tax More Efficient

The Tobin tax will clearly have three desirable effects. It will reduce short-termism and the waste of resources in financial activities. This will work for economic stability and efficiency. The Tobin tax is also a convenient way to tax transnational capital income. This will not only counter, in part, the processes that tend to draw resources from the non-financial sphere to the financial markets; it will also be a step towards a more just and democratic governance of global political economy. Last but not least, the currency transactions tax will create space for national economic policy as well as a new possibility for global democratic self-determination through the supranational body orchestrating the tax.

However, some observers have raised doubts about the effectiveness of the Tobin tax. Most importantly, the doubt concerns the power of the tax to curb volatility and fluctuations. From an empiricist perspective, the misgiving is that 'since Tobin taxes do not exist in practice, there is little empirical evidence to suggest that such taxes would be effective in reducing currency fluctuations'.[61] Of course there is no empirical evidence: a multilateral Tobin tax has never been tried. There will be empirical evidence once the Tobin tax has been worked out in practice. Some of the effects can be analysed, however. Frankel, for instance, argues that the Tobin tax would make the markets less sensitive to changes in the speculators' expectations (political news, etc.) and/or raise the relative amount of real, non-speculative investors in the financial markets. 'Either way, by decreasing the role of destabilizing speculation, the tax would, in this model, result in a lower variance in the exchange rate.'[62]

It can be easily shown that the Tobin tax will bite hard on repeatedly occurring short-term transactions: the actors have to pay the tax every time currencies are exchanged. Tobin uses a simple scheme to calculate the effects of a low rate tax. A 0.2 per cent tax on a round trip to another currency costs 48 per cent a year if transacted every business day, 10 per cent if every week, 2.4 per cent if every month. 'But it is a trivial charge on commodity trade or long-term foreign investments.'[63] Different calculations for a 1 per cent tax are depicted in Table 5.3.

Derivatives may be even more sensitive than spot transactions to increased transactions costs. So the Tobin tax should reduce the volume of transactions quite considerably – the more effectively, the higher it is.

There are also reasons to suspect that a flat-rate Tobin tax alone is not sufficient to tame the volatility and fluctuations of forex markets. Despite these cumulative effects, in the event of significant speculation and drastic volatility, the tax can do little. If the expected short-term, one-shot operation yields are very high, the effective annualised interest comparisons are

TABLE 5.3 The effect of 1 per cent Tobin tax on short-term transactions

Investment horizon	Required foreign yield to attract investor, with a 10% domestic interest rate (by a simple adding up scheme) (%)	Required yield for arbitrage, with a 4% target rate for domestic assets (IMF staff calulations) (%)
One year	11	6.1
One month	22	18.5
One week	62	77.2
One day	260	4016.7

Sources: Constructed on the basis of Frankel 1996, 58; and Spahn 1995: 3, and Appendix 1, 39, for how the IMF figures are calculated.

not helpful. A Tobin tax can hardly stop speculators who for instance anticipate devaluation, say, at the level of 10 per cent or 15 per cent. Even when the tax is high, it is still impotent against expectation of major changes. For instance, the 1992 attack by Soros's Quantum Fund against British sterling implied two currency transactions worth US$15 billion. One per cent of that sum is US$150 million. So had the Quantum Fund paid US$300 million as tax, it would still have obtained almost US$1 billion as profits. In situations such as this, speculation would still pay well. Assuming a non-universal system, in which the tax has to be rather low, at the most 0.1 per cent, the problem would be even more acute.

Hence, to make the Tobin tax more effective against speculation, it could be made into a two-tier tax, as proposed by Spahn.[64] Like the European Monetary System before the advent of the euro, the two-tier Tobin tax would consist of a target rate and an admissible spread or band for any given currency. When the currency is within the band, the low-level underlying currency transaction tax is charged. The exchange surcharge would be applied automatically whenever speculative attacks against currencies occurred, that is, it would be switched on whenever the trading price for a currency passed a predetermined threshold. The exchange surcharge would be much higher, say 2 or 3 per cent, or even more.

In fact, the exchange surcharge does not have to be a fixed percentage. Rather, as in Spahn's proposal, whenever the effective exchange rate transgresses the band, the difference between the band rate next to it and the effective exchange rate could be considered a negative externality and a windfall gain for one of the contracting parties. The difference between the band and the effective rate could be taxed at a high proportional rate,

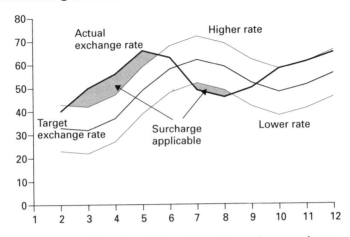

FIGURE 5.1 Illustration of the working of the exchange surcharge

up to confiscating 100 per cent of the windfall gains. This should make currency speculation effectively unprofitable.

Figure 5.1 illustrates how the two-tier system should work. Spahn's proposal for a two-tier tax amounts to a crawling-peg system, which is stabilised, in addition to normal central bank interventions, by a punitive tax against speculation. Even in this kind of a system, acceleration of the rate of depreciation of the exchange rate remains a possibility. To stabilise these fluctuations, as Woodward has suggested,[65] it would be possible to set up a Global Intervention Fund. The money for the Global Intervention Fund should come from the revenues of the Tobin tax.

- The Global Intervention Fund would support exchange rates against speculative pressures, in much the same way that central banks defend the exchange rate (i.e. by using foreign currencies to buy local currency).
- Intervention could be triggered automatically when the reserves reach a certain level (say three months of imports); and the only condition required would be an acceleration of the rate of depreciation of the exchange rate in a crawling-peg system.

The crucial question is whether it is possible to establish the two-tier model as well as the Global Intervention Fund also non-universally. Spahn argues that the absence of some major currencies and financial centres would complicate the system a tad. However, a small underlying tax coupled with an exchange surcharge would also be feasible in non-universal terms. A non-universal, multilateral system would have to define the target rate relative to a basket of currencies (as used to be the case in the European

Monetary System).[66] This link could, however, trigger the exchange surcharge whenever a reference currency in the basket is subject to major volatility, which cannot be excluded *a priori*. Hence, the basket has to be as comprehensive as possible. Moreover, it may be necessary to establish an exception clause: a totally unrelated volatility should not trigger the exchange surcharge for any given currency. 'While not ideal, the unilateral adoption [by a grouping of countries] of the scheme seems to be feasible.'[67]

Box 12 The modified two-phase model of the Tobin tax (version B)

1. In its *first phase*, the system would consist of the EMU and a group of other countries, or a bigger group of other countries without the euro-EU. However constituted, this grouping should establish an open agreement – any state is invited to join at any time – and a supranational body orchestrating the tax and collecting the revenues along the lines proposed above:

- Small underlying transactions tax (10 basis points, at the most). If the counter-party is from outside the Tobin tax zone (TTZ), the actor within the TTZ would have to pay the full amount.
- A relatively high tax on domestic-currency lending to non-residents (only to residents of a country which is not yet part of the tax regime); perhaps twenty times the transactions tax, that is, up to 2 per cent.
- An exchange surcharge triggered by exceptional changes, up to the level of confiscating the windfall gains.
- A higher punitive tax on any capital outflows and inflows to and from non-co-operative tax havens, up to 25 per cent.
- A Global Intervention Fund to stabilise further the exchange rates; a substantial share of the global part of the revenues should be allocated to it.

2. In its *second phase*, which should be carried out when all major financial centres and most other countries have joined the first phase system, a universal and uniform Tobin tax at a higher rate would be gradually applied, coupled with:

- an exchange surcharge as above
- a continuous punitive tax against tax havens
- the Global Intervention Fund

Conclusion

The Tobin tax is technically feasible. Even in the absence of some of the financial centres, and without any co-operation from the most persistent tax havens, it is possible to make the Tobin tax real. Although there are a number of administrative problems to be settled, they do not pose insurmountable problems. Rather, many of them bear also on far-reaching political choices. However, I have argued that a high unilateral tax is not likely to be sustainable.

There are four possible states of affairs. The rate of taxation can be either high or low, and the area of taxation can include major financial centres or exclude some of them. A low global tax is relatively unproblematic. However, the transactions covered by the tax must be defined as comprehensively as possible. Either the supranational body governing the Tobin tax should observe market developments and extend the tax when necessary, or a supranational licence system for actors and transactions should be set up. Since spot transactions and various derivatives can be substitutes for each other, all transactions have to be taxed equally strictly (with the partial exception of swaps and options). The seller should pay one half, the buyer the other half of the tax in all transactions. An electronic routing slip should be attached to any transaction that contains corresponding tax information until the transaction is finally settled. For a number of reasons, it is best to have a national system of taxation. That is, the tax is due to the authorities of the *real* home country of the financial actor.

A higher tax would make a difference in two regards. It would contract the markets more drastically. To avoid triggering a sudden reversal of the financial multiplication process, with unpredictable consequences, it may be a good idea to introduce a tax *gradually*, that is, to start with a lower tax. A higher tax would also render the tax evasion problem more difficult. In effect, it would be likely to necessitate the licence system of legitimate transactions and actors, and make minimalist capital controls necessary. At least, banks can be required to report on the currency positions they hold both for their own and their clients' accounts.

Perhaps the main argument of this chapter is that the Tobin tax is feasible even if some of the financial centres decide to stay out (for the time being). The two-phase model of making the Tobin tax real does not compromise the aim of a universal, global tax, yet it will also allow any grouping of countries to proceed quickly in the absence of the consent of any home country of a major financial centre. For effective multilateral action, a grouping of some thirty countries, covering, say, roughly 20 per cent of forex markets, should suffice. The system would be based on a build-up of political pressure and an open invitation for anybody to join in at any time. It seems, however, that a non-universal tax would have to be rather low. Even a higher tax would not prevent profitable speculation from taking place, particularly at times of exceptional volatility and financial turmoil. The Tobin tax can be made more effective by two means. Within a modified crawling-peg system, a two-tier tax would in effect confiscate all windfall gains from excessive speculation. In addition, a Global Intervention Fund could support the efforts of central banks to avoid an acceleration of change of its exchange rate. These would make the forex markets more stable – at least for those countries deciding to join the Tobin tax regime.

Notes

1. Shome and Stotsky 1995. This is a typical extension of orthodox thinking, which is not content with claiming that only the 'free markets' constitute the best possible world (in most cases, at least); it also believes that it is, ultimately, the only possible world, at least in the long run!

2. Ibid., p. 9.

3. Ibid., p. 11.

4. Eichengreen and Wyplosz 1996: 15.

5. See Stiglitz 1989 for an argument for such taxes; he points out that the Japanese securities tax raised US$12 billion a year (in the late 1980s).

6. Sirkka Hämäläinen, the Director of the Bank of Finland, argued in a public discussion that the Tobin tax is immoral because it is so easy to evade. She may not have thought through the implications of her statement, but I think this Freudian slip of the tongue reveals something essential about the fundamental orientation and disposition of the financial orthodoxy (which most central bankers represent). Hämäläinen was quoted in *Helsingin Sanomat* on 26 October 1999; and is briefly discussed in Patomäki 1999c: 170.

7. This minimalist form of capital control is proposed by Soros (1998: 194).

8. See in particular Chapter 3, section 'Globalising capital and the competition between territorial states', for details. An OECD study has estimated that out of seven categories of regulatory measures – interest rate controls, mandatory reserve requirements, quantitative investment restrictions, capital controls, securities market regulations, restrictions on line-of-business and ownership linkages, and restrictions on foreign bank entry – in only one case has it seemed that deregulation has been carried out because of the direct pressure stemming from the offshores, namely, mandatory reserve requirements. OECD 1996: 5–7.

9. Tobin (1996b) uses the term 'super-efficient markets' (in the narrow technical – not welfare – sense). New innovations come up almost daily. A recent 'e-commerce news' from 6 June 2000 tells that 'seven of the world's leading financial institutions created FXall.com™, which will offer clients low-cost one-stop electronic access to a range of services in foreign exchange (FX), from execution to research. The founding participants are Bank of America, Credit Suisse First Boston, Goldman Sachs, HSBC, J. P. Morgan, Morgan Stanley Dean Witter and UBS Warburg.' FXall.com will offer twenty-four-hour access to the global FX market. Through the use of cutting-edge technology,

FXall.com will create a platform where 'clients can easily access liquidity across a wide range of FX products'. According to the news, Paul Kimball, chairman of FXall.com and co-head of FX at Morgan Stanley Dean Witter, said: 'The efficiencies provided to clients by FXall.com will enable faster and cheaper FX transactions, resulting in an even greater degree of liquidity and transparency across this global market. We believe that FXall.com will be the most powerful application yet of e-commerce to the FX industry worldwide.' From http://www.msdw.com/e-commerce/index23.html (26 June 2000).

10. See Helleiner 1994 for a strong argument against the view that new information technologies have played a crucial role in financial globalisation. Rather, state actions have been central in creating the liberalised framework for the process. Of course, the first part of Chapter 3 of this book makes a similar point, albeit without discussing the technological determinism viewpoint explicitly; however, the second part also emphasises the far-reaching role of the emergent structural properties of the global financial markets.

11. Eichengreen, Tobin and Wyplosz, 1995: 165.

12. Kenen 1996: 122.

13. For an introduction, see, for instance, Jarrow and Turnbull 1996.

14. BIS 1999a: Tables A-1 and A-2, 2.

15. For many, the international forex market is now by definition an OTC market.

16. See Raghavan 1998, following Jan Kregel.

17. Soros 1998: 189.

18. This is clear when financial innovations (i.e. many OTC instruments) are merely attempts to hide or transfer risks. More generally, Stiglitz (1989: 103) argues that many of the new financial innovations have actually made everyone worse off. Financial innovations are costly and speed up and/or complicate the financial process, without actually adding any extra value to the system. The innovators may get, for a short while, a slightly bigger share of the pie. However, they do not increase the size of the pie; yet they force everybody to follow suit. '[...] not only is the social return to this kind of information gathering – getting information slightly earlier than other investors – less than the private return, but this is [also] true of many of the financial innovations [...] that have occurred in the past decade. [...] such financial innovations – to the extent that there are any costs associated with them – actually lead the economy to a Pareto inferior equilibrium. Barring these innovations (were this possible) could actually make everyone better off.'

19. This is a problem that has been pointed out many times (forcefully by John Grahl, for instance, in personal communication), the core of which is that central banks and supervisory bodies require financial actors to register only overnight balance sheet positions. In today's twenty-four-hour global marketplace, foreign exchange traders can hide positions by shifting them between branches in different time-zones to stay continuously within working hours. There are two obvious answers to this. Either it is possible to use the formal, regulated and centralised net settlement system to identify individual transactions independently of the overnight balance sheet positions (see Box 9); or the legislation and registration requirements have to be changed.

20. That is, a forex derivative can be substituted with an instrument derived from assets such as Treasury bills nominated in different currencies; or with interest rates swaps, since currency movements are strongly influenced by differences in interest rates and thus for many purposes can be taken as equivalents. However, many of these substitutes would be costly, and if the tax rate is only 0.05 per cent, there should be no major problems with these rather complicated 'substitutes'. See Kenen 1996: 119.

21. The transaction is tantamount to a surrogate of a tax on capital income.

22. Spahn 1995: 29.

23. As stated, Soros (1998: 190) has proposed a licence system for all financial instruments. It would be better to require a licence for all financial activities. Thereby, democratic surveillance and control of these activities, as well as their taxation, would be facilitated. Moreover, more adequate book-keeping of all daily transactions may be required, not only of overnight balance sheet positions, depending on how the new net settlement system will work (cf. note 19 and Box 9).

24. Kenen 1996: 119.

25. Shome and Stotsky 1995: 9. Italics HP.

26. Felix 1995a, 1995b; and Felix and Sau 1996 give the impression that only spot transactions should be taxed. There seems to be no reason for this assumption.

27. Kenen 1996: 116–19.

28. If and when more major banks will join the FXall.com™ system (see note 9, above), this may become an easy and costless way of taxing also most retail forex transactions.

29. Eichengreen and Wyplosz 1996: 25.

30. Spahn 1995: 28.

31. Ibid., p. 32.

32. Ibid., pp. 113–14.

33. This point is made in a questionnaire.

34. Palan 1998 tends to emphasise the enabling role of the institution of state sovereignty at the expense of real historical processes and power relations, yet he also says that 'many tax havens came about as a result of core countries' covert policies' (Palan 1998: 639).

35. The Continental European states – and the EU – bear their share of responsibility for having allowed Liechtenstein, Monaco, Luxembourg and others to develop their offshore facilities (not only for systematic tax avoidance but also for serious criminal purposes).

36. Since most banks and other financial actors are also extensively utilising offshore facilities by having set up notional banks and companies in the offshore centres and tax havens, all these have to be covered as well. Thus we should talk about the *real* home country, and make the real home base part of the legal definition as well. Given the rate of transnational acquisitions and mergers in the financial industry, a further complication in a non-universal system may stem from companies that are *really* domiciliary in more than one country, at least one of them inside and another one outside the Tobin tax zone. To maximise tax coverage, it is best to make them fully liable to the currency transactions tax.

37. BIS 1996: 20.

38. The economistic theory of law-abidance is, in general, false. In many or most contexts, normative legitimacy as well as cultural values and practices explain legal rule-following behaviour more than the severity of sanctions. However, once, for instance, offshore facilities have become a widely accepted part of everyday practices of financial actors, the first cultural battle is already lost. We may also assume that the collective economic actors (banks, corporations) tend to follow the logic of *homo oeconomicus* at least up to a sufficient extent for these sanctions to work.

39. Felix and Sau 1996: 245. However, they do not consider rates as high as 1 per cent.

40. Eichengreen, Tobin and Wyplosz 1995: 165.

41. Under these kinds of circumstances, hedging may appear more justified. However, the less uncertainty there is, the less the need for hedging. By stabilising the forex markets, a Tobin tax regime may also lead to much less hedging.

It is also worth mentioning that there would be substitutes for the derivatives that are now used to manage currency positions. It would be possible to initiate, by public political actions, insurance instruments against exchange rate fluctuations, preferably backed by a global fund derived from the revenues of the Tobin tax. These regulated insurance markets could also be initiated by the actions of the supranational body in charge of the Tobin tax regime. Any insurance against exchange rate fluctuations would be sold only to actors who could demonstrate a solid connection to non-financial economic activity. These types of insurance could be monitored by, for instance, the national guarantee agencies, or by a global organisation serving as a parent organisation to the national units. The demonstration of a non-financial content of the transaction is no more difficult than meeting the conditions of a car or life insurance. This is only a hypothetical possibility; in practice, an insurance of this kind could be established, if needed, to complement existing possibilities to secure yields. The idea is based on Mann (1998: 3), although she does not discuss it in the context of the Tobin tax.

42. See Box 2 in Chapter 1.

43. Spahn 1995: 12–13.

44. The theoretical idea is that 'liquidity trading' will enhance the efficiency of the markets, and therefore lead towards a general, Pareto-optimal equilibrium, whereas 'noise trading' will lead away from the Pareto-optimal equilibrium (cf. to Stiglitz's argument that all financial innovations amount to 'noise trading', discussed in note 18, above). 'Efficiency' in this argument is understood in a very narrow manner. With many actors each endowed with given preferences, beliefs and assets, the question is whether potential trade would exist that would make each participant in the given market better off, or at least would not make anyone worse off while the situation of one or more improves.

The problems of this yardstick are innumerable (see also Lawson 1997: Chapters 8 and 9). *Even if* there was a unique Pareto-optimal equilibrium *in a given market*, neoclassical models would have nothing to say about how to get there. Besides, if an acceptable specification of a market allows for one specification, it typically allows of many. Even if the specification of the market was based on realistic assumptions, any of these equilibria was Pareto-optimal, and there was a clearly specified way of getting there (none of these conditions is usually fulfilled), the models would say nothing about whether 'efficiency' in this narrow sense in the financial markets would actually enhance the efficiency of the economy as a whole. Keynes's (and Tobin's) point is exactly that it does not! Over-liquid and 'efficient' finance is tantamount to short-termism and irrational investments. Even more fundamentally, the equilibrium theorists themselves do not know what 'effective equilibrium' would designate in the real world (outside the fictitious models). And last but not least, this approach never questions the institutional framework of economic activities. Would there be better-justified beliefs and more desirable ways of organising rules, principles and practices and distributing assets? Lest we forget, the Tobin tax is also about an emancipatory transformation, about democratising globalisation.

45. Most importantly, if the notion of Pareto-optimal equilibrium is totally unclear and does not seem to designate anything in the real world, the whole distinction is unfounded (see note 44, above). But even the distinction between hedging, arbitrage and speculation is blurred. Take the standard *Penguin Dictionary of Economics* definitions

(Bannock et al. 1998). *Arbitrage* is the exploitation of difference between the prices within or between markets by buying where prices are low and selling where they are higher. *Speculation* is about buying and selling with a view to buying and selling at a profit later. The difference between them stems from the risks assumed. Non-speculative arbitrage is said to involve no significant risks, whereas speculation is risky. Take then the category of hedging. *Hedging* is action taken by a buyer or seller to protect his business or assets against a change in prices. It implies that there is a risk unless action is taken. Non-action would be speculative.

It all comes down to assessing the risks of different investments. Most complex trading strategies involve elements of arbitrage, hedging and speculation, as seen from the trader's own point of view. However, prediction is impossible and most financial transactions would be possible only if the buyer and seller made opposing assessments. The risk element is thereby also subjective (despite the existence of such indicators of collective risks as leverage-building, increased short-termism, and rapidly inflated asset-prices). The categories of arbitrage, hedging and speculation are thus very difficult to distinguish empirically.

46. Tobin seems to suppose that the taxation would be implemented at the dealing site. However, when the tax is levied at the booking site, on a national basis, banks cannot avoid it by moving their dealing sites to tax-free locations. More recently, Tobin said in an interview in *Le Monde* (17 November 1998) that he has been thinking a lot about the possibility of a non-universal tax regime, and that he now believes that, to start with, it would be sufficient for twenty countries to introduce the tax. But even in this interview, he seems to indicate that all major financial centres must be included.

47. OECD 1996: 12.

48. Garber and Taylor 1995: 174.

49. Ibid., p. 175.

50. Ibid., p. 174.

51. Garber 1996: 134, 140.

52. Eichengreen, Tobin and Wyplosz 1995: 167.

53. Later, we shall argue that this should be complemented by an organised, global political campaign for a global, universal Tobin tax. The revenues of the first-phase tax could be used to subsidise this campaign (for instance, an advertisement campaign addressed both to the customers of the banks and to the citizens of democratic states).

54. Eichengreen and Wyplosz 1996: 25.

55. 'Malesia lieventämässä pääomaliikkeiden sääntelyä', *Helsingin Sanomat*, 26 January 1999.

56. Many major investors, such as Morgan Stanley Capital International, pulled Malaysia out of their indices immediately following the capital controls. The IMF and major Western governments warned against using capital controls (although they softened their tone later). For other reactions against Dr Mahathir's rhetoric and actions, see Box 1: Paradoxes of Malaysia, in Chapter 1. However, the short-term success *and* the promise quickly to move away the capital controls turned the mode. As *Business Times Singapore* reported in 30 August 1999: 'Even independent strategist David Roche, known for his criticism of Malaysia's policies, has conceded that the Morgan Stanley Capital International move [to reinstate Malaysia in its indices] "may provide an incentive for foreign investors not to repatriate capital trapped by the government's control ... Indeed, much of the world seems to love Malaysia again, with the equity market up over 30 per cent in the year to date."' Moreover, as a surplus country, Malaysia did not have to rely

upon the credit-rating agencies and the IMF; it had some freedom of action. Most states would be more vulnerable to the functioning of global power mechanisms.

57. Eichengreen, Tobin and Wyplosz 1995: 162.

58. For these mechanisms, see Chapter 3; and also Gill 1995a, 1995b.

59. Spahn 1995: 10.

60. Ibid., p. 10.

61. Stotsky 1996 is a representative example of all the standard arguments against the Tobin tax collected together, without any critical reflectivism whatsoever. She even claims that there is no evidence for increased volatility since the 1970s; free markets are working beautifully. This quote is from p. 2.

62. Ibid., p. 72.

63. Tobin 1996a: xi.

64. Spahn 1995: 32–8 and Appendix 3; see also Spahn 1996.

65. Woodward 1999.

66. In a universal, global system the target exchange rates could be defined on an autoregressive basis for each pair of exchange rates.

67. Spahn 1995: 36.

6

Politically Possible? A Two-phase Proposal

Powerful interests are opposing the Tobin tax. Even if it is technically feasible, is perhaps the Tobin tax politically unattainable? Given the opposition, is the best approach for realising the Tobin tax to wait until yet another disaster occurs, such as a major financial crash followed by a global depression? Perhaps only this could cause the anti-Tobinists to shift their ground towards a more positive and co-operative stance. 'Realistically', it is of course possible to continue with the BIS-centred re-regulatory project of filling in the most obvious holes in the system and hope for the 'best', i.e. absence of major troubles.

The sceptical approach implies, of course, that the disciplinary system and undesirable tendencies stemming from the power of finance will persist, perhaps even gain in strength. Moreover, without the possibility of real change, many states are caught in Catch-22 situations. For instance, if the states do not back up the financial actors, crises are more likely to occur and also to be more serious. However, if the states back them up, financial actors are encouraged to take excessive risks, thereby creating conditions for crises. Besides, the states would be paying for the gambling of these financial actors. Regardless of the implicit or explicit promises to the financial actors, it seems that the states and multilateral organisations will have to continue to invest more and more funds in monetary reserves.

There is also the competitive game of regulatory laxity. By deregulating finance or even establishing an offshore centre, in order to gain a relative competitive edge, states seem to be undermining, in the longer run, their own abilities to tax and regulate, and, more generally, to shape their economic fate. Yet, by deciding to defend regulations and taxation unilaterally, they evoke the fear of sanctions of the global financial system. All actors are made visible and transparent *vis-à-vis* the investors; everybody knows that they are being watched and that, indirectly, any deviation from the path towards realising the orthodoxy of economic liberalism may entail immediate punishment. Moreover, by encouraging further transfers of notional activities to offshore, a unilateral defence of financial control may in fact contribute to the entrenchment of the position of the tax havens. Because of these mechanisms and contradictions, also, any unilateral attempt by any single state to set up an equivalent to a Tobin tax is unlikely to make more than a temporary difference. There tends to be a gap between the intention and the result. The intention may be to tax, curb and control democratically, yet anything more than a short-term success is unlikely. The unilateral measure may be defeated by tax evasion or by global power mechanisms. The best way to overcome these contradictions is to organise multilateral global political action. However, mere re-regulation facilitating the free play of global financial markets is also unlikely to resolve the contradictions. The BIS-centric regime may provide, for a while, a more stable regulatory framework for further financial multiplication and expansion. Yet, by facilitating further financial multiplication, this kind of re-regulation may even help in building up the potential for ever more severe and far-reaching crises.

Building on the two-phase model of realising the Tobin tax, in this chapter, I shall argue that the contradictory situations brought on by global finance can be overcome by means of collective, multilateral action aiming at curbing the power of finance and redefining the rights, obligations and accountability of the global financial markets. The two-phase model allows any grouping of states to take the initiative and establish a collective organisation that manages the tax and that could, possibly, also take further actions against tax havens and other initiatives. The present global move-ment for the Tobin tax can prepare the ground for the realisation of the first phase.

Which states could form the group of initiators? I shall discuss two possibilities: the EU countries of the Economic and Monetary Union; and the 'progressive' states together with the 'hard hits'. These are com-plementary rather than exclusive possibilities. The implementation of the first phase presupposes a relatively large grouping of states, some of them home countries for significant financial actors – say at least thirty states together accounting for at least 20 per cent of global currency markets. The more participants there are in the first phase, the better. The tax regime should be as inclusive as possible and encourage others to join in.

Political Opposition

What are the interests opposing the Tobin tax? Obviously, many offshore centres and tax havens would oppose the Tobin tax and related measures of surveillance and regulation. Their market position is based on providing offshore facilities. Switzerland, which established itself as a tax and money-laundering haven as early as in the 1930s, as well as countries such as

Lebanon (Beirut), Morocco (Tangiers) and Uruguay (Montevideo) are unlikely to be among the first to join the Tobin tax regime. Likewise, the anachronistic principals such as Liechtenstein and the numerous island statelets providing offshore facilities will oppose the tax.

However, the most important states expected to oppose the Tobin tax are the US and the UK (Japan may be more ambivalent). A further look at the re-emergence of global finance in the 1960s helps to understand why they would oppose the tax. The re-emergence was made possible and encouraged by intentional state actions. Of course, there were also spontaneous innovations by financial actors, and the process as a whole was not planned by anybody. Yet, in the beginning, the re-emergence of global financial markets was supported and encouraged by these two states and, since then, their interests have been deeply intertwined with those of the globalising financial actors.

After World War II, the British government attempted to restore London's role as the centre of global financial markets. In 1963, the Eurobond market supplemented the dollar-nominated loan market, which was established in the late 1950s. Thereafter, Britain has provided a physical location for the emergent eurodollar markets. US support was crucial, for it had the power to prevent or alter these processes:

> US support was equally important because American banks and corporations were a dominant presence in the market in the 1960s. Although it had the power, the United States chose not to prevent them from participating in the market. In fact, by the mid-1960s, US officials were actively encouraging American banks and corporations to move their operations to the offshore London market.[1]

In the 1970s, the US and the UK initiated a trend towards further financial deregulation and liberalisation. They unleashed 'competitive pressures that indirectly encouraged liberalization and deregulation throughout the system'.[2] In many global forums, they also directly supported the political programme of neoliberal globalisation, later to be known as the Washington consensus. Within the UK, this process culminated in the 1979 UK Banking Act, the first act of the Thatcher government, which removed all distinction between offshore and onshore markets. The City of London became an offshore financial market and perhaps the UK's crucial asset in the global economy. Also, because of the rapid decline of British industrial output in the 1980s, the offshore status of the City of London became an ever more essential element in the British competitive strategy, along with lower wages and cheaper infrastructure.

Moreover, many of the most important offshore centres are either British ex-colonies (Singapore, which became independent from Britain in

1959–63; Hong Kong, which remained under British rule until the late 1990s) or small islands still tied to the British state (Bermuda, the Cayman Islands, the Channel Islands, the Isle of Man, etc.). Many of the most significant offshore activities were established in the 1960s. Moreover, British organisations and expatriates run the bulk of offshore activities in these places.

Mostly, the US supported the British developments. Eventually, the Nixon administration decided to abolish the Bretton Woods system of fixed exchange rates. By the late 1970s, the US Treasury came to the conclusion – with the active encouragement of the New York banking community – that rather than fight the offshore centres, the US could gain by encouraging its own offshore centre. This conclusion fitted well with the neoliberal vision of the new Reagan administration. Consequently, the New York International Banking Facilities (IBF) emerged with the advent of Reaganism. The New York offshore market was established on 1 December 1980.

The London–Wall Street–Washington axis at the turn of the century
Neoliberal globalisation has reinforced the pre-eminent positions of London and New York in the world's financial markets. In 2000, London and New York together account for almost half of the world's forex transactions. They appear to have high stakes in the struggles over de- and re-regulation, and the Tobin tax. Therefore, it is not surprising that there have been very few signs of changes in the positions of the US and the UK. The available evidence from the 1990s reveals a consistent and strong opposition against any measures that would even hint at the possibility of anything like a currency transactions tax. During the Clinton administration, the US Congress has been the ideologically noisy party in the US mission to protect its own sovereignty against any attempt to regulate or tax US citizens and corporations, while simultaneously promoting free market 'globalisation' for the rest of the world. However, it is the US government that has conducted many of the disciplinary acts to silence discussions on global taxes, while pushing for further liberalisation.

The censorship is most obvious in the case of the UN system. In the 1980s, the Reagan and Thatcher governments systematically attacked the UN system, and eventually they succeeded in their attempts to remove North–South relations from the international agenda.[3] The end of the Cold War and the dissolution of the Soviet Union further consolidated these changes. Even under the resulting rather favourable circumstances, in the 1990s, the US was forced to use its direct power to get its own way. The Boutros-Ghali débâcle is a case in point. Towards the end of his 1992–96 term as UN Secretary-General, Boutros-Ghali became increasingly independent from – and critical of – the US. He started to push forward his own vision of the role and possibilities of the UN more forcefully:

In January 1996 I was invited to give a lecture at Oxford University. [...] My lecture stressed the importance of an independent secretary-general, as envisioned by the UN Charter, and the urgent need to find new ways to finance UN operations, since the United States refused to pay its contribution. My words angered the White House and Congress. Staff aides and spokesmen for both parties noted that I had been far too independent over the past five years. My suggestion that a modest levy on international airfares might be used to finance UN expenses was denounced in the Senate as an attempt to impose taxes on American citizens in defiance of the US constitution. Although I was merely repeating an idea first put forward by Pérez de Cuéllar and backed by me five years before, the UN Information Office in Washington used the word 'firestorm' in describing Washington's reaction to my Oxford lecture.[4]

Immediately following this, in 1996, the Helms–Dole bill was introduced in the US Congress (more formally 'Prohibition on United Nations Taxation Act'). The argument for the bill seemed to be, first and foremost, about power relations. 'An international tax would mean that "[the Secretary General would] not be under the daily financial will of the Member States".' Under the conditions of the 1990s, 'the will of the member states' meant, mostly, the will of the US.[5] However, a reference was also made to UNDP's 1994 *Human Development Report*, condemning the idea that 'it is appropriate that the proceeds of an international tax be devoted to international purposes and be placed at the disposal of international institutions'. This was deemed unacceptable.[6] The Helms–Dole bill was intended to prohibit US 'voluntary and assessed contributions to the UN if the UN imposes any tax or fee on US persons or continues to develop or promote proposals for such taxes or fees'.[7] Even remote association with attempts to seize control over globalisation by means of introducing global taxes or fees may thus turn out to be detrimental to the UN.

Later in 1996, the US removed Boutros-Ghali from office. Fourteen votes were cast in favour of a full second term; the United States cast its veto. Despite the resistance of France, the US was eventually able to have its own candidate Kofi Annan nominated. Boutros-Ghali's last accomplishment as Secretary-General was *An Agenda for Democratization*. It can be read also as a reaction to what he perceived as the imperialist behaviour of the US. More than half of this text was dedicated to 'democratization at the international level'.[8] As he explained in his memoirs, 'the fact that a single vote – that of the United States – could dictate the outcome at the

United Nations threatened hopes for increasing democratization on the international scene'.[9]

Under these circumstances, it is not particularly remarkable that, in 1996, the US also suppressed an attempt by the UNDP to circulate a volume of expert papers on the Tobin tax. The collection *The Tobin Tax. Coping with Financial Volatility* – which is, incidentally, rather favourable to the introduction of a currency transactions tax – was eventually published by Oxford University Press as an independent academic text, with no mentioning of the UNDP.[10] The rule was thereby stated. The US has the right to censor discussions on global taxation in the UN system. The episode was repeated after the publication of the UNDP's 1999 *Human Development Report.* This report, commissioned by the UNDP, states on page 13 that 'new sources of financing for the global technology revolution could be investigated, to ensure that it is truly global and that its potential for poverty eradication is mobilized'.[11] The report also mentions the possibilities of a bit tax (essentially a tax on internet e-mail) and a patent tax to raise funds from those who already have access to technology for spreading technology to developing nations.[12]

Although the UNDP has announced, under pressure, that the organisation does not endorse any form of global tax, the report provoked an immediate reaction in Washington. On 16 July 1999, Assistant Secretary of State for International Organization Affairs David Welch sent a letter to UNDP administrator Mark Malloch Brown – naturally, a Brit – reiterating the strong US opposition to any form of international tax and asking for clarification of the UN's stance on global taxes. In Brown's immediate response, he made it clear that the inclusion of the idea for a bit tax in the report does not constitute UN support for any proposals for international taxation. Brown's letter states bluntly that 'UNDP does not advocate and will never advocate the establishment of this or any other kind of global tax'.[13]

Following these and other episodes and developments of the 1980s and the 1990s, the UN system is now almost totally dominated by the US – to the very limits that this is possible in an international organisation within which states are formally equal. Despite its strong hold over the UN system, the US still refuses to pay its due payments. This refusal functions as a constant threat against any attempt at independent thinking at the UN. Moreover, the Helms–Dole bill could also be interpreted as a unilateral prohibition against United Nations personnel recommending or promoting any global taxation – even though it would be levied and collected by member states rather than by the United Nations or its agencies. (According to its Charter, the UN is funded by membership fees and could not collect taxes.) Thus, the legislation was bound to have a dampening effect on any such initiatives from within the UN system.[14] It is telling that a high-positioned, long-term UN civil servant explains in late 1998 that 'nobody at the UN dares even mention the Tobin tax, particularly because of fear of the anti-UN and anti-Tobin tax sentiments in the US Congress'.[15]

The system of silencing non-orthodox voices is extended to all international forums dominated by the US. The situation at the Bretton Woods institutions is certainly no better. The IMF and the World Bank have their headquarters in Washington DC. In both cases, already the system of recruitment is a guarantee against unwanted dissidence. First and foremost, they are looking for mainstream economists from the 'top' US, British and West European universities (in that order). In effect, to qualify, you have to demonstrate your belief in the fundamentals of orthodoxy. The IMF is a bastion of orthodox thinking, and dominated by financial interests.[16] The prevalence of orthodox economics in the World Bank is often likened to the self-assured certainties of fundamentalist theology.[17]

However, lately there have been more signs of independent thinking in the World Bank. In particular, the 1996–99 chief economist, Stiglitz, seemed to be in favour of the Tobin tax, alongside other heterodox ideas. Soon, however (as explained in Chapter 4), he had to resign. The controversy over the year 2000/01 *World Development Report* on poverty is another case in point. The report was intended to be a milestone in the World Bank's new thinking. In April 2000, a draft report was opened for public discussion on the internet. Although 'the draft did not question the importance of the market or the need for reforms', the US Treasury Secretary Lawrence Summers was annoyed by its suggestion 'that no universal prescription of liberalisation would work for poverty reduction'.[18] Since no reservations about the universal validity of orthodox economics are tolerated, the lead author for the report, Ravi Kanbur, had to resign.

There seems to be a division of labour between the US and the UK. Whereas the US takes care of preventing any unorthodox interpretations or initiatives from arising in global forums, the role of the UK has been to block initiatives towards anything like the Tobin tax within the European Union. In the late 1990s and 2000, two episodes have been particularly revealing. The first concerns the so-called savings tax in the EU. The idea of the savings tax is that all citizens resident in a member state of the European Union should pay a uniform tax due on all their savings income. The initiative – that has been discussed for years – is to tax these incomes at the minimum rate of 20 per cent. However, with the support of Luxembourg, the UK has vehemently opposed this initiative on the grounds that it would endanger the position of London as the world's biggest bond market. Instead, in the Helsinki Summit in December 1999, the UK proposed a model of information exchange on bank accounts and savings, also with outsiders.[19] As a compromise, a proposal to allow for two co-existing systems has been made: a direct savings tax or an exchange of information. However, in summer 2000, the UK, worried about its euro-bond industry, wanted an assurance that the tax option would be phased out quickly, preferably within five years. That would be good news also for Cyprus, a candidate for becoming a member, which is the host of some 40,000 holding companies devised merely for tax avoidance purposes.[20] In early December 2000, at the Nice Summit, the UK successfully repeated its insistence on veto-right over all European questions of taxation.

Even more directly to the point is the recent debate and vote in the European Parliament on a Tobin tax initiative. On Wednesday 19 January 2000, Francis Wurtz, president of the GUE Group, obtained the tabling of a debate on the Tobin tax for a plenary session of the European Parliament in Strasbourg. Wurtz was responding to the request of thirty-eight MEPs, members of the Capital Tax, Fiscal System and Globalisation intergroup. The intergroup was launched in 1999 by MEPs Glyn Ford and Harlem Désir and is supported by a number of NGOs such as ATTAC. In a consequent vote, however, the European Parliament rejected, with a margin of only six votes, a resolution 'asking the Commission and the Council to explore new ways to mitigate growing speculation on the world financial markets and to generate revenue for socially valuable invest-ment in environment, education and development across the globe'. Mostly, the vote seemed to illustrate a clear left–right issue, with the conservatives and liberals opposing the resolution and others supporting it. However, the crucial votes against the resolution came from the UK Labour MEPs. French MEP Danielle Auroi, vice-president of the Green/EFA Group, emphasised that 'the UK Socialists obviously accepted an order from Downing Street thus proving that they are more occupied with safe-guarding the interest of the City of London than finding answers to questions of European and global level'.[21]

Any given identity and interest is nothing more than frozen politics. Yet the powerful structures sustaining that identity and related interests of the London–Wall Street–Washington axis appear to be deeply sedimented and not easily changeable. More metaphorically, there might be no heat in sight to melt that frozen entity and turn it into hot politics. Perhaps a Big Crash or, at least, powerful external political forces and historical transformations are needed to create the heat. Although there is nothing eventual or final in the position of the US and the UK, as well as in that of the Bretton Woods institutions, the Washington consensus seems to be the major obstacle working against the realisation of the Tobin tax and other related reforms and re-regulatory measures.

Other social forces opposing the Tobin tax   There are also social forces other than countries, such as the US, the UK, and tax havens, opposing the Tobin tax. The financial industry has its own lobby organisations advocating radical *laissez-faire* policies. They do more than support the basic tenets of the Washington consensus; they lobby for policies that will ensure the continuous flow of further resources and investment opportunities for global financial markets. The Tobin tax and related measures would clearly work against these tendencies. Therefore, we may assume that the British Bankers' Association, the London Investment Banking Association, the Institute of International Finance and many others will fight all attempts to introduce a currency transactions tax. And as these lobby organisations claim themselves, they have a 'unique access' to various governments 'as associations representing the world's leading financial organisations'.[22]

The second major social force working against initiatives such as the Tobin tax are the globalising media. Mass media remain, of course, heterogeneous, and some newspapers and even TV channels can take an explicit stand for reforms such as the Tobin tax. However, the increased privatisation, commercialisation and Americanisation of media is part of the global programme of neoliberal restructuring. These media with a progressively more global reach tend, then, to reinforce the hegemonic self-evidence of orthodox interpretations. The globalising media constitute both a central watchtower of the financial Panopticon in its own right and an element in a complex process that mediates, filters and channels interpretations between the investors and the objects of their gaze.

In the globalising US media, the Tobin tax seems to be among the practically forbidden topics. Ibrahim Warde, a professor at the University of California at Berkeley, recently checked several million media articles in the US and found that the Tobin tax had been mentioned only seven or eight times.[23] It is also noteworthy that when the US media ask for comments on the world economic crisis, they turn to investment bankers – and sometimes to mainstream, orthodox economists – for they are assumed to be the experts on the world's financial problems. In a sense, they are, but it is also clear that one should not expect anything but restatements of the orthodoxy from those sources. And, to repeat, it is particularly the Anglo–American media corporations that have extended their reach globally.

There are also strongholds of orthodoxy within most state bureaucracies. Two of them are particularly powerful: finance ministries and central banks. They have grown relatively more powerful due to globalisation. Insightfully, Cox talks about the 'internationalizing of the state', which is 'the global process whereby national policies and practices have been adjusted to the exigencies of the world economy'.[24] Areas such as nationally based industries and social welfare have become marginalised in state administration at the expense of the growing power of the sectors directly connected to global financial mechanisms.[25] In a 1999 interview, Tobin hit the mark with his suspicion that his proposal for a currency transactions tax may be politically impossible to realise:

I don't think the financial community, including ministers of finance in major countries and the central banks of those countries, have any use for such taxes. They don't want it. Even if somebody else in the government may say good things about it as François Mitterrand did, it won't go through the finance ministry. They are not going to go for it, the International Monetary Fund (IMF) is not going to go for it.[26]

There is no question about it: politically, the Tobin tax is not easy to realise. There are, indeed, powerful social forces opposing reform proposals such as the Tobin tax. This is the challenge that must be overcome.

The Emancipatory Potential of the Two-phase Model

There is no point in speculating on the possible emergence of a universal consent for the Tobin tax. More realistically, an emancipatory vision has to be based on the possibilities opened up by the two-phase approach. Any significant grouping of countries can proceed quickly, despite the resistance of some of the major centres. This model empowers states to work for the tax even without the support of the US, the UK, the International Monetary Fund (IMF) or any given actor opposing the idea. However, the two-phase model would not resolve the problem of will-formation within states. It is my argument that a transnational social movement can influence a sufficient number of governments to initiate the first phase of the two-phase model.

The emergence of a global political movement for the Tobin tax Until the Asian crisis, interest in the Tobin tax has been 'usually triggered by currency crises and died out when the crisis passed from the headlines'.[27] Additionally, in the 1990s, the Tobin tax has been discussed in the context of trying to find alternative sources of funding for the UN system.

Since the Asian crisis, a transnational political movement for the Tobin tax has emerged. ATTAC, organised from Paris, is perhaps the most important building block of that movement. Ignacio Ramonet, the editor of the *Le Monde Diplomatique*, published an article in December 1997 entitled 'Disarm the markets'. According to Ramonet, there are two closely related problems: the volatility and magnitude of global financial markets that 'is causing universal insecurity'; and the threat to democracy posed by global finance. 'Absolute freedom of movement of capital undermines democracy and we need to introduce machinery to counter its effects. [...] Hundreds of billions of dollars are stashed away out of reach of the tax authorities for the benefit of powerful individuals and financial institutions. [...] The power to levy taxes on unearned income is a sine qua non of democracy.'

Consequently, Ramonet proposed three measures to be taken: closing down the tax havens; increasing taxes on unearned income; and levying a tax on currency transactions. He also suggested the establishment of an organisation advocating the Tobin tax. As a result, ATTAC was founded in June 1998. In July 2000, the organisation had 180 local working committees and 24,000 individuals and 1,000 organisations as members in France alone. ATTAC France has quickly become the centre of a transnational network: a number of associations have been formed in Europe (Austria, Belgium, Germany, Ireland, Luxembourg, Netherlands, Portugal, Spain, Switzerland), Latin America (Argentina, Brazil, Chile, Paraguay, Uruguay), North America (Quebec), North Africa (Morocco, Tunis), and Sub-Saharan Africa (Burkina Faso, Cameroon, Ivory Coast, Mali, Senegal). A number of other organisations are closely affiliated with ATTAC, particularly in Asia and Europe.[28]

ATTAC's main focus is on the Tobin tax, but this is only an element in its search for alternatives to attempts at locking-in neoliberalism such as MAI (the Multilateral Agreement on Investments), the NTM (the New Transatlantic Market agreement), and others. It has been able to mobilise tens of thousands of people for demonstrations; organise countless discussions on the problems of global financial markets and neoliberal globalisation; and raise the Tobin tax and other measures on the agendas of the parliament of France, the Council of Europe and the European Parliament.

Other committed civic actors advocating the Tobin tax include:

- the Halifax initiative, a coalition of environment, development, social justice and faith groups in Canada[29]
- CIDSE (International Co-operation for Development and Solidarity), an alliance of fifteen Catholic development organisations from Europe and North America[30]
- War on Want, a campaign against the causes of poverty, in the UK[31]
- Tobin Tax Initiative USA, a project of the Center for Environmental Economic Development (CEED) in the US[32]

These are transnationally, and also very efficiently, networked European or North American coalitions or campaigns for global development and socio-economic justice. Dozens of other national and transnational organisations have included the Tobin tax in their platforms, including the

Box 13 Banning landmines: the power of spontaneous civic activities

In the course of 1991, several NGOs and individuals began simultaneously to discuss the necessity of co-ordinating initiatives and calls for a ban on anti-personnel landmines. Handicap International, Human Rights Watch, Medico International, Mines Advisory Group, Physicians for Human Rights, and Vietnam Veterans of America Foundation came together in October 1992 to formalise the International Campaign to Ban Landmines (ICBL).

Perhaps at the start, the campaign to ban landmines seemed unfeasible in the way that some people may regard the introduction of a Tobin tax and TTO as impossible. However, the concerted efforts made over the years to bring about a complete global proscription of landmines have ultimately amounted to a highly successful process with tangible results. The Ottawa Process and Convention, a cumulative instrument designed by multilateral fora (UN, Red Cross, and Canada, for example) to end the production, sale, transfer and destruction of landmines, has received international recognition, and the 1997 Nobel Peace Prize, for work towards this end.

The Norwegian Nobel Committee stated that the Campaign had changed a ban from 'a vision to a feasible reality'. By the end of the signing ceremony on 4 December 1997, 122 states' parties had formally agreed to the Treaty's strictures. With the fortieth ratification by Burkina Faso, on 16 September 1998, the Treaty officially entered into force six months later on 1 March 1999. The Mine Ban Treaty thus became binding international law more quickly than any other international treaty in history, and pressure grows for other states to join.

It may be argued that the Treaty suffers from the non-inclusion of various producer-states, notably the US, FSU, China, India and Israel. However, with approximately 26,000 landmine casualties each year among non-combatants, the moral force of arguments to ban landmines completely builds year on year. A less than 100 per cent adherence does not make the Ottawa process meaningless. Because of the manifest harm which is done by mines, and the obvious suffering which could be alleviated by all states agreeing to a complete ban, each new signatory builds pressure on those left outside.

Note: This text box is modified from an excerpt that was prepared/edited by Lloyd Pettiford mostly from material available in extended form in Curley et al. (1999). See also the history of campaign as explained in the website of the ICBL at http://www.icbl.org/

Parliamentarians for Global Action and the Commission on Global Governance. Some of them have raised this to the top of their agendas.[33] Moreover, there are also civic actors in Asia struggling for the Tobin tax, in particular the Third World Network based in Malaysia,[34] and the Focus on the Global South based in Thailand (and working also in the Philippines and South Korea).[35] For instance, in early 1999, Martin Khor from the Third World Network circulated a call for action with Andrea Durbin from the Friends of the Earth-US and John Cavanagh from the International Forum on Globalization/Institute for Policy Studies. This call for action included a demand that 'the governments of the world's major currencies should levy a tax on certain international transactions so as to discourage speculative and herd behavior in international capital flows'.[36]

Besides placing the Tobin tax on the agenda of various parliaments (there have been discussions on the topic all over the world), parts of this global social movement have been working to make governments undertake promotion of the Tobin tax. In two cases these attempts have been successful – although only partially. In late 1998, campaigns were started in Canada and Finland. In Finland, the Service Centre for Development Co-operation (Kepa), with the Network Institute for Global Democratisation (NIGD), succeeded in placing the currency transactions tax on the agenda of the March 1999 parliamentary elections.[37] Consequently, after the elections, the new government included 'measures to control financial markets' in its programme. In December 1999, however, the Minister of Finance Sauli Niinistö said in Parliament, in response to an oral question, that because of the lack of political support for related measures in Europe, mostly due to the opposition of the UK, there was no point in trying to promote the much more ambitious global project of a currency transactions tax at this point.[38] In December 2000, a committee organised by the Ministry of Finance, comprising orthodox economists, came unsurprisingly to the conclusion that there are no good reasons for a Tobin tax. With the president and two foreign ministers favourable to the idea of a currency transactions tax, it remains to be seen what the government will make out of this.

In Canada, in a campaign led by the Halifax Initiative, citizens and organisations gave their support to MP Lorne Nystrom's 1998 motion in the House of Commons which stated 'that in the opinion of the House, the government should enact a tax on financial transactions in concert with the international community'. Individuals and groups across the country signed the Citizens' Declaration on the Tobin Tax which was presented to the minister of finance. As a result of widespread public support, the motion passed by an unambiguous margin of 164–83 on 23 March 1999. Canada became the first country in the world to declare its intention to work towards the adoption of a tax to control international currency speculation. Following this, the campaign has continued to make the resistant minister of finance translate this parliamentary commitment into government action.

Although the country-based success has been limited, these campaigns may already have turned the tide even globally, as witnessed by the July 2000 Special Session of the UN General Assembly entitled 'World Summit for Social Development and Beyond: Achieving Social Development for All in a Globalizing World'. Canada and G-77 – the largest Third World coalition in the United Nations – pushed actively for including a paragraph on the currency transactions tax in the final document and, despite the resistance of the US, they succeeded in getting a watered-down formulation, calling for a UN-led study on the topic. However, given the political situation of the UN, it is unlikely that this study will take the currency transaction tax seriously.

Who would take the initiative? Even in the US and the UK, there are campaigns for the Tobin tax. War on Want and the Tobin Tax Initiative USA have been able to bring the issue to the UK Parliament and the US Congress, respectively. Moreover, the UK is a member of the European Union. In a few years' time, it might also join the Economic and Monetary Union. That should also have repercussions on the offshore markets of the City of London, and possibly draw the UK more into the European political processes.[39] Nevertheless, for the time being, both the US and the UK are very likely to continue to oppose any noteworthy version of the currency transactions tax. In the world outside the US and the UK, where 93 per cent of the world population lives, where should we expect the political will for the Tobin tax to emerge most forcefully? In particular, let us consider two, possibly complementary, possibilities: countries participating in the EMU, and the progressivists in countries that have experienced hardships because of recent financial crises.

Will the eurolandia take the lead? In 2000, eleven countries, including Germany, France, Italy and Spain, with a combined US$6 trillion economy, are participating in the third phase of the EMU. This phase will be completed by summer 2002 when national currencies will be replaced by the euro also as notes and coins. Britain, Sweden and Denmark have decided not to participate. Greece has not met the Maastricht criteria. However, Greece is expected to join the euro area possibly before the end of the transition period in 2002. The new euro is likely to be among the strongest currencies in the world, along with the US dollar and the Japanese yen, and possibly the second most important reserve currency after the US dollar.

Because of the joint currency, none of the eleven countries could participate in the Tobin tax regime individually. The first-phase system would 'leak' through the outsider EMU countries. Hence, the EMU countries would have to work together, either as the EU or as an informal grouping of countries. The EU option seems politically unrealistic. However, the EMU countries could form the core of the first phase of the Tobin tax regime.

What are the political implications of the EMU? It is often acknowledged that EMU is ambivalent towards the welfare state and regulations of capitalist markets.[40] On the one hand, it seems to institutionalise the principles of neoliberalism and the Washington consensus in Europe. 'EMU is part of this process in so far as it represents an "internal" structural adjustment programme for Europe.'[41] Yet, it can also be claimed that the EU is 'not causing but [only] exacerbating the problems that the European welfare states are facing'.[42] Further, the unification created by EMU might be necessary for empowering alternative possibilities, as many hope.[43] Or, as I have written elsewhere, (with Petri Minkkinen):

> It is possible to imagine that the single currency and the European Central Bank could introduce, despite EMU's liberalist economic foundations, collective control over liberated capital movements in Europe and perhaps even between the key regions of the world economy. [...] Even a minor streamlet could be the beginning of a mighty river: the global regulation of the speculative capital movements might emerge for instance in the form of an investment tax on capital movements.[44]

In Europe, there seems to be a background and preparedness to do something about the volatile, over-expanded and crisis-ridden global financial markets. Most European countries have not initiated the liberalisation of capital movements; rather, their governments have often felt compelled to liberalise, even against their original intentions and will. In many cases, alternatives have been actively searched for. The EU-Europeans are also much more used to taxing financial transactions, added value and related items. And certainly, there has been more discussion about, and support for, the Tobin tax in Continental Europe than in the UK or the US. Indeed, many European political actors have favoured the idea, including politicians in the crucial Germany–France axis (particularly on the French side). For years, there have been struggles over getting the Tobin tax on the agenda of the EU. The European Parliament has accepted resolutions mentioning the currency transactions tax at least in 1996 (on the Halifax world economic summit, 13 May) and 1997 (on employment, 13 November). In January 2000, the newly formed intergroup almost received approval for its call to explore the possibilities of implementing the Tobin tax. New initiatives will follow.

There are also signs of readiness to go for the Tobin tax option even without the consent of the London–Wall Street–Washington axis. For instance, Martin and Schumann have proposed realising, unilaterally, the currency transactions tax by the European Central Bank. The premise is that 'London and New York are always going to prevent it' from being implemented globally.[45] Similarly, Olivier Giscard d'Estaing has talked about the EMU-model of establishing a tax on speculative transactions. The more resistant countries – the UK in particular – could be left out and the others could take further steps towards a better system of political governance.[46] However, neither Martin and Schumann nor Giscard d'Estaing have explained how the EU could implement the Tobin tax unilaterally; nor have they connected a unilateral European move to global strategy. To complicate matters, a recent Working Paper of the European Parliament summarises the standard view: 'There would need to be agreement on its [the Tobin tax's] application in every financial centre in the world – otherwise foreign exchange markets would move to "tax-free" jurisdictions. The problems of introducing a withholding tax on interest even within the EU alone do not augur well for the chances of such an international agreement.'[47]

This standard view is based on two unsustainable assumptions. First, it presupposes that there should either be a mere currency transactions tax or nothing at all. As explained in Chapter 5, a modified, comprehensive taxation regime, with a low basic rate, is feasible even in the absence of some of the major financial centres. Second, the resistance of the UK is taken for granted and used against any supranational taxation systems. But the UK does not have to be 'in' in the first phase. With other states, the EMU countries can take the initiative also without the consent of the UK. The system must be based on an open invitation for any country to join in at any time, and on the premise that the final aim is a global tax regime.

There is, however, another potential obstacle. Consider Article 73b of the Treaty of the European Union (the Maastricht Treaty). This article seems to make illegal all attempts at regulating global financial markets:

> 1. Within the framework of the provisions set out in this Chapter, all restrictions on the movement of capital between Member States and between Member States and third countries shall be prohibited.
>
> 2. Within the framework of the provisions set out in this Chapter, all restrictions on payments between Member States and between Member States and third countries shall be prohibited.[48]

The Maastricht Treaty takes a strong stand for the freely floating and convertible exchange rate regime and the global, unregulated financial markets. In a sense, it even constitutionalises these principles: the Maastricht Treaty is more difficult to amend than any existing constitution, for any amendment requires unanimity of states. Moreover, at the time when the Treaty of the European Union was concluded, all member states were – and still are – committed to Article VI of the Agreement on the International Monetary Fund. Section 3 of Article VI ('Controls of capital transfers') states that 'members may exercise such controls as are necessary to regulate international capital movements'.[49] The US has been campaigning against this Article,[50] and it seems that the EU countries have voluntarily abandoned this right by a collective, quasi-constitutional agreement.

Does this mean that the EU cannot take any initiative towards establishing the Tobin tax without first changing the Maastricht Treaty? Not necessarily. The Treaty of the European Union (TEU) can of course be revised.[51] However, in the shorter run, it is more relevant that a small, market-friendly transaction tax should not necessarily be counted as a 'restriction' to capital movements. Certainly a small – at the most 10 basis points – basic rate tax is not a 'restriction'. Perhaps only the punitive tax on movements to and from the blacklisted offshore centres would count as a 'restriction'? Yes, it is already an accepted principle that attempts to benefit from tax evasion and money laundering at others' expense is unacceptable.[52] Moreover, Article 73c of the TEU seems to open up the possibility of unspecified 'measures' such as those needed for the first phase of the Tobin tax regime:

> Whilst endeavouring to achieve the objective of free movement of capital between Member States and third countries to the greatest extent possible and without prejudice to the other Chapters of this Treaty, the Council may, acting by a qualified majority on a proposal from the Commission, adopt measures on the movement of capital to or from third countries involving direct investment – including investment in real estate - establishment, the provision of financial services or the admission of securities to capital markets.

Indeed, the measures needed for the first phase of the Tobin tax regime would seem to fall within this category. In the case of more serious difficulties, it might be possible to assume even more 'restrictive' measures without violating the TEU, for Article 73f enables the Union to take 'safeguard measures with regard to third countries for a period not exceeding six months' if, 'under exceptional circumstances, movements of capital to or from third countries cause, or threaten to cause, serious difficulties for the operation of economic and monetary union'.

In sum, there is nothing conclusive in the TEU that would prevent the EMU countries from adopting measures necessary for the first phase of the Tobin tax regime. Even though current interpretations and practices make the TEU support neoliberalist practices and monetarist economic policies, there is also room for alternatives. Given the weight of the eurolandia, the EMU countries could form the core of the first phase.

How could the progressivists and the hard-hits initiate the first phase? Will the strict monetarist vision prevail in the eurolandia for the time being? Or will the EMU countries just be slow in organising any collective action in this regard, while others would like to move forward more quickly? Let me therefore also consider the possibility that some progressive countries, together with those hit hard by the 1997–99 world economic crisis (the hard-hits), would be interested in hurrying up by taking the initiative and moving ahead before the EMU countries.

First, there are countries such as Argentina, Brazil, Indonesia, Malaysia, Mexico, Russia, South Korea and Thailand that have been in deep trouble due to recent financial crises, both economically and politically. Second, there are other states either already experiencing serious problems or immediately threatened by the world economic situation. These countries range from China, Hong Kong, Japan and India to many Latin American countries. And finally, there are those Asian, CIS, Middle Eastern, African and Latin American countries that are facing almost endless deep economic decline, social implosion, and, all too often, political violence. Some of these countries might see a lot of potential in the Tobin tax, not least because of its revenue potential.

By no means do these countries form a politically coherent group. Many are and may remain obedient to the Washington consensus; they are led by social forces still believing in the blessedness of neoliberalist globalisation. Others have decided for, or at least seriously been debating, more national-istic measures to control capital movements and gain some space for autonomous economic policy more generally. In the cases of Malaysia and Russia, for instance, anti-Western social forces have already influenced the political agenda, albeit in different ways (in Malaysia, economic policy and human rights; in Russia, security policy). There are also major cultural and political cleavages within this rather artificial grouping. Yet, it is very encouraging that the G-77 took an explicit stand for the Tobin tax in the July 2000 'World Summit for Social Development' in Geneva. Despite its heterogeneity, the group of hard-hits and poor could work together.

At the moment, Canada is the prime example of a progressive country on the Tobin tax issue. As I have argued elsewhere, the Nordic countries could and should assume this role also, because emancipatory, globally-oriented political action is a condition for the Nordic ideals to be realised and developed further under new circumstances.[53] The Finnish government's approach may be over-cautious,[54] but it is important that all the parties of the coalition government are in favour of the Tobin tax. The problem with the idea of spontaneous Nordic action is that most of the Nordic countries are members of the EU; Finland participates in the EMU and Sweden may well join in at some point soon.[55] As far as Finland is concerned, the first phase has to include all the EMU countries. However, for the other Nordic countries, more independent action is possible. Norway in particular could well take a lead in this matter. It is also important that Canada and the Nordic countries have the economic resources, technical capabilities and the diplomatic credibility for promoting the Tobin tax.

The real challenge for the progressives and hard-hits is not to get the sufficient number of states into the regime (thirty), but to cover a sufficient portion (20 per cent) of the global forex markets. Without the EMU countries, the Asian financial centres – Tokyo, Hong Kong and Singapore – may play a pivotal role. Political and diplomatic efforts are likely to focus on persuading them. However, the global political movement has thus far had few, if any, links with Japan. It may turn out to be crucial to create those links and draw Japan into this new phase of the politics of globalisation.

Whatever the initial coalition of social forces and states will be, it has to be emphasised that all possibilities are complementary rather than exclusive. The larger the base for the first phase, the better the prospects for the Tobin tax regime – economically and, most importantly, politically.

Conclusion

For political possibilities, it is decisive that a non-universal Tobin tax is technically feasible. The modified currency transactions tax regime makes it politically possible to initiate the process of establishing, eventually, a universal, uniform currency transaction tax without the consent of every state. Once started, the process should be self-reinforcing in a number of ways: it stabilises insiders' exchange rates; gives the participating states additional tax revenues; empowers them to take part in deciding on the allocation of the global share of revenues; and penalises outsiders. Due to the success of the regime, soon the outsiders will find themselves dis-empowered, if not isolated.

Indeed, to a large extent, the lack of political will for the Tobin tax comes down to the particular position of the US and the UK in the global financial system, and to the related hegemony of the orthodox economic theory (known also as the Washington 'consensus'). I have argued in this chapter that it is politically possible to establish the Tobin tax regime without the initial consent of the US and the UK, or any given financial centre. Either the EMU countries could assume the role of the initiator, or a coalition of progressivists – Canada and the Nordic countries in particular – with the hard-hits of the latest round of the world financial crises could take the lead.

Whoever proposes negotiations for the first phase, the opening steps to be taken are: to establish the first phase of the Tobin tax regime; to assist in local, national and global struggles over the idea; and to decide about the legitimation and operative principles of the supranational body, including principles for how the revenues should be distributed. The organising principles of the Tobin tax regime will be discussed in detail in Chapter 7.

Notes

1. Helleiner 1994: 82.

2. Ibid., p. 12.

3. See Livingston 1992.

4. Boutros-Ghali 1999: 4.

5. This claim is based on circumstantial evidence: on the fact that the UN headquarters is in the US and subject to the highly biased treatment and conditioning of US society; on the veto-right of the US, and its domination of the Security Council; on the constant financial blackmail of the UN by the US, which has meant in practice that the UN system is responding primarily to the wishes of the US; on the unilateral legislation of the US which implies that the US dictates what the UN can and cannot do; as well as on the implications of the episode of the removal of Boutros-Ghali.

6. Michalos 2000; quoting tax analysts, *Tax Notes Today*, 31 January 1996.

7. This wording is from Congressman John E. Sweeney's 1999 bill, which effectively reintroduced the Helms–Dole bill, but added some further requirements to the UN.

8. Boutros-Ghali 1996: 25–51.

9. Boutros-Ghali 1999: 319.

10. Ul Haq et al. 1996; see Felix 1998: 3.

11. UNDP 1999: 13.

12. Ibid., pp. 10 and 13. The Report also recapitulates the 1994 proposal for a tax on speculative international capital movements, alongside other reform proposals the *Human Development Report*s have made in the 1990s (pp. 18–21). The Report also mentions several times the idea of a world central bank, and in a text box on p. 98 specifically refers to something very similar to Keynes's vision for global governance.

13. Both letters, with a few introductory remarks, can be found at Globalpolicy's website, as 'UN's 1999 Human Development Report Raises International Tax Proposal', at http://www.globalpolicy.org/socecon/glotax/email/usdept.htm (July 2000).

14. Michalos 2000.

15. However, it may be worth mentioning that he continues: '[…] it is good that somebody raises this issue; the initiative must come from the civil society'. Because he prefers to be anonymous, no proper reference is possible here.

16. About IMF's discourse of economism, see Teivainen 1995.

17. About this kind of analysis of the World Bank and its economics discourse, see George and Sabelli 1994. See also Patomäki 1999b.

18. Reddy 2000.

19. Which in turn has been opposed by Austria, which provides secrecy to bank account holders.

20. 'Veroratkaisu vie vuosikausia', *Helsingin Sanomat*, 20 July 2000; 'EU ministers confident euro will rise', *Business Day – News, Information, Analysis*, 18 July 2000, available at http://www.bday.co.za/bday/content/direct/0,3523,631278-6078-0,00.html

21. 'Conservative, Liberal – UK Socialists alliance blocks exploring new ways in taxation policy. Greens deplore rejection of Tobin Tax by the European Parliament', the Green/EFA Group in the EP, Press Release, Strasbourg, 20 January 2000.

22. See Chapter 2 for details.

23. Ibrahim Warde at La Maison de L'Amérique Latine in Paris, 25 January 1999, at a meeting with the public reporting the seminar of international economists on the Tobin tax, organised by the scientific committee of ATTAC.

24. Cox 1987: 253.

25. Cf. ibid., p. 263.

26. Tobin 1999b.

27. Tobin 1996a: x.

28. This list is based on an information sheet sent by Christophe Ventura from International ATTAC on 19 July 2000. Of these countries, ATTAC is in the process of being constituted in Austria, Cameroon, Chile, Germany, Ivory Coast, Mali, Morocco, Paraguay, Tunis and Uruguay. In other countries listed, ATTACs are already formally constituted and active.

29. See http://www.web.net/~halifax/index.htm

30. See http://www.cidse.org/

31. See http://www.waronwant.org/

32. See http://www.ceedweb.org/iirp/

33. Websites and contact information for a number of these can be found at http://ceedweb.org/iirp/camnet.htm

34. See http://www.twnside.org.sg/

35. See http://www.focusweb.org/

36. This call for action is available at http://www.twnside.org.sg/title/ifgcall-cn.htm

37. In November 1998, the campaign was launched by a special section of *Kumppani*, Kepa's magazine, on the Tobin tax (including Patomäki 1998), followed by newspaper interviews and articles. The NIGD Report 'The Tobin Tax: How to Make It Real' (Patomäki 1999a) was published some two weeks before the mid-March 1999 elections, and was reported and discussed widely in the national media. Kepa organised public discussions on the topic and lobbied relevant politicians.

38. The oral question was posed by the Green MP Kirsi Ojansuu (KK 5/2000). The Minister of Finance Sali Niinistö gave an answer in the Finnish Parliament on 7 March 2000.

39. Despite the existence of the London–Wall Street–Washington consensus, the UK might be drawn to the European political processes. How likely is that? Risse et al. (1997: 110–14) argue that deep British beliefs about national identity, sovereignty, and sterling as a symbol of sovereignty will tend to prevent the UK from joining the EMU. However, Diez (1998) claims that the official British discourse has always been less separatist and more in line with the European Commission visions of Europe than usually thought.

After the Labour Party assumed office in 1997, the Bank of England was granted the right to determine interest rates, that is more autonomy along the lines of the Bundesbank. This could be taken as a sign of preparation for UK membership. Further, since the euro was launched on 1 January 1999, there has been a lot of discussion in the UK about whether the UK should, after all, join in. See, for instance, 'The UK warms to the euro. First poll since launch shows record support', *Guardian*, 11 February 1999. However, most of these kinds of analyses fail to address the implications of the EMU to the City of London and its offshore position – and the extent to which the City of London takes part in constituting British interests in the global political economy. Moreover, should the UK join in, it may simply attempt to lock-in the neoliberal economic foundations of the EMU and prevent all changes.

40. See for instance Leander and Guzzini 1997.

41. Gill 1997a: 209.

42. Leander and Guzzini 1997: 160.

43. For different articulations, see Hettne 1993, and Martin and Schumann 1997.

44. Minkkinen and Patomäki 1997a: 10.

45. Martin and Schumann 1997: 104.

46. At the meeting 'Launching Citizens' Century' on 23 May 2000, UNDP Headquarters, NY, in connection with the UN Millennium Forum held on 22–26 May 2000 in New York (as reported by Katarina Sehm Patomäki).

47. Patterson and Galliano 1999: 6.

48. Treaty of the European Union, Article 73b.

49. Articles of Agreement of the International Monetary Fund, Article VI, Section 3.

50. Felix 1998: 3.

51. In my view, ultimately this may well turn out to be necessary, but it would take years and may be too long and contingent a process to form a basis for the first phase of the Tobin tax regime.

52. See Box 10 in Chapter 5.

53. See Patomäki 2000b.

56. Some might say gutless. In the Cold War era, the 'political realism' of Paasikivi and Kekkonen degenerated into a visionless politics of neutrality in the context of concessions towards the Soviet Union and generalised cautiousness about any spontaneous moves or stands. This attitude has also characterised the neoliberal turn to the West of the 1990s. To put it at its crudest, the slave has found a new master to serve, namely the West, and mistakenly believes that placation of the master is vital. See Minkkinen and Patomäki 1997b: 69–71.

55. In January 1999, for the first time, opinion polls in Sweden showed that a majority of Swedes were in favour of joining the EMU, and the Prime Minister Göran Persson scheduled a referendum on the issue. See 'Ruotsi haluaa Emuun kruunun alennusmyynnillä', *Taloussanomat*, 27 January 1999. Following the Danish rejection of the EMU in a referendum in autumn 2000, however, Sweden is unlikely to hold its referendum in the near future.

7

Towards a Democratic Politics of Global Governance

Modern, sovereign states have had a monopoly over taxation. These states could also collect the Tobin tax. However, the Tobin tax would require a global system of surveillance and governance. States would have to collect the tax in concert with, and under the surveillance of, a supranational body. A large share of revenues would go to this supranational body. It would be entitled to allocate the revenues to various global purposes, including a global intervention fund. Would sovereign states be ready and willing to give up aspects of their sovereignty in this way?

In this last chapter, I shall argue that the best way for most states – as well as for the global political movement struggling to democratise global-isation – to regain control over transnational forces and flows is to organise collective action and, thereby, transform existing systems of governance. The Tobin tax regime represents an attempt at such a collective action. There are many ways in which the Tobin tax regime defends sovereign states against the released, and now apparently rampant, forces of neoliberal globalisation. However, the dialectics of emancipation by means of collec-tive action would not leave the state intact either. Rather, this collective action would imply a further transformation of state sovereignty and related international institutions. The first-ever global tax would also raise the whole problematic of political theory into a global context: what are the principles of legitimation of collective organisations? How should they be assessed in terms of material benefits and their distribution, rightful authority, justice and democracy?[1]

Tobin and many of his followers have assumed that the task of orches-trating the tax should be given to the IMF. I shall make an argument for not giving the IMF, or the World Bank, this role. It is not only that the first-phase non-universal tax regime is incompatible with the IMF struc-ture, but also that the IMF seems to lack legitimacy for governing the Tobin tax. Hence, a new supranational body orchestrating the tax must be founded. This Tobin Tax Organisation (TTO) should be independent from any existing organisational structure. Given that it will also have a role in collecting and allocating the revenues, the question is: how can we guarantee accountable and transparent procedures, fair democratic representation in its agenda-setting and decision-making, and the possibility of just outcomes?

When the time for the transition to the second phase approaches, the fate of the TTO has to be decided. Should it remain independent, or, rather, merged with more general systems of governance? I shall argue that the United Nations has a lot of potential in this regard. But the UN system has to be reformed first. To facilitate these reforms, which should both empower and democratise the UN, and also prepare it for the second phase of the Tobin tax regime, I suggest that a share of the revenues should be given to the UN system. I shall discuss in some detail two proposals for reforming the UN. The Commission on Global Governance has suggested that a more representative Economic Security Council should be established alongside the present Security Council. The South Centre, in turn, has proposed that the Economic and Social Council of the UN (ECOSOC) should be reconstructed. Either one could take over the TTO during the second phase.

Sovereign States and Global Taxation

The developments of capitalist money economy, modern bureaucracy and sovereign nation-states gave rise to modern forms of taxation.[2] In the Europe of the seventeenth and eighteenth centuries, taxation became fiscal in the proper sense of the term. For the first time, a recognised public domain of finance and expenditure emerged. Because state sovereignty was taken to imply exclusive control (analogous to ownership) over a territory, modern states have also come to assume monopoly over taxation within their territory. Moreover, a separate and autonomous field of economy – supposedly following its own laws – was constructed, and constituted by private ownership.

Since John Locke and the European colonial expansion, private property rights have been posed as universally valid. Yet, despite the existence of a world economy and the pre-World War I processes of globalisation, during the nineteenth and twentieth centuries it has been common to assume that economies are 'national'. For a national state, taxation has been the way to underwrite the state's expenses by drawing revenues from the field of economy. Moreover, as Giddens correctly observes, with modernisation,

> [...] taxation also becomes closely bound up with the surveillance operations of the state. Tax policies come to be used both to monitor and to regulate

the distribution and the activities of the population, and participate in the burgeoning of surveillance operations as a whole. Taxes, it has been said, 'are used as tools to increase population (tax burden on bachelors; tax reduction for children), to reduce laziness and to force people to work, to check certain human vices, to influence consumption patterns (particularly conspicuous consumption) and so forth. The education or social goals of such taxes characteristically prevail over the fiscal goals.'[3] The revenues of states have been dependent on taxation. Despite recognition of the consequences of financial globalisation, it is likely that states will be jealously guarding their rights in this regard. Moreover, taxation has been associated with the governance of society: it has been used for achieving moral and socio-political purposes. Since the development of parliamentarism (late seventeenth century) and the advent of the notion of peoples' sovereignty (late eighteenth century), more democratic procedures for determining these purposes have been established. Finally, the twentieth-century welfare state emerged – at least in the OECD world – with new ways of spending revenues for social, egalitarian and democratic purposes.

Taxation is thus a deeply political issue which cuts across a number of concerns: state sovereignty, surveillance, governance, shared or imposed values and purposes, democracy and welfare. Is this a problem for the Tobin tax? First, at the turn of the twentieth and twenty-first centuries, there are good reasons to call into question the supposed monopoly of sovereignty by the state. The idea that sovereignty must be located within the state, in a hierarchical and exclusive manner, was based on certain practical, normative and logical presuppositions, which are now quite outmoded.[4] It is more and more common to acknowledge that many social relations defy any strict and exclusive notion of territorial sovereignty. Moreover, the global financial markets seem to have assumed new forms of agency, autonomy and control over most states. Latham, for instance, describes how the re-emergence of the global financial markets and the innovation of new financial instruments opened up a new form of agency for banks and corporations:

> one of the key elements of the new financial markets is the fluid convertibility of capital (e.g. across all sorts of currencies and securities) [...] These engines empower participants, but leave clear lines between insiders and outsiders. They can involve new and evasive practices that are not subject to the reach of state (e.g. offshore corporations). In the end, there is a restricted access and membership, a limited range of allowable actions, meanings, codes – the very limits of which establish the identity of the network in the first place [...] I believe what financial systems and states have in common is social sovereignty not 'stateness', phantom or otherwise.[5]

Financial globalisation has empowered new actors and given rise to new structures. For Latham and many others, these new social structures – originally created by a few leading states – appear to be as sovereign and exclusive as states, but non-territorial. A modern sovereign state is the legal system that defines all the competencies and rules for changing or creating rules; it empowers and constrains. Now, if state A creates, by legislative acts, an offshore haven for banks and firms based in countries other than A, run by non-A-citizens, it empowers those banks and firms by providing them with new opportunities, while constraining other states by making them lose some of their controls – in the form of regulation and taxation – over those very firms. At some point, quantity turns into quality, and suddenly the offshore spaces and related global markets appear as sovereign, instead of states, at least for most states.[6] These emergent financial structures are 'sovereign' in the sense that they empower actors to operate in the autonomous spaces that they have constituted; yet the consequences of these actions forcefully condition actors outside this sphere, not least states. 'In today's world of high capital mobility, even a minor exercise of political autonomy can produce major exchange market pressures.'[7] As was discussed in detail in Chapter 3, many governments of sovereign states seem to be more forcefully and immediately accountable to the financial markets than to their parliaments or people. Under these circumstances, where is sovereignty?

In most contexts, the best way for most states – and for many other political actors as well – to regain control over these forces is to organise collective action. The Tobin tax regime represents an attempt at such a collective action. The Tobin tax is an undertaking to resurrect aspects of the sovereign power of the state. One of the aims of Tobin's original proposal was to create more space for the autonomy of the nation-state, particularly for its economic policies. It may turn out that the increase in autonomy might in practice prove to be only modest, depending on the circumstances,[8] yet it seems that, in the politics of globalisation, the Tobin tax regime sides with the sovereign states. Moreover, the collection of the tax would be carried out at the booking site, on a national basis, and only national authorities can do this. Furthermore, since the implementation of the tax must result from an international agreement, 'participating can be a decision of only sovereign governments'.[9] Although an international body is needed to set the rate of taxation, define taxable transactions, determine exemptions from the tax and undertake monitoring and auditing tasks, as well as collect the revenues from national authorities, the ultimate control and practical implementation would still be – at least partially and collectively – in the hands of governments.

This sounds familiar. New proposals to enhance the powers of the

Bretton Woods institutions or the WTO, or to create new arrangements such as a comprehensive property rights regime or a Multilateral Agreement on Investments (MAI), would deepen states' legal commitment to neoliberal governance, yet states are assumed to remain sovereign and free to decide. Of course, they are free to try to act otherwise, but they have to bear the consequences. The global Panoptican system of control and surveillance works at various levels. Economic globalisation, and the emergence of offshores, non-territorial spaces, and the mobility of banks and firms, have eroded states' capacity to tax capital. Globalisation has also evoked fears about the reactions of economic actors to any attempt to act differently from the standard: neoliberalisation. These fears may sometimes be grossly exaggerated, yet many states have faced powerful constraints against spontaneous actions.[10]

Some of the constraints are legal. Systems of regional and global governance back up their rules and principles with sanctions. Beside the direct, violence- and security-oriented methods of power (crisis management with the help of armed forces, power-balancing policies, alliance-formation, great power management of collective security, etc.), a variety of more sophisticated methods of surveillance have emerged, based on making actors and their intentions transparent by means of systematic data-collection and supervision. The aim of these methods is always to influence the strategic calculations and cost-benefit-analyses of states by making them visible from a certain, standard-setting perspective. There are also so-called decentralised sanctions, resulting from non-centralised sanctions by few or many, which are about the legitimacy of states. One has to live in accordance with the established rules, norms and practices in order to preserve the highly valued relations. Repeated violations of the rules can lead to tit-for-tat responses, delegitimation and, eventually, to exclusion, either contextually or globally.[11]

It is idealism, in the worst sense of the term, to deny the reality of power relations in the global political economy, and to continue to represent state sovereignty as something actually existing and, in most instances, inviolable; or as the exclusive, universal normative ideal all should aspire to, no matter what.[12] Rather, although the autonomy of economic policies of states is an important goal, and although sovereign states should also be defended and developed otherwise, it seems that complementary, future-oriented political responses to globalisation are needed, too.

Like the IMF, the World Bank and the WTO now, or the planned MAI, the body that implements and looks after the Tobin tax must be empowered with surveillance capabilities and sanctions. Moreover, in itself, the tax constitutes a form of social control and regulation. The revenues it creates can be used for social purposes that must be determined globally.

Thereby, the Tobin tax regime would politicise globalisation and revive the normative problems of rightful authority, social justice, and democratic participation and accountability in a new global context.

The Role of the International Monetary Fund

Tobin assumed in the 1970s that the IMF would orchestrate the tax and that 'the tax proceeds could be appropriately paid into the IMF or World Bank'.[13] Why did Tobin make this assumption? Perhaps because the tasks of the IMF appear closer to collecting a global tax than those of any other international organisation; and because the World Bank is the other major, global financial institution. But the implicit idea seems to have been to use the IMF as leverage to enforce a universal regime. Stephanie Griffith-Jones explains this idea as follows: 'rules [for the Tobin tax regime] could be established by an international organization, such as the IMF. Indeed, if there was sufficient agreement among the major member countries, it would be possible to amend the IMF Articles of Agreement so that all countries would have to impose a Tobin tax – as Tobin himself suggested.'[14]

As Griffith-Jones goes on to point out, 'changing the IMF's Articles is a major exercise'. She does not think that it is a good idea to try to implement the tax regime this way.[15] In fact, the two-phase model of establishing the Tobin tax makes the idea of using the IMF as leverage quite unnecessary. In the first phase, there is simply no need for the IMF. Moreover, countries and a management not accepting the rationale for the tax are most likely to remain in control of the IMF. It does not sound reasonable to incorporate this kind of non-universal system of taxation under the auspices of the IMF.

The real question is whether the TTO should be subordinated to the IMF in the second phase. In my opinion, it should not. First of all, the IMF does not have the required expertise in international taxation; in fact, it has often been sceptical and critical about the ease of implementation or, more generally, about the idea as such.[16] Second, and more important, the IMF seems to be lacking legitimacy for taking over the TTO. Since the Asian crisis there has been a vivid transnational and international discussion about the need to reform the IMF. The Bretton Woods institutions seem to have been partially responsible for the Asian crisis and thereby of the legitimation problem (if not crisis) of the Washington consensus. As the founding father of the notion of economic 'shock therapy', Jeffrey Sachs, puts it, with hindsight:

> The International Monetary Fund is currently scoring five out of five – five big rescue packages since mid-1997, and five big failures. [...] The Brazil

debacle follows IMF failures in Thailand (August 1997), Indonesia (November 1997), Korea (December 1997), and Russia (August 1998). [...] The IMF is working with the wrong economic model of the world. And as long as it continues to do so, and to remain protected by a hapless G7 that refuses to call the institution to task for its failures, the rest of the world will continue to wake up to financial shocks that undermine living standards in developing countries and that threaten global stability.[17]

Furthermore, the Bretton Woods institutions themselves are understood to lack transparency, accountability and legitimacy, and to be in need of reform. They are governed in accordance with orthodox economic theory. The hegemony of this false world-interpretation is backed up by the undemocratic principle of 'one dollar, one vote'. In other words, the governance of the Bretton Woods institutions is based on the unjustified and undemocratic domination by a technocratic elite of believers in the orthodoxy, backed up by a few Western governments. In none of the top-down reform proposals is there even a hint that this might be seen as a problem.

There is an alternative. Whatever the alignment of countries that constitute the founding group of the Tobin tax regime, they can build a more democratic and socially responsible regime. They can do this without compromising the ideas of international co-operation and global responsibilities and without undermining global free trade. The governance principles of the TTO could be much more democratic than those of the IMF and the World Bank. Indeed, the IMF and the World Bank may well represent the past. Two countries – the US and the UK – alone created them fifty-five years ago, during World War II. In the twenty-first century, the TTO has the potential to become an exemplar for new global arrangements.

The Tobin Tax Organisation (TTO)

The two-phase model may be the only politically realistic way of establishing the Tobin tax. In the first phase, a new international organisation is needed to set the rate of taxation, define taxable transactions, determine exemptions from the tax and undertake monitoring and auditing tasks, as well as to collect the revenues from national authorities.[18] These are the tasks of the Tobin Tax Organisation. The initiators and the first participants will install the TTO and lay down its basic principles. These should include the following:

• Deciding the location of its headquarters; preferably, in one of the initiating and/or first participating countries.

- Defining the exact levels of first-phase taxes, including the basic tax, the additional surcharge, the extra-domestic lending tax, and the punitive tax on the blacklisted offshore centres.
- Determining the details of the system of mutual crawling pegs, including the way the moving average of the target rate is calculated and the brackets within which the exchange rate can move freely without activating the surcharge.
- Determining the structure and decision-making rules of the TTO. For instance, it could consist of a qualified majority decision-making in the Council of Ministers; and a body representing democratic parliaments and global civil society, with motion-setting rights as well as some budgetary controls and veto-powers.
- Determining whether there should be any exemptions from the tax. Preferably, at least in the beginning, there should be no exemptions, to prevent holes in the system from arising. However, those actors deemed to suffer from this non-exemption could be compensated.
- Determining the national and global shares of revenues. For instance, the OECD countries could get 30 per cent of the revenues they collect, and others 60 per cent. The rest should go to the central fund of the TTO.
- Deciding upon the global intervention fund. What share of the global revenues should be allocated to it, and what exactly would be its principles of operation?
- Setting the basic methods of surveillance and countering tax evasion, and creating the corresponding administrative functions. This part of the TTO needs to be rapid and relatively autonomous in its actions, even if always 100 per cent accountable; changes in electronic codes and routines of the banks as well as national laws about book-keeping might be needed. It has to be verified that booking operations are not transferred to tax-free centres.
- Deciding about the technical and financial support for members who have difficulties in implementing the rules; and sanctions against those members who turn out not to follow the rules of the regime.

Two ethico-political issues surrounding the organising of the TTO are particularly important and delicate. The first concerns the structure and decision-making rules, the second the allocation of resources. Democracy should play a major role in deliberations about the first, while financial stability and social justice seem to be more important considerations in the latter.

At the heart of traditional democratic theory is the idea of an autonomous political community that rightly governs itself and determines its own future. In a world of regional and global interdependencies and internationalised, shared state powers, these are issues that raise questions concerning the nature of consent and legitimacy, the nature of a constituency, the meaning of representation, and the proper form and scope of political participation. How could democratic ideals in the world of globalised power and dependency relations be worked out?

The TTO would be responsible and accountable for potentially huge amounts of money. First, a word or two about estimating the revenues. Researchers make different assumptions about, for instance, the elasticity of foreign currency exchange demand, the average pre-tax costs of foreign exchange transactions, and the likely amount of tax evasion and exemptions. All the existing estimates are based on a global, uniform tax. Michalos discusses some estimates,[19] but, like Felix and Sau,[20] he does not really consider taxes higher than 0.25 per cent. Felix and Sau advise against applying higher tax rates on the grounds that 'such high rates would disrupt foreign exchange trading so much that exchange rate volatility may not be reduced'.[21] These estimates of the revenue from a low-level tax vary from US$70 billion to US$350 billion. Frankel cites Tobin's own estimation of US$1.5 trillion annual revenues from a relatively high 0.5 per cent tax, but he thinks Tobin's calculations are simplistic. However, Frankel claims that, under very cautious assumptions, a 1 per cent tax would yield at least US$500 billion, but may exceed US$1 trillion a year.[22] This too may be an exaggeration; it is hard to imagine who could afford to pay such taxes. Frankel's estimate none the less indicates the size of the revenues.

There seems to be plenty of room for experimentation with the tax and its level, and the TTO should be flexible enough to adjust quickly to the lessons of these experiments. In the first phase, the level of taxation has to be low. In the second phase, it could be raised gradually, if experience shows that to be feasible. Now, assuming that, say, one-third of the world's currency transactions are directly covered by the currency transactions tax in the first phase; and that, in addition, there would be the additional surcharge, extra-domestic lending tax, and the punitive tax on the movements from and to the blacklisted offshore centres, the annual revenues would be around perhaps US$50–100 billion. Obviously, the more countries join the regime, the higher the revenues.

In the second phase, it seems reasonable to assume that the global share of revenues could be up to US$200–300 billion a year. This is five times the GDP of Egypt; two and a half times that of Finland or Norway; half of that of South Korea or Brazil; or a quarter of the GDP of the UK in 1995.[23] It is also between fifty and seventy times more than the annual main budget of the UN. The TTO will also have powers to establish sanctions. It is therefore crucial that the decisions made by the

TTO will be conceived as being legitimate, fair, accountable and, when needed, revisable. That is, they have to be as just and democratic as possible.

It is a basic democratic ideal that suffrage is based on the equality of human beings, not on their inherited privileges, inherited or acquired possessions, nor on the power to threaten others. It also seems that international law no longer holds to the *de facto* approach to statehood and government; mere military control of state institutions does not suffice. There is a tendency to accept only liberal democratic governments as fully legitimate. Should we thus exclude non-democratic states from the TTO?

Even after the 'third wave of democratisation', in the simplest liberal democratic score, a third of states are in no way democracies, and many are – at best – partial democracies. The category of non-democracies includes many economic powers such as China (the fastest-growing economy), Singapore (one of the major financial centres of the world) and Nigeria (accounting for about one-fifth of the population of Sub-Saharan Africa, with its substantial oil revenues and a predatory military state). Also, most of the Islamic world is non- or quasi-democratic, although, it should be emphasised, only in the simple and formal liberal-democratic sense; some of them claim to be different kinds of democracies.[24] Democracy is a contested concept; it is really a process of democratisation rather than a model. In other words, there are no fixed, always and everywhere valid yardsticks.[25] Moreover, any norm that operates by total exclusion is problematic.[26] Exclusion would contradict the universality of international law, and the universalist idea that the TTO must be open to all states.

Instead of any form of exclusion, all states should be invited to join the TTO. Despite obvious deficiencies in the legitimacy of some states, it should be assumed that they represent their populations and weigh the decision-making powers in the TTO accordingly. The votes of states could be weighted roughly in accordance with the size of their respective population, but rather than arithmetically, say, placing them in three categories and with votes from 1 to 3. The rule should be qualified majority decision-making with secret ballots. Whether democratic or not, states would thus make many of the important decisions. However, it is possible to recognise the validity of the emerging international legal norm of democracy in less exclusionary ways and to apply it more imaginatively. The TTO could have two main bodies: the Council of Ministers and the House of Democracy (see Figure 7.1). The House of Democracy should comprise only representatives from those national parliaments whose members are appointed by multi-party elections, and a sample of civil society actors, picked through a screening procedure and lottery. The House of Democracy would thus be the more direct democratic pillar of the system.

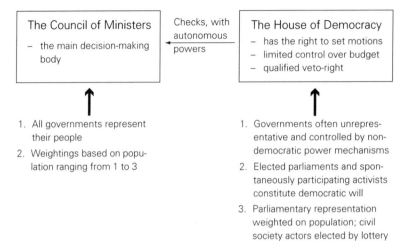

FIGURE 7.1 The structure of the Tobin Tax Organisation

For instance, the House of Democracy could have 600 seats, 350 representing national parliaments, weighted roughly on the population of these countries, and 250 representatives of civil society. The civil society actors should include NGOs, non-national parties, labour unions, transnational religious movements, etc. These actors could also be based in the non-participating or non-democratic countries. The civil society actors would have to apply for a seat. In the screening process, they would have to demonstrate that they are neither artificial products of, nor directly dependent on, states or private corporations, and that they have a sufficient, spontaneous, popular basis. Among the qualified civil society actors, the seats should be distributed through a lottery procedure; and no one actor would be entitled to hold a seat twice in row. Even though the inclusionary, state-centric Council of Ministers would have a stronger say in decision-making, the House of Democracy should be fully empowered to set motions and have limited control over the budget. The House should also have a qualified veto-power over some of the major decisions of the Council. Perhaps there should also be joint decision-making concerning certain important TTO issues.

The first major decision about the revenues concerns the national share. There are three main considerations. States have to be compensated for the administrative costs of organising the tax collection. A generous remuneration might also stimulate enthusiasm among the financial 'great powers' to join the regime and implement its rules. Finally, a deep-rooted sense of justice lies in the principle that nation-states should possess the products of activities that have taken place within their territory.[27] However, this may also be increasingly outmoded in the world of global flows, networks and offshores. As Castells puts it:

> The social construction of new dominant forms of space and time develops a meta-network that switches off nonessential functions, subordinate social groups and devalued territories. By so doing, infinite social distance is created between this meta-network and most individuals, activities and locales around the world. [...] The new social order, the network society, increasingly appears to most people as a meta-social disorder.[28]

If this is a common perception of the world, the metaphors and onto-logical assumptions behind a standard, idealised account of state sovereignty must appear increasingly implausible – except perhaps as a nostalgic reaction against the 'meta-social disorder'. Yet, a persistent common sense national belonging and the notion of state sovereignty have real effects in the world, and should be taken into account in all global political arrangements. Hence, from this conventional point of view, it is also fair that the states will get a direct share of the revenues.

What, then, would be a fair compensation and just share for the participating states? There is no way of calculating this; it is an issue that needs to be agreed upon. I would like to suggest, however, that the OECD countries should get 30 per cent of the revenues they collect and others 60 per cent. This is substantial enough to compensate for administrative costs and to create incentives to join in (also for the poorer states), and it also addresses the conventional notion of justice. Yet it does not violate the idea that the Tobin tax regime is a global and collective endeavour.

The second major decision concerns the allocation of the global fund of revenues. As the existing literature on the Tobin tax reveals, there are many good possible purposes for the spending of these resources. The revenues could be used radically to alleviate poverty in the world or to restructure the debts of the poorest nations; to create stabilising, global investment funds; to establish the basis of global social policy; for medical research and treatment; and for many other socially useful purposes. But instead of making a monological argument for using the money for a particular purpose – it should rather be decided dialogically – let me merely suggest two things.

The Tobin tax regime should from the beginning allocate a slice of the revenues – say US$1–2 billion a year – to the UN basic budget, in order to rescue the organisation from the constant threat of financial disaster. This allocation could also give leverage to more democratic reforms than those currently considered at the UN headquarters. Some additional support could be given also to other, selected parts of the UN system (UNDP,

UNCTAD, etc.). Naturally, funds for certain specific purposes may also be channelled and organised via the UN. This would prepare for a more autonomous and democratic UN to take over the TTO in the second phase. However, the transition should perhaps leave the TTO headquarters in its established location and parts of its structure and functions intact. Moreover, some funds could also be dedicated to an organised, global political campaign for a universal Tobin tax. The revenues of the first-phase tax could be used to subsidise this campaign. For instance, in the first year, some US$500 million could be allocated to an advertisement and publication campaign addressed both to the customers of the banks and to the citizens of democratic states such as the UK and the US. This would possibly include the establishment of more permanent elements of a pluralistic, transnational public sphere: newspapers, on-line publications, virtual TV channels, etc.[29]

The support for the UN system should prepare the organisational structure for the second phase. The political campaign would add to the mounting pressure on the outsiders, although the main pressure should be stemming from the economic incentives built into the regime itself (stability, revenues, decision-making rights, etc.). However, instead of making any further recommendations about the use of funds, I would like to leave these decisions to the participants and democratic processes of the TTO. All decisions about the allocation of revenues would have to follow public, transparent, fair and democratic procedures. The decision-makers should be strictly accountable for their actions both to the member states and the wider, democratising world republic. Only if the participants feel that they are sufficiently involved in determining these decisions on an equitable basis will the decisions and practices of the TTO be legitimate in the longer run. Democratisation does not exhaust issues of social and distributive justice, yet it clearly constitutes an essential ingredient of any just and socially responsible system.[30]

Towards the Second Phase: An Economic Security Council or ECOSOC as the Parent Organisation?

When the time for the second phase of the Tobin tax regime approaches, the future fate of the TTO has to be decided. Should it remain independent or, rather, be merged with a more all-encompassing system of governance? The United Nations has a lot of potential for becoming the governor of the TTO, yet it has to be reformed first. However, we have to acknowledge that this might turn out to be an insurmountable problem.

What is the argument for making the UN the governor of the TTO? The United Nations is the only truly universal organisation. Whereas the perspective of the Bretton Woods institutions is necessarily partial, the UN provides, at least in principle, a more representative and holistic viewpoint for discussions and governance. More than the IMF or the World Bank, it also has certain in-built democratic principles. These include the governing principles of the General Assembly (states are equal in decision-making, which is, despite its problems, more democratic than the 'one dollar, one vote' principle practised at the Bretton Woods institutions), and the commitment to universal human rights (human beings are equal and have thereby civic, social and political rights).[31]

Moreover, the UN organs and specialised agencies form a natural basis for developing global welfare functions further; there are no easy substitutes for them. And all things considered, it may be easier to develop and reform the present UN system than to create a new network of organisations from scratch. In sum, these reasons make a *prima facie* case for the UN to become the governor of the TTO in the second phase of the Tobin tax regime.

The prerequisite is that the UN will be reformed first. UN reform has been on the agenda for decades. Some minor reforms have been carried out, although more far-reaching proposals remain a dead letter. The substance of the proposed reforms has varied with world political constellations and trends. In the beginning of the 1970s, it was the decolonised Third World that took the initiative with proposals such as the New International Economic Order. Since the early 1980s, neoliberal conservatives have defined the content and direction of attempted UN reforms. The time might well be ripe for something else.

In the early 1980s, the Reagan and Thatcher governments launched an attack against the UN. Before the end of the Cold War, they withdrew their support for the UN in a number of ways. Gradually, they and their successors started to push for a financially more accountable UN, i.e. accountable to those who pay the most. 'It is no coincidence that the member states that have done the most to dismantle the welfare state at home, particularly the USA and the UK, have also done most to de-legitimate the claims of the UN to a global role.'[32] After having managed to change the direction of developments, and particularly after the end of the Cold War, these states have concentrated more on using the UN for their own purposes, whenever feasible, and reforming the UN in accordance with their own vision. To summarise, the neoliberal social forces 'are reluctant to concede democratic reform of the UN, and would argue instead for a greater correlation between financial responsibility and influence within the organization – that is, actually enhancing, rather than reducing, the elite privileges contained in the Charter'.[33] The prevailing argument for this course of action was, and still is, that efficiency and democracy are incompatible and that efficiency should be preferred to democracy.[34]

However, under pressure to democratise the UN, and to make recent developments look better in the eyes of the public, neoliberal social forces have granted limited participation in the UN system to certain officially recognised NGOs. This practice represents 'realistic' democratisation. It does not challenge the relations of domination within the UN system, or the content of reforms that attempt to make the UN 'financially more accountable'. Imbalances of the contributions to the UN budget are the means by which reforms are guided. The US and the UK account for 25 per cent and 5 per cent respectively, Japan 12 per cent, and France, Germany and Italy together for 20 per cent of the UN budget. The US has used this leverage in the most straightforward manner. The Kassebaum Amendment (1985) of the US Congress provided that the US could pay no more than 20 per cent of the annual budgets of the UN or any of the specialised agencies, unless the agency had established a system of weighted voting on budgetary matters. Weighted voting was defined as voting strength proportional to a country's share of the total financial burden of the agency. This equals the principle of one dollar, one vote.[35]

In 1997, it was quite appropriate to ponder whether the 'financially more accountable' UN had already passed from being a partially democratic forum to a mere hegemonic instrument.[36] As a report by the South Centre (an intergovernmental organisation closely related to the Group of 77) describes the situation:

> The history of the UN to date has been marked by the ability of a few powerful countries of the North to exercise an overriding influence on its institutional framework and policy direction, in particular by using the 'financial whip'. With the ending of the Cold War, the resulting lopsided balance of power in the Organization has opened the way for some major powers to embark on more vigorous and systematic efforts to shape the United Nations and specialised agencies even more in line with their own interests, priorities and political preferences.[37]

It is for this very reason that those who have envisaged reforms for making the UN both stronger and more democratic have been advocating alternative sources of funding to the UN. Usually, this has meant identifying the most appropriate form of global taxation. There are suggestions ranging from arms sales and travel taxes to the establishment of a UN world lottery and credit card. The Tobin tax is also always mentioned on this list, and often as the most important possibility.

It is my suggestion that the TTO should make, from the beginning, a substantial contribution to the UN budget (perhaps US$1–2 billion a year, which is about half of the basic, annual budget of the UN). By supporting the UN system unconditionally, the TTO may be able to contribute to democratic and socially responsible reforms of the UN. That is, the TTO should facilitate reforms and help to create a political space and momentum for them.

Under current regulations, it may be difficult to find a way of injecting funding from the TTO into the UN system. Moreover, there is no automatic connection between new sources of UN funding and democratic and social reforms of the UN. What would the likely effects of these revenues be? Perhaps the UN representatives and civil servants would feel more encouraged to think independently and consider different, currently prohibited possibilities. Perhaps a number of projects that are now impossible would be facilitated. The financial support of the TTO could also make a difference in the UN by revising the assessment of political possibilities as well as by changing the way the UN is seen – or, often enough, not seen – in the globalising media and by various political actors.

Yet, even after the substantial TTO contribution, things may continue to move in the direction determined by the neoliberal conservatives. The TTO contribution cannot be conditional on desired political reforms. To be effective and in accordance with its democratic aims, the TTO allowance cannot work by conditionality which, in effect, would amount to blackmail. It has to function more indirectly; but how? The best option is to channel funding not only through the basic budget of the UN but also directly to those UN organs and special agencies most in favour of the approach of the TTO and the desired democratic and social reforms. In addition, the member states of the TTO should push for changes. But there is no guarantee that this approach will work.

For one thing, all amendments of the UN Charter have to be approved by the Security Council, whose five permanent members – the US, the UK, France, Russia and China – all have a veto. Any one of them can stop changes from taking place. Even if a clear, absolute and dedicated majority of both states and world population were in favour of a given proposal for amendments, and even if the bulk of the UN budget came from the TTO, the permanent members of the Security Council could still prevent all changes. This is the heritage of World Wars I and II. The globe was divided into re-atomised nation-states, some of which were recognised as 'great powers' with distinctive sets of geopolitical interests that, according to the norm, should be respected. These increasingly anachronistic principles of military power politics were built into the UN Charter conception. Following the logic of these principles, the UN can and should do nothing if resisted by any of the great powers nominated in 1945. Hence, there is no guarantee that the UN can be made more democratic, but it is worth trying. There are, in fact, at least two possible and desirable scenarios describing how things might evolve:

1. The UN will be reformed, and something like an Economic Security Council or a reconstructed ECOSOC will emerge, to complement and revise the existing structures and functions of the UN. Consequently, the TTO can be partially merged with, and legally also subordinated to, this body.

2. The TTO will turn out to be, virtually, the economic security council or new ECOSOC for the UN. It might be more a *de facto* than a *de jure* relationship, but, for instance, many specialised agencies can be linked to it also juridically.

Let us briefly scrutinise these possibilities.

The Economic Security Council of the UN Following the initiative of Willy Brandt immediately after the fall of the Berlin Wall, Ingvar Carlsson and Sridath Ramphal were invited to co-chair the Commission of Global Governance, a group of twenty-eight state leaders, to suggest ways in which the global community 'could better manage its affairs in a new time in human history'. The Commission published a report in 1995 entitled *Our Global Neighbourhood*.[38] In this report, the Commission assumed that 'so far the UN has not provided a satisfactory forum for practical, well-focused international economic discussion'.[39] Given global interdependencies, there is an urgent need for such a forum:

> The time is now ripe – indeed overdue – to create a global forum that can provide leadership in economic, social and environmental fields. It would be more broadly based than the G7 or the Bretton Woods institutions, and more effective than the present UN system. While not having authority to make legally binding decisions, it would gain influence through competence and relevance, and acquire the standing in relation to international economic matters that the Security Council has in peace and security matters.[40]

First and foremost, the Economic Security Council would provide a long-term strategic economic policy framework for governments and major international organisations. Its agenda would be defined in terms of a comprehensive notion of security. For instance, 'shared ecological crises, economic instability, rising unemployment, the problems of transformation in the former Soviet Union, mass poverty, or lack of food security' would constitute the problems it tackles.[41] The Economic Security Council is not intended to be a crisis management forum, but should instead look more generally towards trends in the global economy and should also take preventive measures.

The Economic Security Council would seem to fit well with the idea of governing a currency transactions tax, which is intended to be a preventive measure against global financial volatility, fluctuations and crises. The report also mentions the Tobin tax very positively and urges 'the UN and the Bretton Woods institutions to explore the feasibility of such a system in consultation with the regulatory authorities of the leading financial markets'.[42] Although the report does not specify the relationship between the Economic Security Council and the Tobin tax system, we may well assume that the latter would naturally fall within the authority of the former. In any case, the report argues that the Economic Security Council 'would also be the appropriate forum for studying proposals for financing international public goods by international revenue raising'.[43]

So far, só good. Besides the difficulties of implementing the idea, there are three major problems. First, the proposal of the Commission on Global Governance is based on securitisation of economic, social and ecological issues. This tendency to securitise political issues started in the 1980s but became particularly widespread in the wake of the end of the Cold War. In retrospect, the purpose seems to have been to prioritise these issues by redefining them as matters of security.

It is true that there is a security aspect to many of these issues. However, securitisation as a widespread tendency has to be understood in its specific context: originally it was used both against the Cold War military priorities and practices – to dispel the difference between 'high' and 'low' politics in international relations – and to defend public policies on socio–economic and ecological issues against the criticism of neoliberal conservatives. Soon it assumed new usages and unintended consequences: military organisations such as NATO started to enlarge their agenda, and the logic of national security and military issues was brought into the fields of socio–economy and ecology.

In the case of the Commission on Global Governance, the logic of securitisation led to a proposal for a new, complementary Security Council. As its name indicates, the Security Council was originally intended to deal with issues of peace, war and military security. Its structure – including its veto powers – was devised in the power-political context of 1945. Indeed, the second major problem of the proposal by the Commission is that this may not be the best possible structure for dealing with problems of governing the global political economy of the early twenty-first century.

This is acknowledged also by the Commission. However, the authors of the report do not draw any conclusions from this acknowledgement. They argue that the Economic Security Council must be small to be 'practical and efficient'. It would comprise: the G-7 countries (not Russia, for it would not qualify in terms of its remaining GDP); integration organisations such as the EU, ASEAN and Mercosur; and smaller states, in order to guarantee regional representation. The authors of the report suggest a rotation principle to guarantee better representation. Apparently the rotation would apply only to smaller states – as measured by their GDP. In other words, there would be both permanent (G-7, EU?) and rotating members. Since decisions would be made by consensus only, all states would have the power of veto. And the Commission is very careful in pointing out that 'no major new bureaucratic apparatus is being suggested'.[44]

This structure might be good for discussions and conducting studies, but is not appropriate for governing the Tobin tax. It is not only that it compromises democratic ideals. It would also lack authority and the necessary administrative machinery to govern the tax itself and allocate the revenues from it. Something stronger and more democratic is certainly needed. It is entirely possible, of course, that the Commission of Global Governance would be willing to revise its proposal in order to take into account the requirements of governing a currency transactions tax. That remains to be seen.

The Economic and Social Council (ECOSOC) Originally, the UN was placed at the apex of the emerging system of international organisations, including the Bretton Woods institutions. The Economic and Social Council, ECOSOC, was designed to be the core of this system. Nominally, the specialised agencies are still subject to co-ordination with the UN via the ECOSOC, and the specialised agencies comprise the IMF and the World Bank. In the UN Charter, the ECOSOC is mandated to deal with economic and social issues in the most comprehensive sense of the term.

The ECOSOC consists of fifty-four members of the United Nations elected by the General Assembly. Eighteen members are elected each year for a term of three years. A retiring member is eligible for immediate re-election. Each member of the ECOSOC has one representative, and each member has one vote. According to the UN Charter, decisions of the ECOSOC are made by a majority of the members present and voting. Moreover, the ECOSOC may make suitable arrangements for consultations with non-governmental organisations concerned with matters within its competence.[45] The ECOSOC has the potential to be more democratic than the would-be Economic Security Council. The ECOSOC is also empowered to make real decisions.

It thus seems that: (i) there already is a substitute for the Economic Security Council; (ii) this body is not restrained by securitisation of socio-economic issues; and (iii), even more importantly, this body is designed to be in charge of co-ordinating and supervising the entire system of international organisations. Assuming a more general democratisation of the UN, would this not be the ideal parent organisation for the TTO? It is not even bound to the US: every other of the two bi-annual sessions is held in Geneva.

The Commission on Global Governance is, of course, mostly right in saying 'so far the UN has not provided a satisfactory forum for practical, well-focused international economic discussion'. They should have added only that the UN has not marginalised the ECOSOC; it has been marginalised by other social forces.[46] Yet, despite its *de facto* weaknesses, the ECOSOC has a lot of potential. The revitalisation of the ECOSOC seems to have been on the agenda almost constantly.[47]

In its proposal for a strong and democratic United Nations, the South Centre has firmly emphasised that the ECOSOC 'requires protection against forced erosion from within, as well as demands for its outright abolition'.[48] In addition to the standard demand of making the ECOSOC the entity envisaged in the UN Charter, the South Centre makes a number of suggestions about what the ECOSOC would need urgently:

- An equivalent to a Council of Ministers for long-term planning and actions regarding the trends in the global political economy.
- A new, delegated executive body, with more capabilities for implementing the decisions.
- An enhanced secretariat with rebuilt independent, analytical capabilities.
- Constant sessions, both to develop early warning capabilities, quick actions, and more serious long-term planning.[49]

All of these reforms would require resources, and perhaps those resources could be provided by the TTO. In any case, it seems to me that these reforms – even if in need of further amendments to make the ECOSOC more compatible with the idea, structure and resources of the TTO – would empower the ECOSOC also to govern the currency transactions tax.

The TTO as a focal point of the UN system? Suppose that, despite all tenacious efforts, it will be politically impossible either to establish an Economic Security Council or to empower the ECOSOC. Despite all efforts, the UN will remain undemocratic and incapable of handling the Tobin tax and its revenues. Imagine, further, a scenario where the TTO has none the less supported the UN with a very substantial allowance for years, and where many of the UN organs, special agencies and projects are funded by the revenues from the currency transactions tax.

By the time of its second phase, the TTO would have become a universal and global organisation, and, at that point, it still continues to fund and organise many UN activities. Suddenly, it may appear that the TTO is the focal point of the whole UN system. Perhaps at that moment many actors realise also that, after all, there is in fact no need to construct new bodies or reconstruct old ones. Against all odds, a bottom-up reform would have managed to change the system of governance of the global political economy.

Conclusion

Globalisation has become the theme of politics, with a widespread anticipation of a new era. Financial globalisation is an essential element in the nexus of global power relations and has also transformed state powers and sovereignty. There is a widespread ideological tendency to mystify and reify the powers and requirements of the new financial markets. However, by means of organising collective action, global financial markets can be reformed, transformed and opened up to political conflict. This would simultaneously increase the autonomy of the participating states and result in new, binding supranational arrangements.

In the 1970s, Tobin proposed that the IMF should govern the currency transactions tax. A quarter of a century later, for those looking for a major change in global governance, this may not be legitimate. Moreover, the two-phase model of making the Tobin tax real leaves no role for the IMF and is, in fact, incompatible with the IMF decision-making system. Hence, instead of giving the IMF or any other existing organisation the task of implementing a currency transactions tax, an independent Tobin tax organisation (TTO) should be founded.

Two ethico-political issues of organising the TTO are particularly important and delicate. The first concerns the structure and decision-making rules, the second the allocation of resources. Democracy must play a major role in deliberations regarding the first concern, while financial stability and social justice seem to be more important considerations in the latter. In this chapter, I have proposed a democratic but non-exclusionary system of governance for the TTO. Furthermore, I have suggested that states should keep a fair share – 30 per cent for the OECD states and 60 per cent for the others – of the revenues. The destination of the remaining revenues should be decided democratically.

When the second phase of the Tobin tax regime approaches, the fate of the TTO has to be decided. Should it remain independent or, rather, be merged with a more all-encompassing system of governance? The best option would be the UN system. The problem is that the UN system is dominated by the US and neoliberal conservatives. However, the proposed Economic Security Council would meet some of the criteria for governing the Tobin tax. A reconstructed ECOSOC would be even better. Even with the support of the TTO, however, the chances of democratising the UN may be rather slim. It may thus be that the TTO would have to endure well through into the second phase. In fact, in the twenty-first century, the TTO has the potential to become an exemplar for new global arrangements.

Notes

1. Already the acknowledgement of the power of transnational forces, structures of governance and flows points to the need to discuss these normative fundamentals of politics also in the global context.

2. See Weber 1978/1922.

3. Giddens 1985: 157.

4. Certain assumptions about the nature of persons, states, legal rules and (deontological) logic (in particular, the requirements of asymmetry, irreflexivity and transitivity) led necessarily to the question as to who/what body is not tied by any norms but binds other norms; and this agent or body must be territorially somewhere (inside the state). See Patomäki 1992b: 84.

5. Latham 2000: 10–11.

6. A lot of confusion arises from conflating different meanings of 'sovereignty' (there are a multiplicity of moral/juridical, in contrast to sociological, conceptions of sovereignty; and state sovereignty, in particular, has had internal and external aspects). Cf. Palan 1998: 630, who sees offshores 'as radical redrawing of [state] sovereignty', not as its erosion.

7. Eichengreen, Tobin and Wyplosz 1995: 162.

8. In normal conditions, it would create more space against the volatility based on political news, etc. But the Tobin tax alone cannot give any guarantees against such crises as those of 1992–93, 1994–95, and 1997–99, although it can prevent the build-up of these crises. See Kaul et al. 1996: 6.

9. Ibid., p. 9.

10. See Chapter 3 for details.

11. For a more complete analysis of these power relations, see Patomäki 2000a.

12. In fact, it has always been idealism to represent state sovereignty in this way: it has been a contradictory and counter-factual ideal rather than a blunt description of political realities. Globalisation – in the context of many cultural changes – has only made this more obvious and visible. For different accounts, see Held 1995: 73–140; Walker 1993.

13. Tobin 1978: 159.

14. Griffith-Jones 1996: 149.

15. Ibid., p. 149.

16. See ibid., p. 151.

17. Sachs 1999.

18. Considering only the possibility of a universal and uniform tax, Griffith-Jones (1996: 150–1) argues that it would be useful to complement the operation of an already existing institution (the IMF, the World Bank or the BIS) 'with a small, autonomous intergovernmental global tax commission, in which, for example, proposals for distributing the tax proceeds would be made and discussed. This commission could be established in the context of the UN, but it may need to evoke weighted majority voting.'

In the two-phase scheme, there is no good reason for connections to already existing institutions.

19. Michalos 2000: 25–7.

20. Felix and Sau 1996: particularly 238–40.

21. Ibid., p. 243. Yet, as if to confirm our suspicion that the notion of 'distortion' is derived from the questionable notion of 'Pareto optimal unique equilibrium', in note 20, p. 251, they seem to deny the likelihood of any major 'disruptions'.

22. Frankel 1996: 60.

23. These GDP figures are taken from World Bank 1997: Table 12, 236.

24. See Potter 1997: 3–10, *et passim*. Note also that in Cox's (1997: 63) assessment, 'much of the movement towards democracy noted in recent years must be considered to be what Antonio Gramsci called "passive revolution", i.e. the importing of democratic forms encouraged by external pressures that are embraced by a leading portion of the local populations but without the authentic participation of the local population'. Therefore, this democratising movement is fragile, 'lacking a secure base in a participant, articulated civil society'.

25. See Dryzek 1996.

26. Crawford and Marks 1998: 78–9. Cf. the similar ethico-political criticism of the model of cosmopolitan democracy in Patomäki 2000a.

27. As Beitz (1979: 69) has pointed out, 'perceptions of international relations have been more thoroughly influenced by the analogy of states and persons than any other device', and the standard conception of person, on which this analogy rests, stems from the liberalist political theory of Hobbes, Locke and others; see also Koskenniemi 1989. Now, the Lockean conception of possessive individualism implies that all the products resulting from the work of a person belong rightly to that person; and, in a crucial move, Locke argued that this person can also hire others to work for him, and he still would own the results of that work. By analogy, we may assume that it has been, and still is, a strong moral intuition that all the results of the work occurring within the territory of a state belong to that state (or to the citizens and legal persons constituting it). In a world of global finance and offshore centres, this notion is even more outmoded, yet remains causally efficacious.

28. Castells 1996: 476–7.

29. That is, to create alternatives to the neoliberalist, American global media.

30. See also the discussions about justice and democracy in Chapter 4. Many democratic theorists have been painfully aware of the material and distributional preconditions for democratisation. Some classical republicanists and liberalists have envisaged the diffusion of ownership of property among the many as a condition for democracy (or republic); whereas other, social-democratic, theorists have seen decommodification of labour and fair, transparent and accountable public funding of political activities as a condition for autonomous democratic actions; and some others, calling themselves radical democrats, conceive democratisation to be necessarily linked with the vanguard democratisation of the organisational relations of production. See Esping-Andersen 1990; Held 1996; and Unger 1998.

31. For a discussion, see Archibugi 1995; Held 1995: 83–9.

32. Imber 1997: 223.

33. Ibid., p. 223.

34. Again, an analogy to the domestic political assault on democracy is apt: the

'ungovernability' thesis launched by the Trilateral Commission – close to the elites of the Western (+ Japan) world – in the mid-1970s claimed that too much public demand upon political systems had led to inflation and indebtedness and was beginning to make liberal democracies ungovernable; see Crozier et al. 1975. For an accurate scrutiny of this theory, and a comparison to the rival and rather different neo-leftist 'legitimation crisis' thesis, see Held 1996: 240–53.

35. See Kanninen 1995: 41–2.

36. Imber 1997: 225.

37. South Centre 1997: xv.

38. Commission on Global Governance 1995.

39. Ibid., p. 154.

40. Ibid., p. 155.

41. Ibid., p. 157.

42. Ibid., p. 219.

43. Ibid., pp. 157–8.

44. Ibid., p. 156.

45. See Articles 61–72 of the UN Charter.

46. 'Generous funding has been made available to allow a steady expansion of tasks in the IMF, the World Bank and the WTO, which are considered the most competent institutions whose current working paradigm and governing structures are regarded more favourably. Considerable pressures are exerted to ensure that any remaining activities by the UN in these fields reflect the free market orientation and are supportive of the work of Bretton Woods institutions and the WTO' (South Centre 1997: 206).

47. Cf. the situation in the late 1980s, as described by Kanninen (1995: 81), and in the late 1990s, as illustrated, for instance, by the ECOSOC Press Release 5812, 'Managing Risks of Globalization Great Challenge to Modern Times, Secretary-General Tells Economic and Social Council', 3 February 1999.

48. South Centre 1997: 26.

49. Ibid., pp. 167–70.

8

Concluding Remarks

The Tobin tax has considerable emancipatory potential. If appropriately implemented, there is the potential for better economic policies and global democratisation. A duly implemented Tobin tax would be an essential step towards democratising globalisation and opening up new political possibilities. Having said this, however, two concluding remarks are apt. These remarks should be read as major qualifications of the basic thesis of the book.

First, it is important to acknowledge that it is possible to devise and implement a variation of the currency transactions tax that would *not* challenge the basic tenets of neoliberalism. Such a tax would also not be particularly democratic or emancipatory. Second, even an appropriately implemented Tobin tax would not solve all the problems of the global financial markets. Moreover, our planet suffers, obviously, also from other global problems, which call for emancipatory projects other than those related to the financial markets. A truly democratised globalisation calls for a number of interventions in various areas.

A Reactionary Tobin Tax?

In Geneva, Switzerland, on 1 July 2000, the twenty-fourth Special Session of the UN General Assembly entitled 'World Summit for Social Development and Beyond: Achieving Social Development for All in a Globalizing World', adopted a promising final document.[1] Alongside measures to fight tax avoidance and internationally effective taxation of multinational corporations (MNC), it also proposes that the UN should be 'conducting a rigorous analysis of advantages, disadvantages and implications of proposals for developing new and innovative sources of funding, both public and private, for dedication to social development and poverty eradication programmes'.[2]

Although this subparagraph was rephrased not to mention the Tobin tax directly, John Langmore, the director of the United Nations Division for Social Policy and Development, Department of Economic and Social Affairs, has interpreted the wording as including a study of currency transactions taxation. Accordingly, he says he will form a team also to study currency transactions taxation.[3] On 15 December 2000, Secretary-General Kofi Annan named former Mexican President Ernesto Zedillo to head a high-level panel which will explore ways of fulfilling the finance needs of the world's developing countries. Panel members include Robert Rubin, former Secretary of the Treasury of the United States.

In Geneva in July 2000, the US delegation explained that they could not support even a study on a currency transactions tax, because of the bill that prevents US funding for the UN if the UN develops any imposition of tax on US nationals 'in order to raise funding for the UN or UN agencies'. In order to convince the US delegation, NGOs, the Canadian government, the G-77, and some other actors present in Geneva, tried to argue that there is no reason to oppose a Tobin tax study. They stated that a currency transaction tax is *not a global tax* nor is it meant to raise funds for the UN; rather it can be a set of co-ordinated national taxes.[4] This solution would accord with state sovereignty as the organising principle of world politics.

Although unlikely to succeed in practice, this reinterpretation needs to be scrutinised with great caution. In its extreme, it could mean that a few nation-states would seize all the revenues. Furthermore, in order to make the Tobin tax a mere stabilising device, it is possible to realise a two-tiered version of the currency transaction tax, with a very minimal or zero basic tax rate and an exchange surcharge that would be triggered only during periods of exchange rate turbulence. This solution would accord with the belief in the optimal efficiency of free financial markets almost anywhere at any time, and the tax would be qualified only to take into account exceptional circumstances. It would also allow further growth of the global financial markets, with the increased power to undermine many attempts to conduct independent or spontaneous economic policies by any state. It would also lack any significant redistributional effects. Most certainly, it would not address the quest for global fairness and justice, or democratic self-determination. If the interests of the presently powerful were to dictate the outcome, there is a great risk that this might be the only 'realistic' alternative.

There are good reasons to support a much more comprehensive and emancipatory interpretation of the Tobin tax. These reasons have been spelled out in Chapter 4. To recapitulate, the theory of the optimal efficiency of free, deregulated global financial markets is, in general, false. To counter the disciplinary power of finance and the misallocation of resources it has caused, it is highly desirable to curb and slow down transnational financial flows. Because of the diversity of national economic conditions, it is also important to increase the autonomy of economic policies of states. Moreover, there are values other than economic efficiency. Fairness and a commitment to reduce powerlessness and vulnerability – caused also by the structural power of global finance – vindicate the quest for profound institutional reforms and global redistribution. Equally well, the value of democracy is at stake. Democracy is not only a matter of national self-determination. Transnational practices and power relations based on false beliefs – such as orthodox economics or the theory of hegemonic stability – should also be changed and, ultimately, democratised.

The two-phase model shows how it is possible to realise a more comprehensive and emancipatory Tobin tax regime. Any grouping of countries can initiate a system of taxation at any time, with the background support and pressure of a global social movement. This grouping should establish an open agreement with a supranational body orchestrating the tax and collecting the revenues. Since no universal consent is required, these progressive countries, in close consultation with representatives of civil society, would be freer to decide upon the most appropriate arrangements. Yet, the system does not exclude anybody. Any state is invited to join at any time. The joining states will have a say in further developments of the tax regime, in accordance with the agreed democratic rules and procedures.

Why is the Tobin Tax Not Enough?

The Tobin tax does not suffice for many reasons. Even the most comprehensive version of a substantial, two-tier tax, affiliated with a crawling-peg system and a global intervention fund to back it up, plus a democratic Tobin Tax Organisation, would not address all the problems of the global financial markets. Obviously, there are also many other global issues and reasons for emancipatory aspirations that need to be addressed. At best, the Tobin tax can provide a vehicle for taking a few steps towards a more rational allocation of resources and in empowering the vulnerable, while preparing the ground for other economic reforms and democratic changes.

First, *extra-regulatory financial activities* pose major problems. These activities assume two main forms: off-the-balance-sheet and offshore. These enable the avoidance of both rules and taxes. Rule-avoidance affects (at least potentially) financial stability, whereas tax-avoidance tends to shift the burden of taxation from capital and extreme wealth to ordinary wages and land. Moreover, both forms of avoidance facilitate criminal activities. A comprehensive currency transactions tax would have to tackle some of these problems, at least as far as the forex markets are concerned. For instance, the licence system of financial activities and actors would effectively control some of the off-the-balance-sheet activities. The Tobin tax is also a tax on transnational capital and a comprehensive currency transactions tax would include a punitive tax on offshore activities. Yet, the securitisation of the loans markets, for instance, poses additional problems that the tax regime does not cover. Highly leveraged extra-regulatory financial actors such as hedge funds cause further risks. Moreover, the first phase of the two-phase model would depend, at least partially, on global co-operation on making the offshore centres share information and abide by at least some basic rules.

Second, although a substantial currency transactions tax – coupled with an exchange surcharge – would bite short-term transactions particularly hard, it would not tackle the problem of financial *short-termism* as a whole. For various structural and ideological reasons, short-termism has crowded out other activities in global financial markets. For dealers and investors with short-term horizons, whatever happens to the largely fictitious prices of assets for whatever reasons is in fact quite real, and they have to act accordingly. This stimulates speculation. There is very little room for 'enterprise activities' as 'the activity of forecasting the prospective yields of assets over their whole life'.[5] 'Economic fundamentals' do not weigh in short-term, speculative calculations; only guesses about short-term price movements do. The Tobin tax may make often recurring cross-border transactions involving currency exchange expensive, but otherwise it leaves short-termism intact. Further measures may be needed. For instance, re-regulation of the incentive structures of dealers and a requirement that short-term debts cannot be taken to buy short-term assets might help.

The third major problem is the process of *further flow of resources to financial markets*. As explained in Chapter 2, this is a complex socio-economic process. Evidently, a tax on transnational, short-term financial capital will in turn extract resources *from* the financial markets, also for non-financial uses. However, this would by no means reverse the process as a whole. There are far-reaching developments associated with the rise of a neoliberal risk society, such as the tendency to commodify and privatise the redefined and emergent insecurities, risks and hazards; the increasing concentration of wealth in the hands of a few; funding and privatisation of pensions; the branching out of the insurance companies; and the domination of financial interests over the strategies of non-financial firms. All these developments tend to feed the growth of finance, particularly when coupled with the endogenous process of financial multiplication. The Tobin tax could merely show an initial step in another direction for some of these processes.

What is also at stake is the *governance of credit and investments* in the global political economy. A currency transactions tax would confront this major issue only rather indirectly, by slowing down and curbing cross-border transactions involving forex. This would reduce the influence of the global casino on non-financial investments. However, the Tobin tax would not tackle the asymmetric dependence of most governments on the Bretton Woods institutions or the credit-rating agencies. It would not change major banks' lending practices and procedures. It would also leave intact the tendency towards financial disintermediation and the associated risks.

In a number of crucial ways, even a comprehensive Tobin tax would be only a partial reform of the global financial markets.[6] Moreover, as Chavagneux has pointed out, nobody should be led into the false belief that the Tobin tax – or another regulation mechanism of the financial system – would solve all the world's problems. 'Most of Africa will still be poor or the world's environmental problems will not disappear.'[7] It is also not enough to give more power to the state against the markets. More thorough reforms are needed to make the global economy socially responsible and democratic.

However, in concluding this book, I would like to emphasise that the Tobin tax – and in particular the comprehensive and emancipatory interpretation of it in Chapters 4, 5 and 7 – can be a particularly innovative and far-reaching idea. The beauty of the Tobin tax lies in its potential to give rise to new democratic political constellations. The Tobin tax would, simultaneously, enhance the *de facto* autonomy of states and give rise to new global institutional arrangements which must be legally binding. The argument of this book has been that the best way for states to gain some real autonomy is to collaborate and create new collective forms of organisation. Simultaneously, this will also bind them, but the states would be freer to choose how and by whom and for what purpose. Sovereignty may be further transformed, but more democratically than in the process of neoliberal globalisation.

Indeed, these new institutional arrangements would not hinder the processes of globalisation but would rather politicise and democratise them. This might turn out to be historic. In the irreversible historical processes of structuration, the new phase of globalisation would also inevitably lead to new kinds of political sagas. The Tobin Tax Organisation (TTO) may well play a crucial role in some of these episodes, at least in the beginning. For instance, the TTO may provide a countervailing power and a partial alternative to the Bretton Woods institutions. It can also support democratic reforms of the UN. Even more ambitiously, it can set an example of global organisation more fitting for the conditions of the twenty-first century than the anachronistic institutions that we have inherited from World War II.

Notes

1. The document, including its relevant Part III ('Further actions and initiatives to implement the commitments made at the Summit') is available at http://www.un.org/esa/socdev/geneva2000/docs/index.html

2. Canada proposed the following formulation: 'Further study of the implications of a currency transaction tax, including the potential advantages and disadvantages'; and G-77 the following: 'Further study of the idea of a currency transaction tax, and its potential implications'. The US rejected these. See http://www.un.org/esa/socdev/geneva2000/docs/l5rev33_235.pdf

3. This is based on information delivered in an e-mail message by Jong-Sung You, on 1 July 2000. See also Langmore's (2000) Geneva speech 'A turning point towards global social development?', in which he mentions Canada's initiative, at http://www.un.org/esa/socdev/geneva2000/issues/is9.htm

4. Ibid.

5. The phrases are from Keynes; see Chapter 1, Box 2.

6. One comprehensive proposal for 'a new Bretton Woods agreement' is that by the Robinson College Working Group (1999).

7. Chavagneux 1999: 13.

Appendix 1 Monetarism and the Denial of Reality

Friedman's 1953 essay 'The Case for Flexible Exchange Rates' is a normative argument. Friedman makes the case for a multilateral arrangement different from the regulated Bretton Woods system that was established in the 1940s and developed into practice in the early 1950s. Before long, Friedman's argument was used in justifying the move to floating exchange rates in 1971.

Friedman can be taken to summarise the prevailing justification for deregulated, global financial markets. The development of these markets had two preconditions: freely convertible currencies and the retreat of governments from intervening and controlling financial flows and investments. Equally importantly, Friedman also explicates the dominant Western framework for interpreting the constantly occurring financial crises, according to which instability must be due to problems with domestic 'economic fundamentals'.[1]

Friedman's 'The Case for Flexible Exchange Rates' is framed in the language of 'positive economics'. To understand the argument, it is first necessary to examine the methodology of positive economics.[2]

The Methodology of 'Positive Economics'

Friedman's methodology of 'positive economics' is explicitly meant to defend the orthodox (*laissez-faire*) position.[3] Following Keynes senior, he argues that positive economics is 'a body of systematized knowledge concerning *what is*'. But in line with positivist philosophy, Friedman is in fact deeply sceptical about reality. Indeed, there is nothing about reality – about causality, being and existence – in Friedman's text. 'The Methodology of Positive Economics' is in many ways explicitly anti-realist. For instance, to emphasise his scepticism, Friedman always writes 'reality' in inverted commas. His most important point is to denounce those who criticise economics because of its unrealistic assumptions.

Ambiguously, Friedman seems to hold two positions simultaneously.

On the one hand, he says that the accuracy of these assumptions does not matter; it is enough that they are *sufficient approximations* of how the world is. In that case they could be criticised on the grounds that they are not sufficiently accurate. On the other hand, he also argues that 'truly important and significant hypotheses will be found to have "assumptions" that are wildly inaccurate descriptive representations of reality, and, in general, the more significant the theory, the more unrealistic the assumptions (in this sense)'.[4] He even argues that 'to be important, a hypothesis must be descriptively false in its assumptions'.

What is it, then, that matters, if not the accuracy or truth of the assumptions? Friedman's answer is straightforward: implications, conceived as *predictions*. 'Relevant test of the *validity* of hypothesis is comparison of its predictions with experience.'[5] However, he acknowledges 'if there is one hypothesis that is consistent with the available evidence, there are always an infinite number that are'.[6] Consequently, '*the choice among alternative hypotheses* equally consistent with the available evidence *must be to some extent arbitrary*'.[7] Since Friedman takes assumptions and theories simply as mere instruments for generating predictions, he argues for simplicity and scope of theories or models as the main criteria of their acceptability ('to predict as much as possible with as little as possible').

However, there is the further problem of interpreting evidence: '[E]vidence cast up by experience [...] is far more difficult to interpret. It is frequently complex and always indirect and incomplete. Its collection is often arduous, and its interpretation generally requires subtle analysis and involved chains of reasoning, which seldom carry real conviction.'[8]

Friedman also recognises that facts are theory-dependent.[9] So how is it possible to make rational judgements about the merits and shortcomings of theories? Assumptions can and should be unrealistic; and hypothesis can be descriptively false. It does not help to try to compare them and the world. Simple models may be able to predict a lot, but the same predictions could be derived from many other hypotheses and models equally well. And last but not least, the task of interpreting evidence is always laborious and typically 'does not carry real conviction'.

At this point, Friedman retreats to *epistemological conservatism*. Ultimately, he argues, what matters is a reasonably wide consensus among the qualified economists and the long tradition of Anglo–American economics since David Hume. The skill for making judgements can only 'be learned by experience and exposure in the "right" scientific atmosphere'.[10] The qualified are able to choose assumptions 'on the grounds of their *convenience* in some such respects as simplicity or economy in describing the model, *intuitive plausibility*, or capacity to *suggest*, if only by implication, some of the considerations that are relevant in judging or applying a model'.[11] They also have patience for 'judging conformity of the implications with experience', yet they will also 'be persuaded to accept the hypothesis tentatively by few instances of "conformity"'.[12] However, in reverence to the tradition, the evidence should also be interpreted in accordance with it: 'The [evidence ...] is difficult to document at all comprehensively [...] and tends to become part of the tradition and folklore of a science revealed in the tenacity with which hypotheses are held.'[13] Hence, it is not only the case that Friedman thinks that his favourite theory – quantity theory of money – is supported by extraordinarily strong empirical evidence. More importantly, it seems that he also contends that the Keynesian revolution brought layman's thinking and, thereby, rejection of the quantity theory inside economics, and that this was an unwise and illegitimate thing to do.[14] Only professional, properly trained (Anglo–American) economists should be allowed to make scientific judgements on economic matters; and they should always remember to honour the tradition.

Epistemologically, sociologically and politically, Friedman's rhetorical moves create a *closure*. No contrary evidence could possibly convince Friedman to change his mind; and no 'outside' criticism is legitimate. But what is even more far-reaching is the ontological silence – and the explicit detachment of theory from reality. As a consequence of this epistemological closure and ontological scepticism, it has gone unnoticed for Friedman, and most 'qualified' economists, that they try to apply ideas and methodical tools that would be *suitable only to closed systems* of directly observable phenomena.[15]

Outside astronomy, these systems can be found only in the laboratories of classical, Newtonian physicists. Outside the artificially created existential and causal closures,[16] there are only open systems. In open systems, which moreover typically also include non-observable components and layers, explanation and prediction are *radically asymmetrical*; and meaningful, precise scientific predictions are in general impossible (which does not mean that nothing can be anticipated).[17]

The condition of open systems undermines Friedman's epistemology. If precise, meaningful predictions in open systems are in fact impossible (quite independently of whether this impossibility is recognised), the only thing that is left for an economist assessing hypotheses seems to be *the tradition* and *the consensus among the qualified*. It is not very far-fetched to interpret the 1990s notion of the 'Washington consensus' along these lines. At once, this brings into view the constitutive and legitimising links between a supposedly consensual expert discourse and power. However, it is telling that, even in his attempts to gain the support of the consensus of qualified economists, Friedman has often been in severe difficulties.[18]

In my view, the path that economics should take is that of starting to study reality, in the sense of the agency, everyday practices, social relations and strategic interdependencies of positioned actors. But this is not only excluded, but also ridiculed by Friedman. He says that the behaviour of businessmen need not conform with the 'assumptions' of the theory; and that there definitely is no need for surveys and 'descriptive studies of the decision-making activities of individual firms'.[19] For Friedman, these would amount merely to studying the 'irrelevant question whether businessmen do or do not in fact reach their decisions by consulting schedules, or curves, or multivariable functions showing marginal cost and marginal revenue'.[20] Yet, the clarity and precision brought about by these mathematical tools cannot be a substitute for understanding reality. As Lawson argues:

> [...] the essential point here is that if clarity and precision are not the preserve of formal modellers nor are they anything like sufficient for understanding social phenomena. A farmer may, with as much clarity as any 'theorist', assume that his or her pigs can fly in a definite direction with a determinate velocity. But his exercise is unlikely to help the farmer in understanding the nature, speed or cost etc., of any process whereby pigs can actually be brought to market, unless flying pigs are a real possibility.[21]

The point is to *reclaim reality*.[22] Instead of playing with fictitious models and their formal properties, what political economists should do is to study the real, causally efficacious complexes of actors; their resources; the rules they follow; thus constituted social practices and institutions; and related social relations that produce the outcomes we are interested in understanding and explaining.[23]

The Case for Flexible Exchange Rates

It is noteworthy that Friedman's essay 'The Case for Flexible Exchange Rates', although clothed in the language of 'positive economics', in fact does not strictly follow its tenets. First, in this text Friedman clearly makes a normative argument. He makes a case for changing the world on the grounds of *desirability* of flexible exchange rates (which had never been properly tried by that time). Although mostly grounding his case on broad theory-derived claims and hypotheses about empirical regularities, Friedman in fact assesses the desirability of different possible, multilateral arrangements, some of which were quite hypothetical.[24] Second, Friedman's argument also takes into account a variety of socio-historical changes, and thus goes beyond his 'simple assumptions'. Third, despite his empiricism and epistemological conservatism, he proposed a system that had never been systematically tested. Fourth, the text does *not* contain or discuss any *specific, precise predictions*, but rather discusses general tendencies derived largely from simple and basic neo-classical economic theory. Consequently, in this paper Friedman in fact turns his assumptions and hypothesis into a system that constitutes a *normative ideal*. Ultimately, his task is therefore not to revise the theory to accord with reality, but to realise the theory in practice.

Friedman started this 1953 paper by arguing that the Bretton Woods system is 'ill-suited for current conditions'.[25] In modern, relatively open economies there are manifold tendencies for changes, which create difficulties of adjustment. Elimination of symptoms of underlying tendencies 'by administrative freezing of exchange rates cures none of the underlying difficulties and only makes adjustment to them more painful'.[26]

Friedman frames the problem as that of matching demand and supply of a currency. He distinguishes and assesses four possibilities for reconciling this demand and supply. First, required *changes in domestic prices or income* are impossible in modern societies. Due to modern conditions, 'prices are more flexible upward than downward, but even on the upswing all prices are not equally flexible' and 'wage rates tend to be among the less flexible prices'.[27]

Second, Friedman dismisses direct *controls*, on the grounds that accurate prediction is not possible (thus perhaps casting a shadow of suspicion on the predictive capabilities of both economic actors and theory?). It is true, he says, 'if changes in the composition of imports and exports could be predicted in advance, and if it were technically possible to control selectively each category of imports, exports, and capital transactions, direct controls could be used to produce the required adjustment'.[28] Neither is possible, however, and it is also administratively politically undesirable to have such a system.

Third, although the *monetary reserves* of the central banks can be used for short-term adjustments, Friedman argues that the use of these monetary reserves is not desirable, if possible at all, for countering movements of large magnitude and long duration.[29] Hence, as a permanent solution, they would not do either.

The last possibility for reconciling demand and supply for a currency is *changes in exchange rates*. Governmental devaluation or appreciation of a currency is helpful, but 'each exchange-rate change tends to become the occasion for a crisis'.[30] There is no continuous mechanism for producing required changes and thus other – less desirable – mechanisms must be used. Also, speculation is often a problem, because the future direction of a currency is easy to guess or predict, given visible pressures that a government is struggling with. Friedman thus claims that governmental regulation feeds unnecessary speculation.

Hence, the best and most desirable system is that of flexible exchange rates. Flexible rates 'freely determined in open markets' guarantee automatic adjustments. Also, Friedman presumes that in free markets, speculation – if it is to occur at any significant rate – will help in making the 'necessary adjustments'.

Note the logic of the argument. First, the problem is framed as a supply and demand problem only. Then the argument turns out be an application of the standard axiom of the orthodox economics that prices, which are freely determined in open markets, ensure optimally the reconciliation of supply and demand. Therefore, the most efficient system is that of 'exchange rates freely determined in an open market primarily by private dealings and, like other market prices, varying from day to day'.

In fact, Friedman argues also that 'flexible exchange rates are the logical international counterpart of the monetary and fiscal framework for economic stability that seems to me the most promising'.[31] What is this framework? It is that of a *laissez-faire* system, where it is assumed – for the sake of simplicity and convenience – that the economy as a whole is just an aggregation of atomist market transactions by rational actors, and where governmental intervention is limited to providing the necessary infrastructure and an incrementally increasing supply of money.

Hedging, speculation and stability How does Friedman, then, argue against the standard objections to floating rates? These heavyweight objections were based on the post-1930s fears of uncertainty and instability and constituted the grounds for the Bretton Woods system. The first typical objection is that *flexible rates mean uncertainty about prices for the foreign traders*. Friedman argues that traders can achieve protection through 'hedging in the futures market'. He even claims that 'any uncertainty will be borne by speculators'.[32] Traders have to pay only the cost of hedging. This argument both anticipates and justifies the exponential rise of the futures markets in the 1980s and 1990s.

The second standard objection is that *speculation in freely floating markets tends to be destabilising*. Friedman says 'the special fear in this connection is of capital flight in response to political uncertainty or simply to movements in exchange rate.'[33] He tries to alleviate these fears with two arguments. The theoretical argument is simple: 'People who argue that speculation is generally destabilising seldom realise that this is largely equivalent to saying that speculators lose money.'[34] And since they are (mostly) rational in the strong sense of having all the relevant information about the present and the future (which they can predict), they would not lose money, at least in the longer run.

Moreover, in line with his scepticism concerning evidence and its interpretation, he also argues that there is no convincing empirical evidence for these fears. The widespread belief that speculation is likely to be destabilising 'does not seem to be founded on any systematic analysis of the available empirical evidence'.[35] Nor does Friedman himself provide any analysis of empirical evidence. Hence, his contention that 'speculative' transactions play a positive role both in temporary and permanent adjustment is based merely on simple theoretical reasoning, on the fundamental beliefs of the orthodoxy.

The last standard objection is that *flexible rates mean general instability*. Here, Friedman makes an assertion that has had very far-reaching consequences for the governance of the world economy. He argues that given freely floating rates, changes in the prices of currencies are always due to temporary deficits/surpluses or to 'fundamental factors'.[36]

He contends that if a rate is unstable, 'it is primarily because there is an underlying instability in the economic conditions governing the international trade'.[37] The implication is that if stability is desired, the fundamentals should be corrected and stabilised. In practice this means that measures should be taken to realise the ideals of neo-classical economics in practice: the assumption is that there are 'distortions' as long as there is *unnecessary* governmental regulation and interference.

This assertion about the causes of exchange rate changes and instability is nowhere substantiated. It just follows from Friedman's belief in the generalisation of the standard, simple neo-classical theory (that, as Friedman says, is based on wildly inaccurate descriptive representations of reality). However, once accepted, this contention tells *a priori* how any occurrence of financial instability, or crisis, should be interpreted. If the instability or crisis cannot simply be dismissed as a consequence of temporary deficits/surpluses, *it must be* a matter of 'fundamental factors'.

This system of rhetorical moves and theoretical arguments suggests that there is no need to study reality in concrete instances. The simple theory tells it all. There is only one condition: the theory must be able consistently to predict something deemed decisive – in a world where significant, precise scientific predictions are in fact impossible. The apparent predictive powers are assessed against highly ambiguous evidence. And when the evidence suddenly seems insurmountable, it is always possible to invent *ad hoc* hypotheses that explain the deviations away. In my view, this kind of denial of reality should be unacceptable.

Notes

1. Obviously, there are different views among orthodox economists. But Friedman's argument is not only representative of the logic of translating non-realist economic

models into political practice; he has also been an intellectual leader in the neoliberal movement advocating more orthodox solutions to economic problems, followed by many state leaders from Nixon and Pinochet onwards.

2. 'The Methodology of Positive Economics' is the first essay in *Essays in Positive Economics* that also includes 'The Case for Flexible Exchange Rates'; Friedman 1953a, 1953b.

3. Friedman 1953a: 30.

4. Ibid., p. 14.

5. Ibid., pp. 8–9.

6. Ibid., p. 9.

7. Ibid., p. 10; italics HP.

8. Ibid., p. 10.

9. 'A theory is the way we perceive "facts", and we cannot perceive "facts" without a theory.' Ibid., p. 34. See also his note 3 on p. 5.

10. Ibid., p. 25.

11. Ibid., p. 26.

12. Ibid., p. 30. One wonders what these 'few instances' would be? Take, for instance, the seemingly eternal and unresolved debate about the empirical results of Leontief, whose findings seemed to contradict the basic Ricardian and Heckscher–Ohlin model of comparative advantage in international trade. Instead of revising fundamental assumptions of the theory (except by distinguishing between the 'high-quality US labour and raw foreign labour'), economists labelled this finding as 'Leontief's paradox'; this 'paradox' has for long been presented in all textbooks in international economics as a kind of curiosity that can – possibly! – be explained away with methodological and substantial *ad hoc* explanations. What exactly would be the 'few instances of conformity' that we should accept here? Those supporting the standard theory? Is this kind of selectivity really scientific? See e.g. the rather sharp-sighted treatment of Södersten and Reed 1994: 103–16.

13. Friedman 1953a: 23.

14. Cf. ibid., p. 11, and Friedman 1974: 1.

15. What Friedman's system creates epistemologically – a closure – it presupposes ontologically. In both cases he is wrong. Science can prosper only in contexts of open and mutually critical communication; and social worlds are fundamentally open: (1) the relationship between the causal complexes and those of its external conditions is typically not constant; and (2) change and qualitative variation in the objects possessing causal powers – including social actors – are ubiquitous. See Sayer 1992: 118–38.

16. The point of these artificial closures is to isolate the *mechanisms, laws and explanatory structures* that are also causally efficacious – capable of transfactually producing outcomes – in the open systems of nature.

17. For a discussion, see Bhaskar 1989: 20–36.

18. 'Once again, just as in the debate over the shape of the money demand function, Friedman has tried to saddle his opponents and critics with an extreme assumption and to claim the entire middle ground for himself. In both cases, the truth is that it is his propositions, not theirs, which depend on a special polar case.' Tobin 1974b: 80.

19. Friedman 1953a: 15–16.

20. Ibid., p. 31.

21. Lawson 1997: 112.

22. Again, see Bhaskar 1989.

23. This idea is explained in Patomäki 1991 and 1996; and Patomäki and Wight, 2000.

24. Friedman can always retreat to the claim that his argument is based on *shared values*. Outside a very limited sphere of normative consensus, he seems to think that there can be only a Nietzschean struggle for power. Hence: 'I venture the judgment, however, that currently in the Western world, and especially in the United States, differences among economic policy among disinterested citizens derive predominantly from different predictions about the economic consequences of taking action – differences that in principle can be eliminated by the progress of positive economics – rather than from *fundamental differences in basic values, differences about which men can ultimately only fight*' (Friedman 1953a: 5; italics HP). Of course, he decides, on the basis of his own common sense, what this consensus is all about. See Patomäki 1992a for a criticism of attempts to ground morality on an already existing consensus.

25. Friedman 1953b: 157.

26. Ibid., p. 158.

27. Ibid., p. 165.

28. Ibid., p. 167.

29. Ibid., p. 170.

30. Ibid., p. 163.

31. Ibid., p. 158.

32. Ibid., p. 174.

33. Ibid., p. 175.

34. Ibid., p. 175.

35. Ibid., p. 176.

36. Ibid., p. 162.

37. Ibid., p. 173.

Appendix 2 A Proposal for Monetary Reform: James Tobin, Yale University*

Over the last twenty years economists' prescriptions for reform of the international monetary system have taken various shapes. Their common premise was dissatisfaction with the Bretton Woods regime as it evolved in the 1950s. Robert Triffin awakened the world to the contradictions and instabilities of a system of pegged parities that relied on the debts in reserve currencies, mostly dollars, to meet growing needs for official reserves. Triffin and his followers saw the remedy as the internationalization of reserves and reserve assets; their ultimate solution was a world central bank. Others diagnosed the problem less in terms of liquidity than in the inadequacies of balance of payments adjustment mechanisms in the modern world. The inadequacies were especially evident under the fixed-parity gold-exchange standard when, as in the 1960s, the reserve currency center was structurally in chronic deficit. These analysts sought better and more symmetrical 'rules of the game' for adjustments by surplus and deficit countries, usually including more flexibility in the setting of exchange parities, crawling pegs, and the like. Many economists, of whom Milton Friedman was an eloquent and persuasive spokesman, had all along advocated floating exchange rates, determined in private markets without official interventions.

By the early 1970s the third view was the dominant one in the economics profession, though not among central bankers and private financiers. And all of a sudden, thanks to Nixon and Connally, we got our wish. Or at least we got as much of it as anyone could reasonably have hoped, since it could never have been expected that governments would eschew all intervention in exchange markets.

---

* This paper is Professor Tobin's presidential address to the 1978 conference of the Eastern Economic Association, Washington DC. It was originally published in 1978 in the *Eastern Economic Journal*, 4 (3–4): 153–9, and is reproduced here with the permission of the *Eastern Economic Journal*.

Now after five to seven years – depending how one counts – of unclean floating there are many second thoughts. Some economists share the nostalgia of men of affairs for the gold standard or its equivalent, for a fixed anchor for the world's money, for stability of official parities. Some economists, those who emphasize the rationality of expectations and the flexibility of prices in all markets, doubt that it makes much difference whether exchange rates are fixed or flexible, provided only that government policies are predictable. Clearly, flexible rates have not been the panacea which their more extravagant advocates had hoped; international monetary problems have not disappeared from headlines or from the agenda of anxieties of central banks and governments.

I believe that the basic problem today is not the exchange rate regime, whether fixed or floating. Debate on the regime evades and obscures the essential problem. That is the excessive international – or better, inter-currency – mobility of private financial capital. The biggest thing that happened in the world monetary system since the 1950s was the establishment of de facto complete convertibility among major currencies, and the development of intermediaries and markets, notably Eurocurrency institutions, to facilitate conversions. Under either exchange rate regime the currency exchanges transmit disturbances originating in international financial markets. National economies and national governments are not capable of adjusting to massive movements of funds across the foreign exchanges, without real hardship and without significant sacrifice of the objectives of national economic policy with respect to employment, output, and inflation. Specifically, the mobility of financial capital limits viable differences among national interest rates and thus severely restricts the ability of central banks and governments to pursue monetary and fiscal policies appropriate to their internal economies. Likewise speculation on exchange rates, whether its consequences are vast shifts of official assets and debts or large movements of exchange rates themselves, have serious and frequently painful real internal economic consequences. Domestic policies are relatively powerless to escape them or offset them.

The basic problems are these. Goods and labor move, in response to international price signals, much more sluggishly than fluid funds. Prices in goods and labor markets move much more sluggishly, in response to excess supply or demand, than the prices of financial assets, including exchange rates. These facts of life are essentially the same whether exchange rates are floating or fixed. The difficulties they create for national economies and policy-makers cannot be avoided by opting for one exchange rate regime or the other, or by providing more or different international liquidity, or by adopting new rules of the game of balance of payments adjustment. I do not say that those issues are unimportant or that reforms of those aspects of the international monetary system may not be useful. For example, I still think that floating rates are an improvement on the Bretton Woods system. I do not contend that the major problems we are now experiencing will continue unless something else is done too.

There are two ways to go. One is toward a common currency, common monetary and fiscal policy, and economic integration. The other is toward greater financial segmentation between nations or currency areas, permitting their central banks and governments greater autonomy in policies tailored to their specific economic institutions and objectives. The first direction, however appealing, is clearly not a viable option in the foreseeable future, i.e., the twentieth century. I therefore regretfully recommend the second, and my proposal is to throw some sand in the wheels of our excessively efficient international money markets.

But first let us pay our respects to the 'one world' ideal. Within the United States, of course, capital is extremely mobile between regions, and has been for a long time. Its mobility has served, continues to serve, important economic functions: mobilizing funds from high-saving areas to finance investments that develop areas with high marginal productivities of capital; financing trade deficits which arise from regional shifts in population and comparative advantage or from transient economic or natural shocks. With nationwide product and labor markets, goods and labor also flow readily to areas of high demand, and this mobility is the essential solution to the problems of regional depression and obsolescence that inevitably occur. There is neither need for, nor possibility of, regional macroeconomic policies. It would not be possible to improve employment in West Virginia or reduce inflation in California, even temporarily, by changing the parity of a local dollar with dollars of other Federal Reserve Districts. With a common currency, national financial and capital markets, and a single national monetary policy, movements of funds to exploit interest arbitrage or to speculate on exchange rate fluctuations cannot be sources of disturbances and painful interregional adjustments.

To recite this familiar account is to remind us how difficult it would be to replicate its prerequisites on a worldwide basis. Even for the Common Market countries, the goal is still far, far distant. We do not have to resolve the chicken–egg argument. Perhaps it is true that establishing a common currency and a central macro-economic policy will automatically generate the institutions, markets, and mobilities which make the system viable and its regional economic consequences everywhere tolerable. The risk is one that few are prepared to take. Moreover, EEC experience to date suggests that it is very hard to contrive a scenario of gradual evolution towards such a radically different regime, even though it could well be the global optimum.

At present the world enjoys many benefits of the increased worldwide economic integration of the last thirty years. But the integration is partial and unbalanced; in particular private financial markets have become internationalized much more rapidly and completely than other economic and political institutions. That is why we are in trouble. So I turn to the second, and second best, way out, forcing some segmentation of intercurrency financial markets.

My specific proposal is actually not new. I offered it in 1972 in my Janeway Lectures at Princeton, published in 1974 as *The New Economics One Decade Older* (pp. 88–92). The idea fell like a stone in a deep well. If I cast it in the water again, it is because events since the first try have strengthened my belief that something of the sort needs to be done.

The proposal is an internationally uniform tax on all spot conversions of one currency into another, proportional to the size of the transaction. The tax would particularly deter short-term financial round-trip excursions into another currency. A 1 per cent tax, for example, could be overcome only by an 8-point differential in the annual yields of Treasury bills or Eurocurrency deposits denominated in dollars and Deutschmarks. The corresponding differential for one-year maturities would be 2 points. A permanent investment in another country or currency area, with regular repatriation of yield when earned, would need a 2 per cent advantage in marginal efficiency over domestic investment. The impact of the tax would be less for permanent currency shifts, or for longer maturities. Because of exchange risks, capital value risks, and market imperfections, interest arbitrage and exchange speculation are less troublesome in long maturities. Moreover, it is desirable to obstruct as little as possible international movements of capital responsive to long-run portfolio preferences and profit opportunities.

Why do floating exchange rates not solve the problem? There are several reasons, all exemplified in recent experience. First, as economists have long known, in a world of international capital mobility flexibility of exchange rates does not assure autonomy of national macroeconomic policy. The Mundell–Fleming models of the early 1960s showed how capital mobility inhibits domestic monetary policy under fixed parities and domestic fiscal policy under flexible rates. Moreover, the availability of the remaining instrument of macroeconomic policy in either regime is small consolation. Nations frequently face compelling domestic institutional, political, and economic constraints on one or the other instrument, or on the policy mix.

Second, it may seem that we should welcome an exchange rate regime that increases the potency of monetary policy relative to fiscal policy; after all, monetary policy is the more flexible and responsive instrument of domestic stabilization. But the liberation of domestic monetary policy under flexible rates is in large degree illusory. One reason is the attachment of central bankers to monetarist targets irrespective of exchange rate regimes and the openness of financial markets. More fundamentally, monetary policy becomes, under floating rates, exchange rate policy. The stimulus of expansionary monetary policy to domestic demand is limited by the competition of foreign interest rates for mobile funds. Thus much – in the limit, all – of the stimulus depends on exchange depreciation and its effects on the trade balance, namely on shifting foreign and domestic demand to home goods and services. The depreciation may occur all right, but its effects on the trade balance can be perverse for a disconcertingly long short run, during which further depreciation, perhaps reinforced by speculation, occurs. Meanwhile the effects of depreciation on domestic currency prices of internationally traded goods are inflationary, even for an economy with idle resources and no domestic sources of inflationary pressure.

Furthermore, there are international difficulties in reliance on monetary policy in a floating rate regime. I quote from my 1972 lecture: 'When the export–import balance becomes the strategic component of aggregate demand, one country's expansionary stimulus is another country's deflationary shock. We can hardly imagine that the Common Market will passively allow the US to manipulate the dollar exchange rate in the interests of US domestic stabilization. Nor can we imagine the reverse. International coordination of interest rate policies will be essential in a regime of floating exchange rates, no less than in a fixed parity regime.' The bickering between Washington and Bonn about these issues in the last year is just what I had in mind.

Third, governments are not and cannot be indifferent to changes in the values of their currencies in exchange markets, any more than they did or could ignore changes in their international reserves under the fixed-parity regime. The reasons for their concern are not all macroeconomic; they include all the impacts on domestic industries, export and import-competing sectors, that arise from exchange rate fluctuations originating in financial and capital transactions. The uncoordinated interventions that make floating dirty are the governments' natural mechanisms of defense against shocks transmitted to their economies by foreign exchange markets.

Fourth, another optimistic hope belied by events was the belief that floating rates would insulate economies from shocks to export and import demand. The same Mundell–Fleming-type model that told us the relative impotence of fiscal policies and non-monetary demand shocks under floating rates also implied that trade balance shocks would be absorbed completely in exchange rates without adjustment of domestic output or prices. This will, of course, not be the case if the trade balance moves the wrong way (anti-Marshall–Lerner), or if, for any of the other understandable reasons enumerated above, governments intervene to prevent full exchange rate adjustment. It will not be the case anyway if exchange rate movements have consequences for asset demands and supplies, as they will, either via the capital gains or losses they produce for agents with long or short positions in foreign currency or via the expectations of future exchange rate movements which they generate.

The recent decline of the dollar against the Deutschmark, yen, and Swiss franc illustrates many of the above points. The US, on the one hand, and Germany and Japan on the other, clearly have divergent domestic histories, prospects, and objectives in terms of output growth and inflation. The changes in currency exchange rates have not served, as some proponents of flexible rates might have hoped, to permit these countries to pursue their differing policies without mutual interference. The Germans and Japanese have been reluctant to accept the effects of currency appreciation on their export industries, and so they have intervened to limit the appreciation. The Americans, concerned about the effects of depreciation on price indexes, have tightened monetary policy and raised interest rates in an attempt to stem the anti-dollar tide in the foreign exchange markets.

This history also supports the assertion I made above, that goods 'arbitrage' is very slow relative to inter-currency financial speculation and portfolio shift. The net result of exchange rate movements and domestic price movements over the past few years has been to improve dramatically the competitive position of the US *vis-à-vis* Germany and Japan. This is true when wholesale prices indices, converted to a single currency at prevailing exchange rates, are compared. Our trade-weighted real exchange rate is about 5 per cent below 1977 and March 1973, and more than 7 per cent below 1976. Germany's is 7 per cent above 1973, though still below 1976 and 1977. Japan's is 3 per cent above 1973, 7 per cent above 1976, and 2 per cent above 1977. The change is even more spectacular when labor costs are similarly compared. In 1970 US hourly labor costs, including fringe benefits, were the highest in the world, 67 per cent above Germany, 300 per cent above Japan. In 1977 five countries had higher costs at exchange rates prevailing in December. Our costs were 16 per cent below Germany, and now only 55 per cent above Japan.[1] The US is now a low-wage country! Yet we are suffering from the worst trade deficits in history.

I do not wish to be misunderstood. I think the hysteria over the recent decline of the dollar is greatly overdone, and that the panicky pressure on our government to defend the dollar – pressure from European governments, from financial circles here and abroad, from the media – has been most unjustified. Moreover, anyone who thinks that the pre-1971 system of pegged rates would have handled better the recent flight from the dollar into marks, yen, and Swiss francs has a very short memory. Things would have been lots worse, with greater impacts on US domestic policies and greater disruptions to international markets. My message is not, I emphasize again, that floating is the inferior regime. It is that floating does not satisfactorily solve all the problems.

One big reason why it does not is that foreign exchange markets are necessarily adrift without anchors. What we have is an incredibly efficient set of financial markets in which various obligations, mostly short-term, expressed in various currencies are traded. I mean the word 'efficient' only in a mechanical sense: transactions costs are low, communications are speedy, prices are instantaneously kept in line all over the world, credit enables participants to take large long or short positions at will or whim. Whether the market is 'efficient' in the deeper economic-informational sense is very dubious. In these markets, as in other markets for financial instruments, speculation on future prices is the dominating preoccupation of the participants. In the ideal world of rational expectations, the anthropomorphic personified 'market' would base its expectations on informed estimates of equilibrium exchange rates. Speculation would be the engine that moves actual rates to the equilibrium set. In fact no one has any good basis for estimating the equilibrium dollar–mark parity for 1980 or 1985,[2] to which current rates might be related. That parity depends on a host of incalculables – not just the future paths of the two economies and of the rest of the world, but the future portfolio preferences of the world's wealth-owners, including Arabs and Iranians as well as Americans and Germans. Reasonable economists and traders, not to mention unreasonable members of both species, can and do have diverse views. In the absence of any consensus on fundamentals, the markets are dominated – like those for gold, rare paintings, and, yes, often equities – by traders in the game of guessing what other traders are going to think.

As a technical matter, we know that a rational expectations equilibrium in markets of this kind is a saddle point. That is, there is only a singular path that leads from disequilibrium to equilibrium. If the markets are not on that path, or if they don't jump to it from wherever they are, they can follow any of a number of paths that lead away from equilibrium-paths along which, none the less, expectations are on average fulfilled. Such deviant paths are innocuous in markets – as for rare coins, precious metals, baseball cards, Swiss francs – which are sideshows to the real economic circus. But they are far from innocuous in foreign exchange markets whose prices are of major economic consequence.

This suggests that governments might contribute to exchange market efficiency by themselves calculating and publicizing estimates of equilibrium exchange rates, rates expected some years in future. The floating of the Canadian dollar in the 1950s was probably an empirical episode of considerable intellectual importance in solidifying economists' acceptance of the theoretical case for flexible rates. Floating rates had acquired a bad reputation, rightly or wrongly, in the interwar period. The Canadian experiment seemed to show that market speculation was stabilizing; certainly there were no gyrations greatly disturbing to Canadian–US economic relations or to the two economies. One reason, among others, appears to have been a general belief in a long-run equilibrium not far from dollar–dollar parity, an equilibrium that accorded both with the interconnected structures of the two economies and with the policy intentions of the Canadian government. Those who extrapolated from the model to the world-wide floating of the 1970s have been disappointed. It is scarcely conceivable that the various OECD countries could individually project, much less agree on, much less convince skeptical markets of, a system of equilibrium or target exchange rates for 1980 or 1985. So I must remain skeptical that the price signals these unanchored markets give are signals that will guide economies to their true comparative advantage, capital to its efficient international allocation, and governments to correct macroeconomic policies.

That is why I think we need to throw some sand in the well-greased wheels. Perhaps one might have hoped that the volatility of floating rates would do that automatically; given the limitations of futures markets, uncovered risks might permit wedges between national interest rates and currency diversification might limit intercurrency movements of funds. In my 1972 excursion into this subject I was skeptical on this point, and events since have vindicated my skepticism. I said, 'Increasing exchange risk will help, but I do not think we should expect too much from it. Many participants in short term money markets can afford to take a relaxed view of exchange risk. They can aim for the best interest rate available, taking account of their mean estimate of gain or loss from currency exchange. Multinational corporations, for example, can diversify over time. They will be in exchange markets again and again: there are no currencies they cannot use.'

Let me return to my proposed tax, and provide just a few more details. It would be an internationally agreed uniform tax, administered by each government over its own jurisdiction. Britain, for example, would be responsible for taxing all inter-currency transactions in Eurocurrency banks and brokers located in London, even when sterling was not involved. The tax proceeds could appropriately be paid into the IMF or World Bank. The tax would apply to all purchases of financial instruments denominated in another currency – from currency and coin to equity securities. It would have to apply, I think, to all payments in one currency for goods, services, and real assets sold by a resident of another currency area. I don't intend to add even a small barrier to trade. But I see offhand no other way to prevent financial transactions disguised as trade.

Countries could, possibly subject to IMF consent, form currency areas within which the tax would not apply. Presumably the smaller EEC members and those ldc's which wished to tie their currency to a key currency would wish to do this. The purpose is to moderate swings in major exchange rates, not to break links between closely related economies.

Doubtless there would be difficulties of administration and enforcement. Doubtless there would be ingenious patterns of evasion. But since these will not be costless either, the main purpose of the plan will not be lost. At least the bank facilities which are so responsible for the current troublesome perfection of these markets would be taxed, as would the multinational corporations.

I am aware of the distortions and allocational costs that can be attributed to tariffs, including tariffs on imports of foreign-currency assets. I don't deny their existence. I say only that they are small compared to the world macroeconomic costs of the present system. To those costs, I believe, will be added the burdens of much more damaging protectionist and autarkic measures designed to protect economies, at least their politically favored sectors, from the consequences of international financial shocks.

I do not want to claim too much for my modest proposal. It will, I think, restore to national economies and governments some fraction of the short-run autonomy they enjoyed before currency convertibility became so easy. It will not, should not, permit governments to make domestic policies without reference to external consequences. Consequently, it will not release major governments from the imperative necessity to coordinate policies more effectively. Together the major governments and central banks are making fiscal and monetary policy for the world, whether or not they explicitly recognize the fact. Recently, it is quite clear from the differences and misunderstandings among the so-called three locomotives, they have not been concerting their policies very successfully. I would hope that, relieved of the need to stay in lockstep in order to avoid large exchange rate fluctuations, these governments might approach the task of policy coordination with a longer-range and more global view of their responsibilities.

Notes

1. For these calculations, made at the Institut der Deutschen Wirtschaft, Koln, I am indebted to Professor Herbert Giersch.

2. As above.

References

The list of references is divided into two categories. 'Academic Publications' includes all works published in conventional academic journals or book series or as papers of research institutes. All other sources are in the second category, 'Other References', including analytic mimeos, papers published only on the web, documents, newspaper articles and more popular books. The distinction does not imply any value judgement. Many of the most important sources, both first hand and analytical, belong to the second category. The distinction is merely a conventional organising device.

Academic Publications

Abbott, Jason (1999): 'Mahathir, Malaysia and the Labuan International Offshore Centre: Treasure Island, Pet Project or Ghost Town?', in M. P. Hampton and J. P. Abbott (eds): *Offshore Finance Centres and Tax Havens. The Rise of Global Capital* (London: Macmillan), pp. 192–211.

Agenor, P., J. Bhandari and R. Flood (1992): 'Speculative Attacks and Models of Balance of Payments Crises', *IMF Staff Papers*, 39, pp. 357–94.

Amin, Ash (ed.) (1994): *Post-Fordism. A Reader* (Oxford: Blackwell).

Archibugi, Daniele (1995): 'From the United Nations to Cosmopolitan Democracy', in D. Archibugi and D. Held (eds): *Cosmopolitan Democracy. An Agenda for a New World Order* (Cambridge: Polity Press), pp. 121–62.

Arestis, Philip and Malcolm Sawyer (1997): 'How Many Cheers for the Tobin Transactions Tax?', *Cambridge Journal of Economics*, 21(6): 753–68.

Ashley, Richard K. (1984): 'The Poverty of Neorealism', *International Organization*, 38(2): 225–86.

—— (1989): 'Imposing International Purpose: Notes on a Problematic of Governance', in E.-O. Czempiel and J. Rosenau (eds): *Global Changes and Theoretical Challenges. Approaches to World Politics for the 1990s* (Lexington, MA: Lexington Books), pp. 251–90.

Bainbridge, Timothy, with A. Teasdale (1997): *The Penguin Companion to European Union* (London: Penguin).

Baker, Dean, Gerald Epstein and Robert Pollin (eds) 1998: *Globalization and Progressive Economic Policy* (Cambridge: Cambridge University Press).

Bannock, Graham, R. E. Baxter and David Evan (1998): *Penguin Dictionary of Economics*, 6th edn (London: Penguin).

Baudrillard, Jean (1993): 'The Evil Demon of Images and the Precession of Simulacra', in T. Docherty (ed.): *Postmodernism. A Reader* (New York: Prentice Hall), pp. 194–9.

Bauman, Zygmunt (1997): *Postmodernity and Its Discontents* (Cambridge: Polity Press).

Beck, Ulrich (1992): *Risk Society. Towards a New Modernity*, trans. M. Ritter (London: Sage).

Beddoes, Zanny Milton (1999): 'The International Financial System', *Foreign Policy* (Autumn 1999): 16–26.

Beitz, Charles (1979): *Political Theory and International Relations* (Princeton, NJ: Princeton University Press).

Bhaskar, Roy (1986): *Scientific Realism and Human Emancipation* (London: Verso).

— (1989): *Reclaiming Reality* (London: Verso).

— (1994): *Plato Etc. The Problems of Philosophy and Their Resolution* (London: Verso).

Bowles, Samuel and Herbert Gintis (1998): *Recasting Egalitarianism. New Rules for Communities, States and Markets. The Real Utopias Project, Volume III*, ed. E. O. Wright (London: Verso).

Brenner, Robert (1998): *The Economics of Global Turbulence*, special issue, *New Left Review*, 29.

Castells, Manuel (1996): *The Rise of the Network Society. The Information Age. Vol. I: Economy, Society and Culture* (Oxford: Blackwell).

Chavagneux, Christian (1999): 'On the Tobin Tax as a Bad Idea and Why It Should be Supported', in H. Patomäki (1999a): 'The Tobin Tax: How to Make It Real', UPI Working Papers 13 (Helsinki: UPI), pp. 12–13.

Collier, Andrew (1994): *Critical Realism. An Introduction to Roy Bhaskar's Philosophy* (London: Verso).

Cox, Robert W. (1987): *Production, Power, and World Order. Social Forces in the Making of History* (New York: Columbia University Press).

— (1997): 'Economic Globalization and the Limits to Liberal Democracy', in A. McGrew (ed.): *The Transformation of Democracy?* (Cambridge: Polity Press in association with the Open University), pp. 49–71.

Crawford, James and Susan Marks (1998): 'The Global Democracy Deficit: An Essay in International Law and Its Limits', in D. Archibugi, D. Held and M. Köhler (eds): *Re-imagining Political Community. Studies in Cosmopolitan Democracy* (Cambridge: Polity Press).

Crozier, M., S. Huntington and S. Watanuki (1975): *The Crisis of Democracy. Report on the Governability of Democracies to the Trilateral Commission* (New York: New York University Press).

Curley, Melissa, Frank Faulkner and Lloyd Pettiford (1999): 'Does the Security Debate Have to be Presented Polemically?: Landmines and the Case for a Micro-Security Approach', *Journal of Low Intensity Conflict*, 8(3): 1–21.

Deacon, Bob (1997): *Global Social Policy. International Organizations and the Future of Welfare*, with M. Hulse and P. Stubbs (London: Sage).

— (1999): 'The Tobin Tax and Global Social Policy', in H. Patomäki (1999a): 'The Tobin Tax: How to Make It Real', UPI Working Papers 13 (Helsinki: UPI), pp. 84–6.

Diez, Thomas (1998): 'Speaking "Europe": The Politics of Integration Discourse', COPRI Working Paper 26/1998.

Dreyfus, H. L. and P. Rabinow (1982): *Michel Foucault. Beyond Structuralism and Hermeneutics* (Brighton: Harvester Wheatsheaf).

Dryzek, John S. (1996): *Democracy in Capitalist Times. Ideals, Limits and Struggles* (Oxford: Oxford University Press).

Edey, Malcolm and Ketil Hviding (1995): 'An Assessment of Financial Reform in OECD Countries', OECD Economics Department Working Papers 154, OCDE/GD(95)60.

References 243

Edwards, Franklin R. (1999): 'Hedge Funds and the Collapse of Long-term Capital Management', *Journal of Economic Perspectives*, 13(2): 189–210.

Eichengreen, Barry and Albert Fishlow (1998): 'Contending with Capital Flows: What is Different About the 1990s?', in M. Kahler (ed.): *Capital Flows and Financial Crises* (Manchester: Manchester University Press), pp. 23–68.

Eichengreen, Barry and Charles Wyplosz (1996): 'Taxing International Financial Transactions to Enhance the Operation of the International Monetary System', in M. ul Haq et al. (eds): *The Tobin Tax. Coping with Financial Volatility* (Oxford: Oxford University Press), pp. 15–40.

Eichengreen, Barry, A. Rose and C. Wyplosz (1996): 'Contagious Currency Crises', *Scandinavian Journal of Economics*, 9(4): 463–84.

Eichengreen, Barry, James Tobin and Charles Wyplosz (1995): 'Two Cases for Sand in the Wheel in International Finance', *Economic Journal*, 105(1): 162–72.

Elster, Jon and Karl Ove Moene (1989): *Alternatives to Capitalism* (Cambridge: Cambridge University Press).

Esping-Andersen, Gøsta (1990): *The Three Worlds of Welfare Capitalism* (Cambridge: Polity Press).

Felix, David (1995a): 'The Tobin Tax Proposal: Background, Issues and Prospects', policy paper commissioned by UNDP for the World Summit for Social Development, Copenhagen, March 1995 (New York: UNDP Division of Public Affairs).

— (1995b): 'Financial Globalization versus Free Trade: The Case for the Tobin Tax', UNCTAD Discussion Papers 108 (Geneva).

Felix, David and Ranjit Sau (1996): 'On the Revenue Potential and Phasing in of the Tobin Tax', in M. ul Haq et al. (eds): *The Tobin Tax. Coping with Financial Volatility* (Oxford: Oxford University Press), pp. 223–54.

Fleetwood, Steve (ed.) (1989): *Critical Realism in Economics. Development and Debate* (London: Routledge).

Foucault, Michel (1979): *Discipline and Punish. The Birth of the Prison*, trans. A. Sheridan (London: Penguin Books).

Frankel, Jeffrey (1996): 'How Well Do Foreign Exchange Markets Work: Might a Tobin Tax Help?', in M. ul Haq et al. (eds): *The Tobin Tax. Coping with Financial Volatility* (Oxford: Oxford University Press), pp. 41–81.

Friedman, Milton (1953a): 'The Methodology of Positive Economics', in M. Friedman: *Essays in Positive Economics* (Chicago: University of Chicago Press), pp. 3–43.

— (1953b): 'The Case for Flexible Exchange Rates', in M. Friedman: *Essays in Positive Economics* (Chicago: University of Chicago Press), pp. 157–203.

— (1974): 'A Theoretical Framework for Monetary Analysis', in R. J. Gordon (ed.): *Milton Friedman's Monetary Framework. A Debate with His Critics* (Chicago: University of Chicago Press), pp. 1–62.

Garber, Peter M. (1996): 'Issues of Enforcement and Evasion in a Tax on Foreign Exchange Transactions', in M. ul Haq et al. (eds): *The Tobin Tax. Coping with Financial Volatility* (Oxford: Oxford University Press), pp. 129–42.

Garber, Peter and Mark P. Taylor (1995): 'Sand in the Wheels of Foreign Exchange Markets: A Sceptical Note', *Economic Journal*, 105(1): 173–80.

George, Susan and Fabrizio Sabelli (1994): *Faith and Credit. The World Bank's Secular Empire* (London: Penguin).

Giddens, Anthony (1985): *The Nation-State and Violence. Volume Two of a Contemporary Critique of Historical Materialism* (Cambridge: Polity Press).

— (1990): *Consequences of Modernity* (Cambridge: Polity Press).

— (1991): *Modernity and Self-Identity* (Cambridge: Polity Press).

— (1998): *The Third Way. The Renewal of Social Democracy* (Cambridge: Polity Press).

Gill, Stephen (1994): 'Knowledge, Politics, and Neo-Liberal Political Economy', in R. Stubbs and G. Underhill (eds):*Political Economy and the Changing Global Order* (London: Macmillan), pp. 75–88.

— (1995a): 'Globalisation, Market Civilisation and Disciplinary Neoliberalism', *Millennium: Journal of International Studies*, 24(3): 399–423.

— (1995b): 'The Global Panopticon?: The Neo-Liberal State, Economic Life and Democratic Surveillance', *Alternatives*, 20(1): 1–49.

— (1997a): 'An Emu or an Ostrich? EMU and the Neo-liberal Economic Integration: Limits and Alternatives', in P. Minkkinen and H. Patomäki (eds): *Politics of Economic and Monetary Union* (Dordrecht: Kluwer), pp. 207–31.

— (1997b): 'Analysing New Forms of Authority: New Constitutionalism, Panopticism and Market Civilization', paper presented at the conference 'Non-State Actors and Authority in the Global System', Warwick University, 31 October–1 November 1997.

— (1999): 'The Constitution of Global Capitalism', paper presented at the Annual Conference of the British International Studies Association, University of Manchester, 20–22 December 1999.

Gilpin, Robert (1981): *War and Change in World Politics* (Cambridge: Cambridge University Press).

Gowan, Peter (1999): *The Global Gamble. Washington's Faustian Bid for World Dominance* (London: Verso).

Grahl, John (1991): 'Economies Out of Control', *New Left Review*, 185: 170–83.

Griffith-Jones, Stephany (1996): 'Institutional Arrangements for a Tax on International Currency Transactions', in M. ul Haq et al. (eds): *The Tobin Tax. Coping with Financial Volatility* (Oxford: Oxford University Press), pp. 143–58.

Grunberg, Isabelle (1990): 'Exploring the "Myth" of Hegemonic Stability', *International Organization*, 44(4): 431–77.

Guzzini, Stefano (1993): 'Structural Power: The Limits of Neorealist Power Analysis', *International Organization*, 47(3): 443–78.

Hampton, M. P. and J. P. Abbott (eds) (1999): *Offshore Finance Centres and Tax Havens: The Rise of Global Capital* (London: Macmillan).

Harmes, Adam (1998): 'Institutional Investors and the Reproduction of Neoliberalism', *Review of International Political Economy*, 5(1): 92–121.

Harvey, David (1990): *The Condition of Postmodernity* (Oxford: Blackwell).

Held, David (1995): *Democracy and the Global Order. From the Modern State to Cosmopolitan Governance* (Cambridge: Polity Press).

— (1996): *Models of Democracy*, 2nd edn (Stanford, CA: Stanford University Press).

Helleiner, Eric (1994): *States and the Reemergence of Global Finance* (Ithaca, NY: Cornell University Press).

Henwood, Doug (1997): *Wall Street. How It Works and For Whom?* (London: Verso).

Herman, Edward S. and Robert W. McChesney (1997): *The Global Media. The New Missionaries of Corporate Capitalism* (London: Cassell).

Hettne, Björn (1993): 'Neo-Mercantilism: The Pursuit of Regionness', *Cooperation and Conflict*, 28(3): 211–32.

Hills, Richard (1996): *Hedge Funds. An Introduction to Skill Based Investment Strategies* (Leighton: Rushmere Wynne).

Hirst, Paul and Grahame Thompson (1999): *Globalization in Question*, 2nd edn (Cambridge: Polity Press).

Hodgson, Geoffrey (1988): *Economics and Institutions* (Cambridge: Polity Press in association with Blackwell).

Holesovsky, Vaclav (1977): *Economic Systems. Analysis and Comparison* (New York: McGraw-Hill).

Hudson, Alan C. (1998): 'Placing Trust, Trusting Place: On the Social Construction of Offshore Financial Centres', *Political Geography*, 17(8): 915–37.

Ikenberry, John G. (1992): 'A World Economy Restored: Expert Consensus and the Anglo-American Postwar Settlement', *International Organization*, 46: 289–321.

Imber, Mark (1997): 'Geo-Governance without Democracy? Reforming the UN System', in A. McGrew (ed.): *The Transformation of Democracy?* (Cambridge: Polity Press in association with the Open University), pp. 201–30.

Jarrow, Robert and Stuart Turnbull (1996): *Derivative Securities* (Cincinnati, OH: South-Western College Publishing).

Kahler, Miles (1998): 'Introduction: Capital Flows and Financial Crises in the 1990s', in M. Kahler (ed.): *Capital Flows and Financial Crises* (Manchester: Manchester University Press), pp. 1–22.

Kanninen, Tapio (1995): *Leadership and Reform. The Secretary-General and the UN Financial Crisis of the Late 1980s* (The Hague: Kluwer).

Kant, Immanuel (1983/1793): 'On the Proverb: That May be True in Theory, But is of No Practical Use', in I. Kant: *Perpetual Peace and Other Essays*, trans. by Ted Humphrey (Indianapolis: Hackett Publishing Company), pp. 61–92.

Kaul, Inge, Isabelle Grunberg and Mahbub ul Haq (1996): 'Overview', in M. ul Haq et al. (eds): *The Tobin Tax. Coping with Financial Volatility* (Oxford: Oxford University Press), pp. 1–12.

Kenen, Peter B. (1996): 'The Feasibility of Taxing Foreign Exchange Transactions', in M. ul Haq et al. (eds): *The Tobin Tax. Coping with Financial Volatility* (Oxford: Oxford University Press), pp. 111–28.

Keohane, Robert O. (1980): 'The Theory of Hegemonic Stability and Changes in International Economic Regimes 1967–1977', in O. R. Holsti et al. (eds): *Change in the International System* (Boulder, CO: Westview Press), pp. 131–62.

Keynes, John Maynard (1961/1936): *The General Theory of Employment, Interest and Money* (London: Macmillan).

Kindleberger, Charles P. (1981): 'Dominance and Leadership in the International Economy: Exploitation, Public Goods and Free Riders', *International Studies Quarterly* 25(2): 242–54.

Korten, David C. (1997): *Maailma yhtiöiden vallassa* [When Corporations Rule the World], trans. T. Norkola (Helsinki: Like).

Koskenniemi, Martti (1989): *From Apology to Utopia. The Structure of International Legal Argument* (Helsinki: Lakimiesliiton Kustannus).

Krugman, Paul (1979): 'A Model of Balance of Payments Crisis', *Journal of Credit, Money and Banking*, 11: 311–25.

— (1999a): *The Return of Depression Economics* (London: Allen Lane/Penguin).

Kymlicka, Will (1999): 'Citizenship in an Era of Globalization: Commentary on Held', in I. Shapiro and C. Hacker-Cordón (eds): *Democracy's Edges* (Cambridge: Cambridge University Press), pp. 112–26.

Latham, Robert (2000): 'States, Globalization and Social Sovereignty', *Theory, Culture and Society*, 17(4): 1–18.

Lawson, Tony (1997): *Economics and Reality* (Routledge: London).

Leander, Anna and Stefano Guzzini (1997): 'Economic and Monetary Union and the Crisis of European Social Contracts', in P. Minkkinen and H. Patomäki (eds): *The Politics of Economic and Monetary Union* (Dordrecht: Kluwer), pp. 133–63.

Leyshon, Andrew and Nigel Thrift (1997): *MoneySpace. Geographies of Monetary Transformation* (London: Routledge).

Livingston, Steven G. (1992): 'The Politics of International Agenda-Setting: Reagan and North–South Relations', *International Studies Quarterly*, 36(3): 313–30.

McCloskey, Donald (1986): *The Rhetoric of Economics* (Brighton: Wheatsheaf).

Martin, Hans-Peter and Harald Schumann (1997): *The Global Trap. Globalization and the Assault on Democracy and Prosperity*, trans. Patrick Camiller (London and New York: Zed Books).

Martin, Pierre (1994): 'The Politics of International Structural Change: Aggressive Unilateralism in American Trade Policy', in R. Stubbs and G. Underhill (eds): *Political Economy and the Changing Global Order* (London: Macmillan), pp. 439–51.

Marx, Karl (1980/1894): *Pääoma 3. Kapitalistisen tuotannon kokonaisprosessi*, trans. A. Tiusanen (Moscow: Progress).

Maynes, Charles William (1999): 'US Unilateralism and Its Dangers', *Review of International Studies* 25(3): 515–18.

Michalos, Alex C. (1997): *Good Taxes. The Case for Taxing Foreign Currency Exchange and Other Financial Transactions* (Toronto: Dundurn Press).

Minkkinen, Petri and Heikki Patomäki (eds) (1997a): *The Politics of Economic and Monetary Union* (Dordrecht: Kluwer).

— (1997b): *Yhdentymisen ja rahaunionin politiikkaa. Suomi ja Emu globaalissa poliittisessa taloudessa* (Helsinki: Like).

Minsky, Hyman P. (1982): *Can 'It' Happen Again?* (Armonk, NY: M. E. Sharpe).

Obstfeld, M. (1996): 'Models of Currency Crises with Self-Fulfilling Features', *European Economic Review*, 40: 1037–47.

O'Neill, Onora (1991): 'Transnational Justice', in D. Held (ed.): *Political Theory Today* (Cambridge: Polity Press), pp. 276–304.

Ormerod, Paul (1994): *The Death of Economics* (London: Faber and Faber).

Palan, Ronen (1998): 'Trying to Have Your Cake and Eating It: How and Why the State System Has Created Offshore', *International Studies Quarterly*, 42(4): 625–44.

— (1999a): 'Offshore and the Structural Enablement of Sovereignty', in M. P. Hampton and J. P. Abbott (eds): *Offshore Finance Centres and Tax Havens. The Rise of Global Capital* (London: Macmillan), pp. 18–42.

— (1999b): 'Offshore', in H. Patomäki (1999a): 'The Tobin Tax: How to Make It Real', UPI Working Papers 13 (Helsinki: UPI), pp. 42–4.

— (forthcoming): *International Relations in the Age of Offshore: Fictional Spaces and the Market for Sovereignty*.

Patomäki, Heikki (1991): 'Concepts of "Action", "Structure" and "Power" in "Critical Social Realism": A Positive and Reconstructive Critique', *Journal for the Theory of Social Behaviour*, 21(2): 221–50.

— (1992a): 'From Normative Utopias to Political Dialectics: Beyond a Deconstruction of the Brown–Hoffman Debate', *Millennium: Journal of International Studies*, 21(1): 53–75.

— (1992b): *Maailmamme rajat* (Tampere: Rauhantutkimusyhdistys).

— (1992c): 'Scientific Realism, Human Emancipation and Non-Violent Political Action', *Gandhi Marg*, 14(1): 30–51.

— (1996): 'How to Tell Better Stories About World Politics', *European Journal of International Relations*, 2(1): 105–33.

— (1999a): 'The Tobin Tax: How to Make it Real', NIGD Project Report, prepared in co-operation with Katarina Sehm Patomäki and C. Chavagneux, B. Deacon, A. Harnes, M. Montes, R. Palan and D. Woodward. UPI Working Papers 13 (Helsinki: UPI).

— (1999b): 'Good Governance of the World Economy?', *Alternatives*, 24(1): 119–42.

— (1999c): *Tobinin veron toteutus. Kohti oikeudenmukaisempaa ja demokraattisempaa globaalia taloutta* (Helsinki: Like).

— (2000a): 'Republican Public Sphere and the Governance of Global Political Economy', in M. Lensu and J.-S. Fritz (eds): *Value Pluralism, Normative Theory and International Relations* (London: Macmillan), pp. 160–95.

— (2000b): 'Beyond Nordic Nostalgia: Envisaging a Social/Democratic System of Global Governance', *Cooperation and Conflict*, 35(2): 115–54.

— (2000c): 'The Tobin Tax: A New Phase in the Politics of Globalisation?', *Theory, Culture and Society*, 17(4); reproduced in H. Hakovirta (ed.): *Globalism at the Crossroads. Wedges into Global Theory and Policy* (Helsinki: Finnish Political Science Association), pp. 166–84; a translation of an earlier version was published in Indonesian, as 'Pajak Tobin: Sebuah Fase Baru dalam Politik Globalisasi', in *Wacana*, 4 (1999): 96–116.

Patomäki, Heikki and Christer Pursiainen (1999): 'Western Models and the Russian Idea: Beyond Inside/Outside in the Discourses on Civil Society', *Millennium: Journal of International Studies*, 28(1): 53–77.

Patomäki, Heikki and Colin Wight (2000): 'After Post-Positivism: The Promises of Critical Realism', *International Studies Quarterly*, 43(2): 213–37.

Patterson, B. and M. Galliano (1999) 'The Feasibility of an International "Tobin Tax"', European Parliament Working Papers 107, Economic Affairs Series, Luxembourg.

Petras, James and Morley Morris (2000): 'Contesting Hegemons: US–French Relations in the "New World Order"', *Review of International Studies*, 26(1): 49–67.

Picciotto, Sol (1999): 'Offshore: The State as Legal Fiction', in M. P. Hampton and J. P. Abbott (eds)*Offshore Finance Centres and Tax Havens. The Rise of Global Capital* (London: Macmillan), pp. 43–79.

Polanyi, Karl (1957/1944): *The Great Transformation. The Political and Economic Origins of Our Time* (Boston, MA: Beacon Press).

Potter, David (1997): 'Explaining Democratization', in D. Potter et al. (eds): *Democratization* (Cambridge: Polity Press), pp. 1–40.

Rawls, John (1958): 'Justice as Fairness', *Philosophical Review*, LXVII: 164–94.

— (1973): *A Theory of Justice* (Oxford: Oxford University Press).

Risse, Thomas et al. (1997): 'Identity Politics in the European Union: The Case of Economic and Monetary Union', in P. Minkkinen and H. Patomäki (eds): *The Politics of Economic and Monetary Union* (Dordrecht: Kluwer), pp. 105–32.

Robertson, J. (1999): *The New Economics of Sustainable Development: A Briefing for Policy Makers* (London: Kogan Page).

Robinson College Working Group (1999): 'An Agenda for a New Bretton Woods', *International Papers in Political Economy* (University of East London), 6(1).

Sayer, Andrew (1992): *Method in Social Science. A Realist Approach*, 2nd edn (London: Routledge).

Shome, Parthasarathi and Janet G. Stotsky (1995): 'Financial Transactions Taxes', IMF Working Papers/95/77 (August).

Sinclair, Timothy (1994): 'Passing Judgement: Credit Rating Processes as Regulatory Mechanisms of Governance in the Emerging World Order', *Review of International Political Economy*, 1(1): 133–59.

Singh, Ajit (1999): '"Asian Capitalism" and the Financial Crisis', in J. Michie and J. G. Smith (eds)*Global Instability. The Political Economy of World Economic Governance* (London: Routledge), pp. 9–36.

Singh, Kavaljit (1999): *The Globalisation of Finance. A Citizen's Guide* (London: Zed Books).

Södersten, Bo and Geoffrey Reed (1994): *International Economics*, 3rd edn, rev. G. Reed (London: Macmillan).

Spahn, Paul Bernard (1995): 'International Financial Flows and Transactions Taxes: Survey and Options', IMF Working Papers 95/60 (June).

— (1996): 'The Tobin Tax and Exchange Rate Stability', *Finance and Development*, 33(2), downloaded from http://www.worldbank.org/fandd/english/0696/articles/0130696. htm

Stiglitz, Joseph E. (1989): 'Using Tax Policy to Curb Speculative Short-Term Trading', *Journal of Financial Services Research*, 1(3): 101–15.

— (1992): 'Capital Markets and Economic Fluctuations in Capitalist Economies', *European Economic Review*, 36: 269–306.

Stiglitz, Joseph E. and Andrew Weiss (1981): 'Credit Rationing in Markets with Imperfect Information', *American Economic Review*, 71(3): 393–410.

— (1983): 'Incentive Effects of Terminations: Applications to the Credit and Labor Markets', *American Economic Review*, 73(5): 912–27.

Stotsky, Janet G. (1996): 'Counterpoint. Why a Two-Tier Tobin Tax Won't Work', *Finance and Development*, 33(2), downloaded from http://www.worldbank.org/ fandd/english/0696/articles/0140696.htm

Strange, Susan (1986): *Casino Capitalism* (Oxford: Blackwell).

— (1987): 'The Persistent Myth of Lost Hegemony', *International Organization*, 41(3): 551–74.

— (1998): *Mad Money* (Manchester: Manchester University Press).

Teivainen, Teivo (1995): 'Politics of Economism and Containment of Changes in the Global Political Community', in H. Patomäki (ed.): *Peaceful Changes in World Politics* (Tampere: Tapri), pp. 81–121.

Thrift, Nigel J. (1983): 'On the Determination of Social Action in Space and Time', *Environment and Planning D: Society and Space*, 1(1): 23–57.

Tobin, James (1974a): *The New Economics One Decade Older. The Eliot Janeway Lectures in Honour of Joseph Schumpeter* (Princeton, NJ: Princeton University Press).

— (1974b): 'Friedman's Theoretical Framework', in R. J. Gordon (ed.): *Milton Friedman's Monetary Framework. A Debate with His Critics* (Chicago: University of Chicago Press), pp. 1–62.

— (1978): 'A Proposal for International Monetary Reform', *Eastern Economic Journal*, 4(3–4): 153–9.

— (1993): 'Price Flexibility and Output Stability: An Old Keynesian View', *Journal of Economic Perspectives*, 7(1): 45–65.

— (1996a): 'Prologue', in M. ul Haq et al. (eds): *The Tobin Tax. Coping with Financial Volatility* (Oxford: Oxford University Press) pp. ix–xviii.

— (1996b): 'A Currency Transactions Tax, Why and How?', *Open Economies Review*, 7: 493–99.

— (1997a): 'Foreword', in Stephany Griffith-Jones: *Global Capital Flows. Should They Be Regulated?* (London: Macmillan), pp. xi–xv.

— (1998a): *Money, Credit and Capital* (Boston, MA: McGraw-Hill).

Tuathail, Gearóid Ó (1996): *Critical Geopolitics. The Politics of Writing Global Space* (London: Routledge).

Ul Haq et al. (eds) (1996): *The Tobin Tax. Coping with Financial Volatility* (Oxford: Oxford University Press).

Unger, Roberto Mangabeira (1987): *Social Theory: Its Situation and Its Task* (Cambridge: Cambridge University Press).

— (1998): *Democracy Realized. The Progressive Alternative* (London: Verso).

Useem, Michael (1989): *Investor Capitalism. How Money Managers are Changing the Face of Corporate America* (New York: Basic Books).

Valdez, Stephen (1997): *An Introduction to Global Financial Markets*, rev. edn (London: Macmillan).

Veseth, Michael (1998): *Selling Globalization. The Myth of the Global Economy* (Boulder, CO: Lynne Rienner).

Walker, R. B. J. (1993): *Inside/Outside: International Relations as Political Theory* (Cambridge: Cambridge University Press).

Walter, Andrew (1993): *World Power and World Money*, rev. edn (Brighton: Harvester Wheatsheaf).

Weber, Max (1978/1922): *Economy and Society. Volume One*, ed. G. Roth and C. Wittich (Berkeley, CA: University of California Press).

Weiss, Linda (1998): *The Myth of the Powerless State* (Ithaca, NY: Cornell University Press).

Woodward, David (1999): 'Global Intervention Fund', in H. Patomäki (1999a): 'The Tobin Tax: How to Make It Real', UPI Working Papers 13 (Helsinki: UPI), pp. 54–6.

Other References

Antweiler, Werner (2000): 'Pacific Exchange Rate Service' at http://pacific.commerce.ubc.ca/xr/

Bello, Walden, Kamal Malhotra, Nicola Bullard and Marco Mezzera (1999): 'Notes on the Ascendancy and Regulation of Speculative Capital', paper prepared for the conference on Economic Sovereignty in a Globalizing World, Chulalongkorn University, Bangkok, 23–26 March 1999.

BIS (Bank for International Settlements) (1996): *Central Bank Survey of Foreign Exchange and Derivatives Market Activity 1995* (Basle: BIS/Monetary and Economic Department, May 1996).

— (1999a): *Central Bank Survey of Foreign Exchange and Derivatives Market Activity 1998* (Basle: BIS/Monetary and Economic Department, May 1999).

— (1999b): *Bank for International Settlements 69th Annual Report 1 April 1998–31 March 1999* (Basle: BIS, 7 June 1999).

Boutros-Ghali, Boutros (1996): *An Agenda for Democratization* (New York: United Nations).

— (1999): *Unvanquished. A U.S.–U.N. Saga* (London: I.B.Tauris).

Brown, Gordon (1998): 'Statement by the Hon. Gordon Brown, Governor of the Fund and Alternate Governor of the Bank for the United Kingdom, at the Joint Annual

Discussion of the IMF', downloaded from http://www.imf.org/EXTERNAL/ AM/ 1998/speeches/PR54GBE.pdf

Business Day – News, Information, Analysis, 'EU ministers confident euro will rise' (18 July 2000), available at http://www.bday.co.za/bday/content/direct/0,3523,631278–6078–0,00.html

Bustelo, Pablo (1998): 'The East Asian Crisis: An Analytic Survey', mimeo, available at http://www.ucm.es/info/icei/asia/bwp98.pdf

Chossudovsky, Michel (1998): ' "Financial warfare" Triggers Global Economic Crisis', mimeo, available at http://www.twnside.org.sg/souths/twn/title/trig-cn.htm

Clinton, Bill (1998): 'Remarks by the President to Opening Ceremony of the 1998 International Monetary Fund/World Bank Annual Meeting', White House Press Release, 6 October 1998.

Commission (of the European Communities) (1970): *Report to the Council and the Commission on the Realisation of the Stages of Economic and Monetary Union in the Community* (the Werner Report), Supplement to Bulletin 11–1970 of the European Communities.

Commission on Global Governance (1995): *Our Global Neighbourhood. The Report* (Oxford: Oxford University Press).

ECOSOC, 'Managing Risks of Globalization Great Challenge to Modern Times, Secretary-General Tell Economic and Social Council', ECOSOC Press Release 5812, 3 February 1999.

Friedman, Thomas (1999): *The Lexus and the Olive Tree* (London: HarperCollins).

de Goede, Marieke (1999): 'Finance, Gambling and Speculation: The Politics of Risk and Uncertainty', paper presented at the LSE conference 'The Politics of Financial Globalisation', 20 September 1999.

The Green/EFA Group in the EP (2000): 'Conservative * Liberal - UK Socialists alliance blocks exploring new ways in taxation policy. Greens deplore rejection of Tobin Tax by the European Parliament', press release, Strasbourg, 20 January.

Hayat, Khalid H. (1999): 'International Financial Liberalisation: Implications for Social Democratic Economic Policy', mimeo (University of Warwick), 1 September, presented at the LSE conference 'The Politics of Financial Globalisation', 20 September 1999.

Hayward, Helen (1999): 'The Global Gamblers. British Banks and the Foreign Exchange Game', mimeo, printed and distributed by War on Want, London.

— (2000a): 'Costing the Casino. The Real Impact of Currency Speculation in the 1990s', mimeo, printed and distributed by War on Want, London.

— (2000b): 'Offshore Financial Markets', mimeo, printed and distributed by War on Want, London.

Heong, Chee Yoke (1998): 'Malaysia: Mahathir Counts on Asia Amid Capital Controls', *IPS*, 18 December 1998.

IMF (International Monetary Fund) (1998a): *Annual Report 1998* (Washington, DC: IMF).

— (1998b): *World Economic Outlook* (Washington, DC: IMF, May 1998).

— (1999): *World Economic Outlook* (Washington, DC: IMF, October 1999).

James, Barry (2000): 'Tax Havens Face OECD Threat of Sanctions', *International Herald Tribune*, 14 June 2000.

Khor, Martin (1998): 'Hedge-fund crisis shatters myths', *Third World Economics*, 195 (16–30 October), available at http://www.southside.org.sg/souths/twn/title/myths-cn.htm

Krugman, Paul (1998): 'What Happened to Asia?', mimeo, available at http://web.mit. edu/krugman/www/DISINTER.html

— (1999b): 'Deflationary Spirals', mimeo, available at http://web.mit.edu/krugman/ www/spiral.html

Langmore, John (2000): 'A turning point towards global social development?', speech delivered at Geneva UN Summit, June 2000, available at http://www.un.org/esa/ socdev/geneva2000/issues/is9.htm

McLean, Bethany (1998): 'Everybody's Going Hedge Funds', *Fortune*, 8 June 1998, pp. 177–84.

Mann, Catherine L. (1998): 'The IMF, Moral Hazard, and Market-oriented Solutions to International Financial Crises' (Washington, DC: Institute for International Economics), 11 September 1998.

Michalos, Alex (2000): 'A Handful of Sand in the Wheels of Financial Speculation', paper for the conference 'New Rules for the New Millennium' (sponsored by Mani Tese), Florence, 18–19 March 2000; an earlier version appeared in B. K. McLean (1999) (ed.): *Out of Control: Canada in an Unstable Financial World* (Toronto: Canadian Centre for Policy Alternatives and James Lorimer and Co.), pp. 145–59, available at http://www.attac.org/fra/list/doc/michalos05.htm

OECD (1996): 'Government Policies Towards Financial Markets', OECD Working Papers, IV(83) (Paris: OECD).

Patomäki, Heikki (1997): 'Yhden viidesosan yhteiskunta' [One-Fifth Society], book review of Swedish edn of Hans-Peter Martin and Harald Schumann: *Globalizierungsgefälle*, *Helsingin Sanomat*, 5 August 1997.

— (1998): 'Tobinin vero iskee spekulaatiotalouteen' [Tobin Tax Hits the Core of the Speculative Economy], *Kumppani*, 6(98): 10–12.

Plender, John (2000): 'High Anxiety. Economists See People as Automata. But in Financial Crises We Can be All Too Human', *Financial Times Weekend*, 1 January 2000, pp. 29–31.

Raghavan, Chakravarthi (1998): 'BIS Banks Kept Shovelling Funds to Asia, Despite Warnings', *Third World Economics*, 177, 16–31 January 1998.

Ramonet, Ignacio (1997): 'Désarmer les marchés', *Le Monde Diplomatique* (December).

Reddy, C. Rammanohar (2000): 'Development: A Leopard and Its Spots', *The Hindu*, redistributed via South–North Development Monitor SUNS in the stop-IMF e-mail discussion list on 16 July 2000.

Roubini, Nouriel (1999): 'Chronology of the Asian Currency Crisis and Its Global Contagion', available at http//www.stern.nyu.edu/~nroubini/asia/AsiaHomepage. html

Sachs, Jeffrey (1999): 'Going for Broke. After Repeated Financial Fiascos, It's Time to Bring the IMF to Book', *Guardian*, 16 January 1999.

Schmidt, Rodney (1999): 'A Feasible Foreign Exchange Transactions Tax', paper written for the North–South Institute, available at http://sierraclub.com/canada/national/ halifax/Issues_info/Tobin_Tax/currspec.htm

Soros, George (1998): *The Crisis of Global Capitalism. Open Society Endangered* (New York: Public Affairs).

South Centre (1997): *For a Strong and Democratic United Nations. A South Perspective on UN Reform* (London: Zed Books in association with South Centre).

Stevenson, Richard W. (1999): 'Outspoken Chief Economist Leaving World Bank', *New York Times*, 25 November 1999.

Stiglitz, Joseph E. (1998a): 'More Instruments and Broader Goals: Moving Toward the Post-Washington Consensus', WIDER Annuel Lectures 2 (Helsinki: UNU/WIDER), available at http://www.wider.unu.edu/plec981.htm

— (1998b): 'Must Financial Crises be This Frequent and This Painful?', the McKay Lecture in Pittspurgh, Pennsylvania, 23 September 1998, available at http://www.worldbank.org/html/extdr/extme/js-092398/index.htm

Tobin, James (1997b): 'Why We Need Sand in the Market's Gears', Editorial, *Washington Post*, 21 December 1997.

— (1998b): 'Lutter contre cette idée que le marché fera tout bien, en toutes circonstances. James Tobin, Prix Nobel d'économie', interview, *Le Monde*, 17 November 1998.

— (1999a): 'What kind of Socially Responsible Economy Do We Want?', a videoconferenced talk in a 'Parliamentarians–NGOs Conference', 'Market-Oriented Society, Democracy, Citizenship and Solidarity: An Area of Confrontation?', Strasbourg, 31 May–1 June 1999, published in the proceedings, Council of Europe Publishing: Strasbourg, pp. 42–5.

— (1999b): 'Reigning in the Markets', an interview with James Tobin, *Information Access Company/UNESCO (France) Courier*, 1 February 1999; available also at http://www.igc.apc.org/globalpolicy/socecon/glotax/currtax/cur7_2.htm

Toh, Eddie (1999): 'The Jury is Still Out on the Malaysian Experiment', *BT (Business Times Singapore) Online*, 30 August 1999.

UNCTAD (1998): *Trade and Development Report, 1998. Financial Instability, Growth in Africa* (New York: UN).

— (1999): *World Investment Report. Foreign Direct Investment and the Challenge of Development* (New York: UN).

UNDP (1999): *Human Development Report 1999* (New York: UNDP and Oxford University Press).

Watson, Matthew (1998): 'The "Common Sense" of "Market Rationality": Neo-liberal Lock-in Effects and the "Privatisation" of Debt-financed Growth Regimes', paper presented at the Annual BISA Conference, University of Sussex, Brighton, 14–16 December 1998.

Weiss, Linda (1999): 'Beyond Neoliberal Globalism: Review Article', *New Left Review*, 238, November/December 1999: 26–40.

World Bank (1997): *World Development Report. The State in a Changing World* (Oxford: Oxford University Press).

Articles from

AFP News, The Banker, Business Times Singapore, The Economist, Financial Times, Guardian, Helsingin Sanomat, Investors Chronicle, Taloussanomat, Wall Street Journal

Index

Index

This book is also available in the following countries

Bangladesh
The University Press Ltd
Red Crescent Building, 114 Motijheel C/A, PO Box 2611, Dhaka 1000
tel: 880 2 956 5441; fax: 880 2 956 5443

Fiji
University Book Centre
University of South Pacific, Suva
tel: 679 313 900; fax: 679 303 265

Ghana
EPP Book Services
PO Box TF 490, Trade Fair, Accra
tel: 233 21 773087, fax: 233 21 779099

India
Segment Book Distributors
B-23/25 Kailash Colony, New Delhi
tel: 91 11 644 3013; fax: 91 11 647 0472

Mozambique
Sul Sensacoes
PO Box 2242, Maputo
tel: 258 1 421974; fax: 258 1 423414

Nepal
Everest Media Services
GPO Box 5443, Dillibazar, Putalisadak Chowk, Kathmandu
tel: 977 1 416026; fax: 977 1 250176

Pakistan
Vanguard Books
45 The Mall, Lahore
tel: 92 42 735 5079; fax: 92 42 735 5197

Papua New Guinea
Unisearch PNG Pty Ltd
Box 320, University, National Capital District
tel: 675 326 0130; fax: 675 326 0127

South Africa
Institute for Policy & Social Research
41 Salt River Road, Salt River 7925, Cape Town
tel: 27 21 448 7458; fax: 27 21 448 0757

Tanzania
TEMA Publishing Co Ltd
PO Box 63115, Dar Es Salaam
tel: 255 51 113608; fax: 255 51 110472

Thailand
White Lotus
GPO Box 1141, Bangkok 10501
tel: 66 2 741 6288; fax: 66 2 741 6607

Uganda
Aristoc Booklex Ltd
PO Box 5130, Kampala Road, Diamond Trust Building, Kampala
tel/fax: 256 41 254867

Zambia
UNZA Press
PO Box 32379, Lusaka
tel: 260 1 290409; fax: 260 1 253952

Zed Titles on Globalization

The ongoing headlong rush towards an economically much more integrated world – which is usually referred to as globalization – is intimately connected to the changing nature of capitalism and to one strand of economic theory and policy which is currently dominant, neoliberalism. Zed Books has published an extensive and growing list of titles which explore these processes and changes from a variety of perspectives.

Samir Amin, *Capitalism in the Age of Globalization: The Management of Contemporary Society*

Robert Biel, *The New Imperialism: Crisis and Contradictions in North–South Relations*

Walden Bello, Nicola Bullard, Kamal Malhotra (eds), *Global Finance: New Thinking on Regulating Speculative Capital Markets*

Christian Comeliau, *Impasses of the Market Society*

Carlos M. Correa, *Intellectual Property Rights, the WTO and Developing Countries: The TRIPS Agreement and Policy Options*

Peter Custers, *Capital Accumulation and Women's Labour in Asian Economies*

Bhagirath Lal Das, *An Introduction to the WTO Agreements*

Bhagirath Lal Das, *The WTO Agreements: Deficiencies, Imbalances and Required Changes*

Bhagirath Lal Das, *The World Trade Organization: A Guide to the New Framework for International Trade*

Diplab Dasgupta, *Structural Adjustment, Global Trade and the New Political Economy of Development*

Wim Dierckxsens, *The Limits of Capitalism: An Approach to a Globalization without Neoliberalism*

Graham Dunkley, *The Free Trade Adventure: The WTO, the Uruguay Round and Globalism: A Critique*

Terence Hopkins and Immanuel Wallerstein et al., *The Age of Transition: Trajectory of the World-System, 1945–2025*

Francois Houtart and Francois Polet (eds): *The Other Davos: The Globalization of Resistance to the World Economic System*

Arthur MacEwan, *Neo-Liberalism or Democracy? Economic Strategy, Markets, and Alternatives for the 21st Century*

Hans-Peter Martin and Harald Schumann, *The Global Trap: Globalization and the Assault on Prosperity and Democracy*

Jan Nederveen Pieterse (ed.), *Global Futures: Shaping Globalization*

Saral Sarkar, *Eco-Socialism or Eco-Capitalism? A Critical Analysis of Humanity's Fundamental Choices*

Harry Shutt, *The Trouble with Capitalism: An Enquiry into the Causes of Global Economic Failure*

Kavaljit Singh, *The Globalisation of Finance: A Citizen's Guide*

Kavaljit Singh, *Taming Global Financial Flows: Challenges and Alternatives in the Era of Financial Globalisation*

Amory Starr, *Naming the Enemy: Anti-Corporate Social Movements Confront Globalization*

Bob Sutcliffe, *A 100 Ways of Seeing an Unequal World*

Oscar Ugarteche, *The False Dilemma: Globalisation: Opportunity or Threat?*

David Woodward, *The Next Crisis? Foreign Direct and Equity Investment in Developing Countries*

For full details of this list and Zed's other subject and general catalogues, please write to: The Marketing Department, Zed Books, 7 Cynthia Street, London N1 9JF, UK or e-mail: sales@zedbooks.demon.co.uk

Visit our website at: http://www.zedbooks.demon.co.uk